COLONIAL
DELAWARE

A HISTORY

A HISTORY OF THE AMERICAN COLONIES
IN THIRTEEN VOLUMES

GENERAL EDITORS:
MILTON M. KLEIN & JACOB E. COOKE

JOHN A. MUNROE

COLONIAL DELAWARE

A HISTORY

kto press

A DIVISION OF KRAUS-THOMSON ORGANIZATION LIMITED
MILLWOOD, NEW YORK

First printing

Printed in the United States of America

Library of Congress Cataloging in Publication Data

Munroe, John A., 1914–
  Colonial Delaware.

  (A History of the American colonies)
  Bibliography: p. 265
  Includes index.
  1. Delaware—History—Colonial period, ca. 1600–
1775. 2. Delaware—History—Revolution, 1775–1783.
I. Title. II. Series.
F167.M84   975.1′02   78-18738
ISBN 0-527-18711-9

TO
STEPHEN, CAROL, AND MICHAEL

CONTENTS

ILLUSTRATIONS

EDITORS'
INTRODUCTION

The American colonies have not lacked their Boswells. Almost from the time of their founding, the English settlements in the New World became the subjects of historical narratives by promoters, politicians, and clergymen. Some, like John Smith's *General History of Virginia,* sought to stir interest in New World colonization. Others, such as Cotton Mather's *Magnalia Christi Americana,* used New England's past as an object lesson to guide its next generation. And others still, like William Smith's *History of the Province of New-York,* aimed at enhancing the colony's reputation in England by explaining its failures and emphasizing its accomplishments. All of these early chroniclers had their shortcomings but no more so than every generation of historians which essayed the same task thereafter. For it is both the strength and the challenge of the historical guild that in each age its practitioners should readdress themselves to the same subjects of inquiry as their predecessors. If the past is prologue, it must be constantly reenacted. The human drama is unchanging, but the audience is always new: its expectations of the past are different, its mood uniquely its own.

The tercentenary of John Smith's history is almost coterminous with the bicentenary of the end of the American colonial era. It is more than appropriate that the two occasions should be observed by a fresh retelling of the story of the colonization of English America not, as in the case of the earliest histories, in self-justification, national exaltation, or moral purgation but as a plain effort to reexamine the past through the lenses of the present.

Apart from the national observance of the bicentennial of American independence, there is ample justification in the era of the 1970s for a modern history of each of the original thirteen colonies. For many of them, there exists no single-volume narrative published in the present century and, for some, none written since those undertaken by contemporaries in the eighteenth century. The standard multivolume histories of the colonial period—those of Herbert L. Osgood, Charles M. Andrews, and Lawrence H. Gipson—are too comprehensive to provide adequate treatment of individual colonies, too political and institutional in emphasis to deal adequately with social, economic, and cultural developments, and too intercolonial and Anglo-American in focus to permit intensive examination of a single colony's distinctive evolution. The most recent of these comprehensive accounts, that of Gipson, was begun as far back as 1936; since then a considerable body of new scholarship has been produced.

The present series, *A History of the American Colonies,* of which *Colonial Delaware* is part, seeks to synthesize the new research, to treat social, economic, and cultural as well as political developments, and to delineate the broad outlines of each colony's history during the years before independence. No uniformity of organization has been imposed on the authors, although each volume attempts to give some attention to every aspect of the colony's historical development. Each author is a specialist in his own field and has shaped his material to the configuration of the colony about which he writes. While the Revolutionary Era is the terminal point of each volume, the authors have not read the history of the colony backward, as mere preludes to the inevitable movement toward independence and statehood.

Despite their local orientation, the individual volumes, taken together, will provide a collective account that should help us understand the broad foundation on which the future history of the colonies in the new nation was to rest and, at the same time, help clarify that still not completely explained melodrama of 1776 which saw, in John Adams's words, thirteen clocks somewhat amazingly strike as one. In larger perspective, *A History of the American Colonies* seeks to remind today's generation of Americans of its earliest heritage as a contribution to an understanding of its comtemporary purpose. The link between past and present is as certain as it is at times indiscernible, for as Michael Kammen has so aptly observed: "The historian is the memory of civilization. A civilization without history ceases to be civilized. A civilization without history ceases to have identity. Without identity there is no purpose; without purpose civilization will wither."*

Delaware was the neglected member of England's colonial family. Many fellow colonists were seemingly unaware of the separate status of this tiny colony, which was also largely ignored by imperial authorities. Indeed, during the colonial period what would become "Delaware" did not even have a proper name, but was referred to as the "Territories of Pennsylvania," the "Three Lower Counties on the Delaware," or merely the "Lower Counties."

American historians have similarly slighted Delaware's early history, an oversight that is no longer pardonable. Compensating for some two centuries of neglect, John A. Munroe demonstrates in this volume that the history of Delaware's formative era is richly varied and historically consequential. It is also unique, in the sense that it is the story of a successful struggle not only for political autonomy but also for political identity.

In the seventeenth century Delaware seemed to merely be a shuttlecock in the game of European diplomacy. Successively an appendage of New Netherland, New Sweden, and New York, Delaware was finally joined to Pennsylvania in the munificent land grant that the English monarch awarded to William Penn. The political union between Delaware and Pennsylvania was from the outset fragile, and it broke early in the eighteenth century when Penn granted the Lower Counties their own assembly. The two provinces continued to share a common governor and proprietor and the smaller, still nameless, colony remained an economic and intellectual satellite of Philadelphia, but for all practical political purposes Delaware was henceforth a separate proprietary colony.

Delawareans were troubled neither by their colonial nor proprietary status. Uniquely among American colonists, they respected rather than resisted their proprietary ties. While the more populous and vastly larger colony of Pennsylvania might ponder the advantages of exchanging a profit-seeking proprietor for a royal master, the Lower Counties regarded their connection with the Penn family as beneficent. Alone among the colonies, Delaware was more vulnerable to the assaults of its neighbors than it was menaced by proprietary and imperial restrictions.

---

* Michael Kammen, *People of Paradox* (New York, 1972), p. 13.

These restraints were so mild as to be scarcely felt at all. No other American colony more successfully contrived to run its own affairs. Nor did it particularly matter that what Munroe describes as the "rewards of obscurity" were primarily attributable to Delaware's "inconsequence in the grand pattern of an expansive and expanding empire." There were, in sum, advantages in smallness and Delaware made the most of them.

The fortunate result was that "politically and culturally" the colony "had reached maturity decades" before it enlisted in the movement for American independence. Why should such a singularly contented colony have done so? Although Delawareans would have found the notion of English tyranny hard to credit, they nevertheless felt imperilled. As Professor Munroe explains, their "great fear was of losing their identity, of forfeiting the large measure of independence they had attained under the proprietors and the Crown." So it was that Penn's Lower Counties unhesitatingly entered a war that confirmed rather than established their independence. Delaware's colonial history, viewed in conjunction with the histories of the other twelve colonies, thus clarifies the meaning of a revolution whose inception, however fortuitous, produced consequences so momentous that they live with us still.

MILTON M. KLEIN
JACOB E. COOKE

PREFACE

In a prefatory note (dated February 1887), to his original, extensive, comprehensive, but often inaccurate volumes on Delaware, J. Thomas Scharf expressed his surprise that no one had heretofore written a history of this colony and state though 256 years had passed since its first settlement by a literate people. As far as the history of the colonial period is concerned, the situation has not changed much since Scharf's time. A number of writers have copied him, but the only volume dealing specifically with the entire colonial period is Henry Clay Reed's *The Delaware Colony*, an excellent book in style and content, but a short work (just over one hundred pages) aimed at a youthful audience, though good reading for anyone.

Fortunately for latter-day historians compelled to lean on the work of their predecessors, good scholars have illuminated several aspects of Delaware's colonial past. Foremost among them is Amandus Johnson, whose studies of New Sweden are still authoritative, although the greatest and earliest of them, *The Swedish Settlements on the Delaware*, was published sixty-six years ago. More recently Clinton A. Weslager has earned the gratitude of historians of colonial Delaware through a series of books and articles on the aborigines, the Dutch, and the early English settlers. The essays of Judge Richard S. Rodney throw light on the history of New Castle and on Delaware as an English colony, but the demands of his professional life restricted the time spent on what was for him only an avocation. Particularly for the late colonial period, Harold Hancock has been producing a series of works based on thorough examination of the sources. Although other good studies are noted in the bibliography, great dark gaps remain in the colonial history of Delaware, particularly for the mid-eighteenth century, where surviving records await analysis.

The neighboring colonies, especially Pennsylvania and New York, which once had intimate ties with Delaware, naturally attract the interest of the Delaware historian. But historians of colonial Pennsylvania from Robert Proud to Gary Nash and Joseph Illick are primarily looking at Penn's province and not at the "territories appended thereto." Historians of New Netherland and of ducal New York similarly give only casual attention to the settlements on the west shore of the Delaware.

Small as the Delaware colony was, it had a long history and an involved one. Its study is instructive in demonstrating how the vagaries of political organization in the old British empire permitted the accidental development of a remarkably independent commonwealth, even of so small an extent and population as these three counties which lacked a proper name, other than the awkward title, "Government of the Counties of New Castle, Kent, and Sussex on Delaware." It is the hope of this author that he has provided a long-needed sketch, in modest detail, of this history, that he has incorporated results of the best work done to date, and that this book will encourage and provide a basis for future analyses of the forgotten and ignored past of this colony.

A word of caution is necessary about the dates used in this study. In the seventeenth century the Dutch employed the new Gregorian calendar, whereas the Swedes and the English still did not. Hereafter, when an account is being related from the viewpoint of the Dutch, the dates are given in what is generally referred to as New Style. These dates are ten days later, in the seventeenth century, than the Old Style dates employed when the focus is on Swedish or English history. From 1700 to 1752, when England finally adopted the new calendar, the difference was eleven days.

Footnotes are not commonly used for scholarly citations in the series of which this book is a part. The author, however, intends to deposit a brief list of citations in the Morris Library of the University of Delaware for the use of interested scholars. He has also taken particular pains with the bibliography in the hope of encouraging those beginning work on any phase of the history of colonial Delaware.

He owes and gladly acknowledges a debt of gratitude to the personnel of the Historical Society of Delaware, the Delaware Division of Historical and Cultural Affairs, the Eleutherian Mills-Hagley Foundation, and particularly the Morris Library of the University of Delaware. So many persons at these institutions have been helpful over so many years that he is sure he would forget some who gave valuable assistance, perhaps six or eight years ago. For this reason he hopes they will accept *en masse* this statement of his appreciation. By occasional leaves and in other ways the University of Delaware has been generally supportive of this work and deserves the author's thanks.

Individuals who have helped solve various scholarly problems include Raymond A. Callahan, the Rev. Edward B. Carley, Anna J. De Armond, Leon de Valinger, Jr., Paul Dolan, the late Arthur R. Dunlap, William P. Frank, George F. Frick, Harold B. Hancock, Mrs. Thomas Herlihy, Jr., Chief Justice Daniel Herrmann, Anthony Higgins, Carol E. Hoffecker, the Rev. Theodore L. Ludlow, William E. McDaniel, the late Ernest J. Moyne, Edward H. Rosenberry, Clinton A. Weslager, and W. Emerson Wilson, as well as the series editors, Jacob E. Cooke and Milton M. Klein, who offered stimulating criticism. The author is grateful to his colleague Russell Remage for providing a refuge on Lake Winnipesaukee when the text was being revised and to Constance P. Weber for her thoughtful, intelligent work as typist. The copy editor asked searching questions and saved the author from many errors and infelicities of expression. Domestically, he was humored and spoiled as he always has been; otherwise this book could not have been written.

Newark, Delaware   John A. Munroe
August 17, 1977

COLONIAL
DELAWARE

A HISTORY

1

SWANENDAEL AND NEW SWEDEN

The discovery of the Delaware River and Bay comes late in the chronicle of European exploration of America. Almost a century earlier, Balboa reached the Pacific at Panama and other Spanish adventurers conquered Mexico and Peru. Long before the Delaware estuary appeared on maps, the coasts of Baffin Island in the far north and of the Carolinas to the south had been delineated. Settlements were being planted, not always successfully, from Florida to Maine, while the fertile valley of the Delaware still remained unknown to Europeans.

Perhaps one of the earliest European explorers did enter Delaware Bay. No clear report of any such entry survives, though it seems possible that Giovanni da Verrazzano in 1524 saw the capes at the mouth of this bay. The truly significant discovery, the discovery that led to important consequences, was made by Henry Hudson, an Englishman, who was in command of a Dutch ship, the *Half Moon*, when he entered Delaware Bay in 1609. Searching for a northwest passage that would provide a route to the Far East, Hudson was examining the American coast north of Cape Charles when on August 28 he rounded Cape Henlopen and, in the words of his mate, Robert Juet, "found the Land to trend away North-west, with a great Bay and Rivers." The bay was tidal and so full of shoals that they feared to explore further and left after a night at anchor.

Brief as the visit was, it was quite long enough to convince Hudson that this broad estuary was probably not the entrance to the strait he sought. "Hee that will thoroughly Discover this great Bay," to quote Juet again, "must have a small Pinnasse [a pinnace, or tender], that must draw but foure or five foote water, to sound before him."

This brief visit was also enough to call the bay to the attention of the Dutch and the English, for Hudson, after a much more extended exploration of New York Bay and its main tributary, made port in England on his return and was prevented from going on to Holland. His ship, however, with part of his small Dutch-English crew and his reports, went on to Amsterdam, and thereby the Dutch maritime world learned of his discoveries. The captain himself was furnished with an English ship and the money to make a new search for a northwest passage, a search that led him to his death in what was thereafter called Hudson Bay.

Other European sailors were soon frequenting the portion of the Atlantic Coast that Hudson had explored. The first bay he had entered, Delaware Bay, was bordered by a low, flat land called by a Dutchman "beautifully level." Great variety of animals, birds, and marine life abounded on the land and in the waters—deer and beaver, wildcats and bear, rattlesnakes and eagles, grouse and wild turkeys, oysters and crabs, and sturgeon and shad that swam upstream seasonally to breed. Flights of wild pigeons sometimes covered the sky. In 1632 a party of Dutch sailors found that by one cast of their seine in Delaware Bay they could catch enough fish to feed thirty men.

The western shore that was to become the State of Delaware was sandy near the ocean with a few stands of tall pine trees. Upstream the sand gave way to marsh and to reedy islands until well up the river some fast land appeared. In the interior the land was densely forested, although occasionally there were clear fields where the natives planted corn, beans, and squash. In the fall they set fire to the forests and the thickets to aid themselves in their hunting; the fragrance of sweet-smelling herbs and trees, such as the sassafras, was carried far to sea by the westerly winds.

The natives themselves, the Delaware Indians, though from one viewpoint Stone Age savages, possessing no knowledge of textiles, glass, or metal, having no beasts of burden and no knowledge of the wheel, appear to have been, in comparison with other men, a gentle, peaceable folk. They dwelt in bark huts (or wigwams) in semipermanent villages, supporting themselves by a mixed life of fishing, farming, and hunting.

To the best of our knowledge, they seem, like many other Indian tribes, to have had no central government, power residing wholly in the village community and its leader, or sachem. They called themselves Lenni Lenape, or "original people," and they were so decentralized and loosely organized that it is difficult to speak of them as a tribe or a nation. One important element of the culture that these river people shared was their language, though significant dialectic differences existed among them in vocabulary and pronunciation. The language belonged to the prevailing coastal linguistic group, called Algonkian, and was therefore related to the tongue spoken by most of their neighbors.

A significant exception to this linguistic relationship existed to the north and northwest, regions dominated by tribes of the Iroquoian linguistic family. In the early seventeenth century, when Europeans first came to know the Lenape, they were engaged in a defensive war with one of these Iroquoian tribes, the Minqua, who from their homeland in the Susquehanna valley (they were also called the Susquehannock) often sent war parties to the lower Delaware to attack Lenape villages. The Appoquinimink Creek and the Christina River were favorite routes for Minqua invaders, and the latter stream became known to the Dutch as the Minqua Kill. Many Lenape moved to the east bank of the Delaware, in flight from the Minqua, and in time the Minqua established a sort of suzerainty over the southern Lenape, while the northernmost Lenape became similarly subject to the powerful Iroquoian tribes of the Five Nations, who controlled the head waters of the Delaware.

Algonkian-speaking tribes to the southwest of the Delaware Indians included the Nanticoke and Choptank, dwelling on tributaries of the Chesapeake. They too were oppressed by the Minqua and possibly also by the Five Nations, till they finally withdrew in the 1740s from the Delmarva Peninsula, as the Eastern Shore of the Chesapeake is called, to seek refuge from European civilization among their old native enemies on the Susquehanna. Only a remnant of these tribes, and of some Assateague, who had settled on Indian River, remained on the peninsula.

The Lenape, in their gradual retreat, followed the same path westward into Pennsylvania but then split, some continuing west into the Mississippi valley while others went northwestward into Canada. Their numbers, which are estimated at over ten thousand in the time of the first explorers, may have dropped to less than half that by 1671. Hardship and adaptation gave the Delaware Indians a changed and more militant posture by the time they became known in the Indian wars of Ohio and the trans-Mississippi plains. After two centuries, descendants of the people whose lives were interrupted on the Delaware were prominent among the hardy scouts who accompanied Kit Carson and John C. Frémont across the Rockies to California.

The name given the Indians and the river they lived on owes it origin to the second European sea captain known to have visited Delaware Bay. This was Samuel Argall, a veteran of the Newfoundland fisheries who was employed by the Virginia Company, when on August 17, 1610, blown from his course on a voyage from Virginia to Bermuda, he took refuge from the weather behind Cape Henlopen, arriving a year almost to the day later than Hudson. The headland, nameless, indeed nonexistent, on his charts, and the bay behind it he named for his master, Thomas West, Baron De La Warr, the governor of Virginia. The headland lost this name, but the bay retained it, and from the bay the name traveled to the river that fed it, to the Indians on its banks and, later, to the state formed of the three lower counties on the western shore.

For the time being, however, it was not the English but the Dutch who most often frequented these waters and who first settled this land. The first sailor to penetrate beyond the bay and into the Delaware River may have been Cornelis Hendricksen, who was there at least as early as 1616, when he reported his discoveries to authorities in the Netherlands. The name of Cape May commemorates the explorations of Cornelis Jacobsen May, who was in the area in 1620 and possibly earlier.

Fishing was what had drawn the Dutch to the sea in the first place, and they noted the abundance of fish in America. But fish were to be found nearer home; it was furs—particularly beaver skins—that attracted their ships increasingly to this coast and to its two river valleys which they claimed—the Hudson, called the North River, and the Delaware, their South River. When the Dutch formally established a colony in this area, a beaver was the central figure on its seal.

In 1614 the whole area was named New Netherland by the Dutch legislature, the States General, which incorporated a group of Amsterdam and Hoorn merchants as the United New Netherland Company and gave them a three-year monopoly on trade in the area between Virginia and New France. (Jamestown and Quebec existed, though they were hardly flourishing, but New England had no permanent settlements yet.) In 1618 the charter of this company expired, but in 1621 a greater enterprise, the West India Company, was chartered and given a monopoly on Dutch trade with the west coast of Africa and all of the New World. The company was not fully organized until 1623, but soon thereafter it planted the first settlements on the Delaware, a colony of Walloons (French-speaking refugees from southern Belgium), probably on Burlington Island, and a small palisaded trading post called Fort Nassau, at Gloucester. Neither settlement was permanent and neither was in the present state of Delaware.

The Dutch West India Company never cared much about developing the New Netherland. Its orientation was toward war and the spoils of war; its incorporation was hastened by the resumption, after a twelve years' truce, of the long Dutch struggle for independence from Spain, and the directors and stockholders of the company looked toward the Spanish Main and South America for richer treasures than the furs Indians could gather along the Hudson or the Delaware.

Responsibility for New Netherland was assigned by the company to the most important of its five boards of directors, the Amsterdam chamber, a group of twenty of the principal stockholders of the company from Amsterdam, by this time the largest, wealthiest, and most powerful city in the Netherlands. Under these auspices several trading posts were established in the colony, but they remained weak, and those on the Delaware—the Walloon colony and Fort Nassau—were soon abandoned. On the other hand, two settlements in the Hudson valley—Fort Orange, at the site of modern Albany, and New Amsterdam, on the tip of Manhattan Island—persisted, and the latter became the seat of a governor or director who, with his appointed council, became the chief authority of the colony *in situ*.

Meanwhile both English and French ships had entered the Delaware, and it became clear that the Dutch claim to this area, as well as to all the New Netherland, was insecure. Even the war party among Dutch merchants wished to retain control of New Netherland because they saw it as one more base for raids on the Spanish. A plan was therefore devised to bring private initiative to the fore and to encourage establishment of a number of private colonies that would strengthen the Dutch presence in New Netherland. This was a charter of "Freedoms and Exemptions" prepared by the West India Company in 1628 and approved, with modifications, by the States General in 1629.

The charter encouraged independent settlers by promising them a gift of as much land as they could cultivate properly. But a special incentive was reserved for stockholders in the West India Company. Any stockholder who would settle fifty adults in America might arrange privately to buy from the Indians a tract sixteen miles long on one shore of a river or eight miles long on both shores, running inland as far as was practical. In this tract of land (it could be larger if the settlers numbered more than fifty) the controlling stockholder had the powers, roughly, of a manor lord, and he was given the hereditary title of patroon, equivalent in meaning to the English "patron" but grander in concept. His colonists were to be tax free for ten years but could not leave the land except with the patroon's written consent. The patroon could fish and trade all along the coast between Florida and Newfoundland, but all imports and exports must pass through New Amsterdam and the fur trade remained a monopoly of the company wherever the company had an agent. The manufacture of cloth in New Netherland was forbidden.

Few independent settlers took advantage of the "Freedoms and Exemptions," but an interconnected group of large stockholders sought to establish patroonships not only in New Netherland but also in the West Indian islands and in South America. Among them was a Walloon named Samuel Godyn (also written Godijn and Godin), president of the Amsterdam chamber of the company, who, in association with two other stockholders—Samuel Blommaert, a leader in the Baltic copper and grain trade, and Kiliaen Van Rensselaer, a diamond merchant—sent two agents to America to purchase land in 1629 before the "Freedoms and Exemptions" had been announced publicly. On Godyn's behalf one of these agents, Gillis Hossitt, a seaman, using trade goods such as cloth and axes as a medium of exchange, bought from the Indians in the "south corner of the Bay of the South River" a tract of land that was called Swanendael (or, in modern Dutch, Zwaanendael) because of the number of swans in the area. Blommaert and Van Rensselaer took shares in the enterprise, as did Albert Coenraetsen Burgh, a fur merchant, and, eventually, half a dozen other Dutch merchants and sailors. Godyn became a partner in the patroonships planned by Blommaert on the Connecticut and by Burgh on the east side of Delaware Bay, both of which perished unborn, and also in Van Rensselaer's successful patroonship on the Hudson. Godyn authorized his agents to purchase furs with whatever trade goods remained in their hands after the land transactions. Enemies said this fur transaction was more than incidental to the enterprise, for Hossitt and his partners brought back to Amsterdam a fur shipment equal to about one-twelfth of the West India Company's annual imports.

Since the "Freedoms and Exemptions" allowed him only four years to settle his land, Godyn wasted little time in getting an expedition to sea, having the assistance of David Pietersen de Vries of Hoorn, a sailor of wide experience who for his knowledge, not for money, was made a partner in the patroonship. Peter Heyes, experienced in the Greenland fishery, was given command of the eighteen-gun *Whale* (in Dutch, *Walvis*), which, accompanied by a yacht (a Dutch term for a small, swift vessel with a sharp prow), set out from Holland in December 1630, carrying, besides colonists (all men) and crew, a cargo of lime, brick, tiles, horses, cows, ammunition, provisions, merchandise, and equipment not only for farming but also for whaling. Godyn and his associates were eager to get a supply of whale oil from the whales they were told frequented Delaware Bay.

After an adventurous voyage, twenty-eight men disembarked in Delaware Bay and immediately began construction of a brick house, surrounded by a wooden palisade, on the bank of Lewes Creek. Gillis Hossitt commanded the settlement, the first by Europeans in what is now Delaware. It was soon slightly enlarged, and in May Hossitt and Captain Heyes purchased another tract of land on the east side of Delaware Bay, registering their purchase at New Amsterdam with Director Peter Minuit and his council on June 3, 1631.

Godyn had hoped that the *Whale* would return with a valuable cargo of furs, whale oil, or commodities purchased or seized from the Spanish in the West Indies. But the West India Company's vigilance in insisting on its monopoly of the fur trade prevented Hossitt from sending home another shipload of pelts, and the only oil Captain Heyes loaded was a sample from a dead whale found on the shore. He arrived too late in the year for the whale fishery, Heyes explained, and he had no West Indian cargo either, probably because he took a northern route home. "This was a losing voyage to us," wrote David de Vries, with sarcasm, "because this captain . . . durst not sail [back] by way of the West Indies with only one ship of eighteen guns, where he must have made good the expense of this voyage."

Dutch merchants looked for quick profits, but Godyn encouraged his partners not to give up. A second expedition was fitted out, this one to be commanded by De Vries himself, who presumably would not fear the

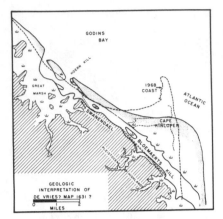

A recent map of the coastline at Lewes and Cape Henlopen superimposed by Professor John C. Kraft on an early seventeenth-century map of the area. The Cape has grown sharper as the ocean shore has receded, but the site of Swanendael remains beside a stream, as it was in 1631.

Aerial view of a portion of Delaware Bay and shoreline, with Roosevelt Inlet (center), Broadkill Creek (top), and Lewes Creek, today the Lewes and Rehoboth Canal (bottom). The site of Swanendael is on the left side of Lewes Creek, just north of modern Lewes. This photograph and the map above are used by courtesy of Professor John C. Kraft. From *The Evolution of Lewes Harbor*, by John C. Kraft and Robert L. Caulk (*Technical Report No. 10*, November 1972, College of Marine Studies, University of Delaware).

dangers of the Caribbees. The plan was to leave in the spring, allowing for adventures in the West Indies and arrival in Delaware waters before winter, when the whales were said to come to this coast.

Before the expedition sailed, Godyn and company heard of tragedy at Swanendael, the news probably brought by Peter Minuit, returning from New Amsterdam, where he had been serving as director of New Netherland. The settlers had been massacred by Indians, killed to the last man.

Nevertheless Godyn went ahead with plans for the second expedition to the Delaware, altering only his intent to send additional settlers and supplies to Swanendael. The mission of this second expedition, consisting again of the *Whale* and a yacht, was whaling primarily, as far as the Delaware was concerned. After leaving Holland in May and experiencing various adventures in the West Indies, the two vessels arrived off Cape Henlopen on December 3, 1632.

At Swanendael De Vries found the burnt remnants of the house and palisades, with the bones of the thirty-two murdered settlers and the skulls of their horses and cattle lying here and there. At first the Indians kept out of sight, but in a few days De Vries enticed them aboard and heard from them the story of the destruction of the settlement. The settlers had fastened a tin Dutch coat of arms on a column. All metals being great rarities to men who could not smelt ores, an Indian stole this tin piece to make a tobacco pipe. The Dutch made a great to-do about the theft as an insult to their country, and in consequence some of the Indians killed the thief. The Dutch were disturbed that the Indians had taken such quick vengeance, but this was not the end of the affair. The slain Indian's friends blamed the Dutch for what had happened and one clear day, when most of the Dutch were at work in the fields, these Indians came to Swanendael, pretending to be bringing furs to barter. When the chief Dutch trader came down from his loft with trade goods an Indian smashed his head with an axe. The Indians killed a sick man in the house and then stole up on the Dutchmen at their work, killing every one. A dog chained by the house may have offered the greatest resistance, for the Indians shot twenty-five arrows into him before they were satisfied he was dead.

Wisely, De Vries decided there was no point in prolonging the dispute by taking vengeance on the Indians, even if he could find the guilty ones. After reestablishing peace, he had his men set up a cauldron for whale oil and a wooden shelter on Lewes Beach, and while they proceeded with the whale fishery in the bay, De Vries sailed up the Delaware in his yacht, the *Squirrel*, hoping to buy corn from the Indians. In two voyages up the river—the second lasting a month because he was caught in the ice—De Vries had many adventures and learned much about the geography of the Delaware valley but had little success in obtaining food for his men, for the Delaware Indians were themselves on short rations and in flight from raiding parties of Minqua.

In desperate need of provisions for the voyage home, De Vries sailed to Virginia, thinking it more likely he would find an ample supply there than at New Amsterdam and also probably intrigued with the idea of learning something about the English settlement and the possibility of developing trade with it. He was well received at Jamestown, where the English were eager to learn more about the Delaware, which they claimed as England's. They had, in fact, sent a sloop there in September 1631, with seven or eight men, but it had not returned. De Vries could explain this disappearance; in his voyage up the Delaware he had seen Indians wearing English jackets and had been told that an English sloop had been captured recently and the men killed.

On returning from Virginia, De Vries was disappointed with the progress of the whale fishing at Swanendael. Seventeen whales had been struck by the inexperienced Dutch harpooners, but only seven had been secured, and the amount of oil collected was meager. The whales had now left this coast, so De Vries gave up the enterprise and started back to Holland on April 14, 1633.

En route, he called at New Amsterdam and was greatly annoyed when the new governor there, Wouter (or Walter) Van Twiller, sought to examine his cargo. Aboard were some furs, as well as some oil, plus salt that had been loaded in the West Indies, so the voyage was not a complete loss. Still, two expeditions to Swanendael had proved so unprofitable that the proprietors had no heart for more, and in 1635 they were glad to sell their land, with all the patroonship privileges, to the West India Company.

One of the partners of the patroonship reported that forty thousand guilders were lost on Swanendael and implied that stronger management might have avoided this loss, possibly by reestablishing the settlement. Godyn, he said, retained "but the bare name of patroon, permitted as many as ten people to share in the management, whereupon the business ran into great expense on account of the many directors, one wanting this and another something else, and had to be sold at a loss." Perhaps something more would have been done had Godyn not died in September 1633, only two months after De Vries returned from Swanendael.

Though the Swanendael colony of 1631–33 was a failure, its brief existence prevented Delaware, or at least southern Delaware, from being adjudged part of Maryland. The latter colony came into being in 1632 when King Charles I granted Cecilius Calvert, the second Lord Baltimore, a magnificent tract of land running north from the Potomac River to the fortieth parallel and east to the Delaware. However, the preamble to the charter stated that the grant was to land "hitherto uncultivated," the phrase being understood to apply only to Europeans, not to Indians. Since the land at Swanendael had been seeded by the Dutch and was covered with a fine crop in 1631, a year prior to the Maryland charter, an argument could be made for excluding the land along Delaware Bay from Lord Baltimore's claim. For the sake of the eventual independence of Delaware, however, it was important that early Maryland settlers on the Eastern Shore found numerous good plantation sites with fine landings along the many estuaries of the Chesapeake; for several decades, consequently they had little temptation to move into the forested interior of the peninsula separating the two bays, the Chesapeake and the Delaware.

Another English claim that encompassed Delaware was New Albion, a colony planned by Sir Edmund Plowden, an ambitious, contentious man with a rich wife whose money he may have used in purchasing a vast tract along the Atlantic seaboard in 1634. Plowden set out for the Delaware in 1642 but was taken to Virginia by error. It is possible that he did reach the Delaware River late in 1643, but by that time his followers had abandoned him and he was powerless to make good his claim.

Before Plowden left America for good in 1648, an interest in the fur trade led some New Haven Colony merchants, calling themselves the Delaware Company, to purchase Indian lands in Pennsylvania, New Jersey, and Delaware. Though active in New Jersey, they never attempted to settle their lands in Delaware, which by this time had been claimed by the Swedes.

The Swedish settlement of Delaware came about as a result of Dutch interest in the area. Seventeenth-century Sweden was a kingdom renowned for great military prowess but of limited commercial development. Swedish armies had won control of most of the shores of the Baltic Sea, but the trade of the area was dominated by the Dutch. In the late sixteenth century 55 percent of the ships entering the Baltic were Dutch, and they carried 75 percent of the cargoes. When King Gustavus Adolphus of Sweden founded the city of Gothenburg (Göteborg in Swedish) in 1619 in order to have an Atlantic port (outside the Danish-controlled entrance to the Baltic Sea*), the new city was so Dutch dominated that ten of the eighteen members of the first city council were Dutch, and the Dutch language was accepted on equal terms with Swedish.

The Dutch influence in Swedish commercial life explains how it was that Dutch merchants went to Sweden for a charter empowering them to develop an American trade outside the monopoly of the Dutch West India Company. The first of these men was William Usselinx, an Amsterdam merchant born in Antwerp and a principal founder of the Dutch West India Company who became disenchanted with the company soon after its founding because he felt his services were insufficiently rewarded.

After accepting an appointment in Danzig as agent for Dutch grain merchants, Usselinx traveled to the Baltic city via Gothenburg. While Usselinx was in Gothenburg, Gustavus Adolphus met him and heard his proposals for a Swedish trading company. At just this time a rare interval of peace in Gustavus's wars allowed the Swedish king to concentrate on the economic development of his country, and he was sufficiently impressed with Usselinx's ideas to see to it that by 1626 a company on Usselinx's model was chartered for foreign trade. Nothing much came of it, however. The South Company, as this new enterprise was called, never sent an expedition to America. When they failed to raise enough money for large-scale foreign ventures, its directors became interested in such other enterprises as a glassworks, a shipyard, and a ropewalk, and sent some small fleets to European ports. Gustavus Adolphus's death on the battlefield in 1632, as well as the absorption of Swedish energies in war, dealt the company a further blow. Its affairs were liquidated in 1640, long after Usselinx had severed his connection with it.

Meanwhile the Dutch-Swedish commercial connection had produced another corporation interested in American trade—the New Sweden

---

* The southern provinces of present-day Sweden, those nearest to Copenhagen, Denmark, did not become Swedish until 1658.

Company. Chartered in 1637, this company sponsored the expedition that resulted in the permanent settlement of Delaware in March 1638.

Though Christina, daughter and heir to Gustavus Adolphus, was the nominal ruler of Sweden, she was only six when her father died and twelve in the year the American colony was founded. A council of regents, dominated by Count Axel Oxenstierna, the chancellor, ran the country in her name. Oxenstierna, Admiral Klas Fleming, president of the board of trade, and Peter Spiring, Baron Silfverkrona (a Swedish nobleman but son of a Dutch merchant) were the chief Swedish members of the New Sweden Company, and their principal Dutch associates were Samuel Blommaert and Peter Minuit.

Swedish officials became acquainted with Blommaert in 1632, when they sought to market their mineral resources—mainly copper and iron—to support their political and military ambitions. Blommaert at first proposed a joint Dutch-Swedish effort to sell copper for gold on the Guinea coast of Africa, where he knew the Dutch had begun such a trade, and in 1635 Oxenstierna himself, returning from a diplomatic mission in France, visited Amsterdam and discussed this proposal with Blommaert.

The latter's eagerness to establish a Dutch-Swedish enterprise arose because he, like Usselinx earlier, was dissatisfied with the conduct of the Dutch West India Company, of which he was a director in the Amsterdam chamber. By chance, in the year in which Oxenstierna conferred with Blommaert, the latter was also approached by a former colonial governor, Peter Minuit, who aroused in Blommaert a renewed interest in North America.

Minuit, a veteran adventurer of fifty-five, had recently been dismissed as director general of New Netherland, apparently on suspicion of favoring the interests of individuals over those of the company. German born, but of French or Walloon descent, Minuit had gone to New Netherland, probably as a merchant, when the original settlements were being made, had quickly been given positions of authority in West India Company service, first as a councillor and then as director general, had helped make Manhattan Island the center of Dutch authority, and had there registered the patroonships claimed by Godyn, Blommaert, and others. He therefore was well aware of the failure of the plans of all the patroons except Van Rensselaer, and he influenced Blommaert to turn his negotiations with the Swedes in the direction of American rather than African trade and colonization.

With Oxenstierna's acquiescence, plans went forward rapidly. The New Sweden Company was chartered with power to trade along the American coast from Newfoundland to Florida and perhaps to do much else that is not certainly known today because the charter is lost. Before the year was out an expedition was prepared and under way to found a colony in America for the greater glory of Sweden and the profit of its Swedish and Dutch supporters.

The foundation of New Sweden in 1638 is correctly viewed as an extension of Dutch commercial imperialism, though as the years passed the enterprise lost its Dutch character and became more properly what its name indicated. The two ships—the *Key of Kalmar* (*Kalmar Nyckel*) and the *Griffin* (*Vogel Grip*)—that set out from Gothenburg in November 1637 as the first expedition to New Sweden were Swedish vessels, flying the Swedish flag, operating under a Swedish charter, and carrying Swedish colonists. But a former Dutch colonial official (Minuit) was in command, Dutch skippers and a crew that was half Dutch manned the vessels, a good part of the cargo was Dutch, an area claimed by the Dutch was the destination, and half of the financing came from Dutch sources. The Swedish investors were Oxenstierna and two members of his family, along with Admiral Fleming and Spiring. Blommaert was responsible for one-half of the Dutch investment, and some associates of Blommaert promised the rest, though Blommaert finally advanced much of the money.

Heavy storms in the North Sea delayed the ships, and after securing repairs and some additional cargo (including goods and six settlers for Van Rensselaer's patroonship on the Hudson), a new start was made from North Holland on December 31. In mid-March they arrived in Delaware Bay, which looked so good to these adventurers that they named a promontory, where they first landed, Paradise Point. From there they proceeded according to instructions up the Delaware and into the Christina River, the Minquas Kill to the Dutch. Here, after reconnoitering the stream, Minuit met with Indians and purchased lands from Duck Creek (the southern boundary of New Castle County) to the Schuylkill. Here too a site was picked for a settlement that was called Fort Christina. It was at the Rocks, "a wharf of stone" on the Christina about two miles

Monument by Carl Milles at The Rocks, Wilmington, commemorating the landing of
the first Swedish settlers in 1638 and the construction by them of Fort Christina. The
decorated black granite shaft, surmounted by a representation of the *Key of Kalmar*, was a
gift from the people of Sweden at the three hundredth anniversary of the landing. A
duplicate stands prominently on the waterfront of Gothenburg, Sweden, departure point
of the first expedition. Courtesy of the Historical Society of Delaware, Wilmington.

from the Delaware River and above the junction of the Christina and its main tributary, the Brandywine, on the east side of the present city of Wilmington.

While a palisaded square fort surrounding a storehouse and a dwelling house was being constructed, Minuit made two trips up the Delaware. At Fort Nassau, reoccupied by the Dutch, he was challenged by its commander. But this was no more than Minuit expected. The Dutch were too weak to do much beyond protest, even if affairs in Europe, where the Swedish army occupied the attention of Holland's enemies, had not discouraged Dutch aggression. Minuit and his colleagues had purposely planned their settlement in an agreeable and almost unoccupied valley of the New World, an area claimed by the Dutch but hardly utilized by them, a region with a promising fur trade not yet exhausted. Even the specific site on the Christina was a wise choice because the river offered a route westward to the interior, where furs were more abundant than on the Delaware.

While Minuit explored the Delaware, the *Griffin* was sent off on trading missions, first to Virginia and then to the West Indies. Neither was successful. The Virginians were uncooperative, and the only substantial outcome of the long West Indies voyage was the purchase of a black man who was left at Fort Christina in April 1639, the first of his race on the Delaware, before the *Griffin* returned to Sweden.

Meanwhile Minuit had left Måns Kling in charge of Fort Christina and twenty-four colonists in June 1638, when he sailed away on the *Key of Kalmar*. En route via the West Indies, where he still hoped to find a rich cargo, Minuit perished when a Dutch ship on which he was visiting at St. Kitts was blown to sea and lost in a hurricane.

The *Key of Kalmar,* however, continued to Holland, where its cargo of seven hundred beaver, otter, and bear pelts was sold as the share of the Dutch investors. (Later, fifteen hundred pelts from the *Griffin* arrived in Holland via Gothenburg.) The Dutch West India Company was disturbed at this manifest invasion of its monopoly of American trade, particularly the fur trade, and had the *Key of Kalmar* seized some time after its arrival in October 1638. To this company it was clear that independent Dutch merchants were circumventing the law, buying furs in Dutch colonial territory and selling them in Dutch markets, all in collusion with Swedes by virtue of a Swedish charter. But Blommaert and company got away with it. Spiring, as Swedish representative in the Netherlands, intervened, and the *Key of Kalmar* was freed to return to Gothenburg with its remaining cargo: tobacco consigned to the Swedish sponsors.

Blommaert and his associates had found a way to circumvent the legal corporate monopoly of the Dutch West India Company, but the scheme did not pay. The Dutch investors had no interest in exalting the glory of Sweden through development of a colonial empire, nor were they moved by dreams of spreading the gospel among the heathen and increasing the prosperity of all Europe. Minuit, of course, had been interested in finding a new colonial role for himself, but he was dead, and his Dutch associates were in the Swedish company only to make money. When the first expedition failed, they became squeamish and might have withdrawn at once except for their eagerness to recover the funds they had invested in the company. Their situation was also complicated by the unfriendliness of the Dutch West India Company, in which they were stockholders. They could put up with this jealousy if they were making money, but a losing proposition was something else again.

When a second expedition was sent to New Sweden, the Dutch associates wanted little to do with it. They finally agreed to share half the cost of the cargo and provisions purchased in the Netherlands but refused to help with the other expenses of the voyage. Another Dutchman was found to take charge of the colony, but this man, Peter Hollander Ridder, was already in Swedish service as an officer in the Royal Navy. The *Key of Kalmar* was again the ship employed, leaving Holland in February 1640, and arriving at Fort Christina in April.

Rumors were heard in Holland that the settlers, now two years in America, had agreed with William Kieft, Dutch director general of New Netherland, that they would abandon Fort Christina and move to New Amsterdam in early June 1640 if no relief arrived for them before that. The *Key of Kalmar* arrived in the nick of time, but Dutch desires to see the Swedish colony given up may have fathered the rumor. There was apparently some ill-feeling between the Swedes and the Dutchmen employed as soldiers at Fort Christina, and on the voyage some of the Dutch sailors, including the skipper, tormented a "Swedish priest" aboard, probably as much because he was a Lutheran (and not of the Reformed Church) as because he was a Swede. Besides this clergyman— the Reverend Reorus Torkillus, the first Lutheran pastor in America— and the new officers of the colony, little is known of the passengers brought on this second voyage of the *Key of Kalmar*. They probably included the first women and children; also the first farmers (other than the men employed primarily as soldiers) came at this time. Ridder did not find his colonists very handy, for he complained he had no one capable of building a "common peasant's house."

Måns Kling, the commander of Fort Christina, returned on the *Key of Kalmar*, which arrived in Gothenburg in July with its cargo, primarily furs. Almost as soon as the ship reached Europe another expedition left Amsterdam for Fort Christina. Largely a Dutch affair, it did not originate with the Dutch stockholders in the New Sweden Company but with a group of dissatisfied farmers in the province of Utrecht who wished to move to the New World to better their lot. Repulsed by the West India Company, they appealed through Blommaert and Spiring to the Swedes, who were doubtful about further diluting their colony with Dutchmen and yet eager to populate the land they claimed. An agreement was eventually drawn up to admit these Dutch colonists to New Sweden and to give them land and privileges near Fort Christina. Two or three shiploads were expected, but only about fifty Utrecht farmers finally migrated.

Little is heard of them after their arrival on November 2, 1640, and within a few years they probably relocated in Dutch territory. The Dutch West India Company made clear its intention of seizing the property of anyone attempting to trade within the territory it claimed, excepting only, in courtesy to Swedish allies, the Christina River. If pressed, the company would necessarily make larger exceptions for Swedes, but hardly for Dutchmen unless Swedish arms protected them.

The embarrassing and unprofitable position of the Dutch stockholders in the New Sweden Company came to an end in 1641 when the Swedes bought them out. Funds for the purchase came from the old South Company that Usselinx had promoted fifteen years earlier. By its amalgamation with another Swedish enterprise, the South Company had acquired a number of vessels, one of which was now sold for the money needed to buy out the Dutch investors in the New Sweden Company. A reorganization, involving an infusion of new money, was carried through, and when it was completed in 1642 the South Company was responsible for one-half of the capital of the New Sweden Company, the Swedish crown was responsible for one-sixth, and five individuals—Chancellor

Oxenstierna and two of his relatives, together with Admiral Fleming and Peter Spiring (Baron Silfverkrona)—were responsible for the remaining one-third.

Not all of the individual subscriptions were ever paid in full, but these particular stockholders were immensely important to the company, for all of them except Spiring sat in the council of state that ran Sweden. It was easy for them, therefore, to give the reorganized company some financial encouragement by assigning it a monopoly of tobacco imports into Sweden. New Sweden was expected eventually to become the main source of tobacco, fitting the mercantilist conception of the function of a colony to produce raw materials not produced at home. But for the time being most of the tobacco imported by the New Sweden Company was purchased in Holland.

Admiral Fleming acted as head of the company and injected some vigor into its affairs until he was killed in 1644. He was succeeded by Oxenstierna, who became distracted by his other more pressing responsibilities. Company affairs and affairs of state became closely intermingled. Some employees of the company were given tasks for the government without any additional compensation. Government officials, on the other hand, often performed company business. To all intents and purposes, the New Sweden Company had become an arm of the Swedish government.

During the period of new vigor following the reorganization of the New Sweden Company, an army officer, Lieutenant Colonel Johan Printz, temporarily without assignment, was asked to go to New Sweden and take over its government from Peter Ridder, who returned to his duties in the Swedish navy. The departure of Ridder in 1643 marked the end of direction of the company by Dutchmen. A year earlier, Blommaert had severed his last tie with the company by ceasing to act as its agent in Amsterdam. Of course, Dutchmen still continued to play some role in the colony, but the dominant role thereafter was played by Swedes.

A good many of the Swedish colonists, however, were really Finns. Finland and Sweden had been closely related for four centuries, with Swedes settling in Finland and Finns moving to Sweden. Finnish family names frequently were changed to Swedish, the two languages being very different, so that the Finnish origin of a family might be hidden, just as Irish names are often written in their English equivalent. (The relationship of Finns to Swedes had a similarity to that of the Irish and Scots to the English, and also to the relationship of the Walloons to the Dutch.)

In the seventeenth century Finns had been encouraged to take up vacant land in central and northern Sweden, where they experienced conditions roughly similar to those found by pioneers in North America. When a fourth expedition to New Sweden was being prepared in 1641 to develop an agricultural colony and difficulty was encountered in finding farmers willing to emigrate, the former commandant at Fort Christina, Måns Kling, who was himself about to return to America, was directed to recruit some Finns. He managed to obtain some Finnish foresters. One of the two vessels carrying this fourth expedition, which reached Fort Christina in November 1641, was the *Key of Kalmar*, making its third and final voyage to America.

It was something more than a year later, in February 1643, that the new governor, Johan Printz, reached Fort Christina. Printz, accompanied by his second wife and at least some of his six children, brought with him many things needed in the colony such as grain and peas, clothing, muskets, livestock and hay for their feed, wine and malt, paper and wax. He also brought additional soldiers and colonists, some of the latter being criminals, debtors, and army deserters, including some Finns.

The new supplies and the additional personnel, especially the new governor, gave renewed life to New Sweden. As a colonial executive, fifty-year-old Printz proved to be in many ways a good choice. He was the son of a minister and had been born in Småland in southern Sweden, unlike most of the colonists, who generally came from Upland, near Stockholm, and from other provinces of central and western Sweden. Educated for the Lutheran ministry in Sweden and at German universities, Printz while still a young man was shanghaied by a troop of mercenary soldiers. Attracted by the military life, he entered the Swedish army in the period of its greatest repute, during the Thirty Years War. In this service, in 1640, Printz was forced to surrender the ruins of the Saxon city of Chemnitz. Though cleared by a court-martial, his military career was temporarily interrupted, and he retired to a country estate until new opportunity to advance his career arose in the form of the governorship of New Sweden.

Printz arrived in America not just as an agent of the New Sweden

Portrait of Johan Printz, governor of New Sweden from 1643 to 1653. Artist unknown. Copy from original in Sweden. Courtesy of the Historical Society of Pennsylvania, Philadelphia.

Company but as a salaried official of the Swedish government armed with careful instructions that gave him great power, authorities having heard of previous altercations arising from division of responsibility in New Sweden. Printz remained in New Sweden for ten years, his governorship extending through most of the short history of this little colony.

The first half of Printz's term as governor was a period of vigorous leadership and of optimism regarding the future of the colony. Relief expeditions arrived with regularity in 1644, 1646, and 1647, and though they brought few colonists, they did provide needed supplies, including seeds, clothing, household and farm implements, and goods for trade with the Indians. In turn, furs—mainly beaver skins—and tobacco were sent back to Sweden.

Most of the tobacco was purchased in New Sweden from Englishmen who carried it by ship from their settlements on the Chesapeake. However, a significant amount was grown along the Delaware, and Printz was proud of having encouraged farming, both by freemen and by servants of the New Sweden Company. Some of the tobacco exported was raised on land Printz appropriated for himself.

By purchases from the Indians Ridder had extended the bounds of New Sweden from Cape Henlopen to the falls at Trenton, and Printz purchased land on the Jersey shore from Cape May nearly to Fort Nassau. When ordered to build a fort so situated as to enable the Swedes to control all shipping on the Delaware, Printz constructed Fort Elfsborg on the Jersey shore, south of Salem Creek. With this exception Swedish settlement was altogether on the west side of the river and till the very last years of the colony was confined to the area between the Christina and the north shore of the Schuylkill. On or near the Schuylkill, a good site for Indian trade, Printz eventually constructed a blockhouse, a fort, and a water mill. Farther down the Delaware on Tinicum Island, he built another fort and a home for himself. For a decade this place was the capital of the colony. Another settlement, with a blockhouse, developed at Chester, but the commercial center of the colony remained at Fort Christina, the chief port.

In the early years of the colony, many of the settlers died. Printz believed that the numerous deaths which occurred in 1643, including that of the first clergyman, were due to lack of sufficient food, and making the farms productive was one of his major successes. Printz claimed Ridder misled him by arguing that one man could grow enough

Indian corn to feed eight others, but in the first year nine men grew only enough for one. In time, however, the ratio of labor to farm product vastly improved. Rye and barley—crops the Swedes were used to at home—were introduced, and the livestock—cattle, sheep, pigs, and goats—gradually multiplied. A brewery was established and some boats were built, but the hopes of the colony's directors for the production of salt and silk and for a whale fishery were unrealistic.

In the long run, the Swedes and Finns proved peculiarly well fitted as colonists in the Delaware valley. They were accustomed, unlike the English and Dutch, to a land densely forested, sparsely settled, and with long cold winters, though Printz, a tall and very stout man, declared such cold as he felt in America was unknown in central or southern Sweden. A number of these settlers, especially the Finns, had actually lived as pioneers in the old country, pushing the frontiers of settlement northward and westward into the Scandinavian backwoods. They knew how to make houses of logs and kept themselves warm in cozy quarters, while winter winds blew through the frailer walls of their English neighbors.

It has been said that in the log house these settlers introduced in America what became the archetypal home of the pioneer east of the Missouri. But this is only the most famous instance of their adaptability. Some of them, at least, had experience in clearing fields of trees, in making shoes of bark, and in using wood splinters to illuminate their homes. An adage is still popular to the effect that every Finn is a carpenter, so the production of wooden goods from plates to flails to furniture was no great problem.

The great problem was to find hands to do the work and realize the possibilities of this new land. Printz begged for more people—soldiers to man his forts, farmers to till the soil, and especially women. There were, he reported in 1647, twenty-eight freemen settled on their own farms, with livestock, but they lacked wives. With wives and children and farms of their own, the settlers would be content in the New World; otherwise most colonists wanted to return to Sweden.

For one reason or another—war, lack of population pressure, the perilous voyage—these appeals for colonists went unanswered. In 1647, after nine years of settlement, there were but 183 men, women, and children in the whole of New Sweden, which was a weak array of farms and forts strung along the Delaware.

Yet this frail Scandinavian colony survived, or at least its people did, though stronger and more promising colonies were abandoned or destroyed. Some of the colonists did desert to the English or the Dutch, and most or all would willingly have gone home to Sweden at one time or another if they could have. But in America they thought themselves a people apart, with their own customs, language, and religion. The cultural unity of the settlers was fortified by the presence of Swedish Lutheran pastors sent to America in an unending series until after the American Revolution.

The first Lutheran church seems to have been built at Fort Christina by 1643. One of the early pastors, Johan Campanius Holm, distinguished himself by acquiring some competence in the Delaware Indian language, of which he prepared a vocabulary and phrase book. In his zeal for converts, he was the first Protestant minister in America to translate a catechism into an Indian tongue. When he returned to Sweden, Campanius was succeeded by Lars Karlsson Lock, who was later viewed as a troublemaker by the English.

These Swedish pastors were expected to be teachers of more than religion, and thanks to them the population did not surrender to illiteracy. In the years of New Sweden there were usually two clergymen serving less than two hundred persons, so despite the scattered nature of the settlements, the clergy could exert considerable influence.

While Printz ruled the colony, the government of New Sweden was both arbitrary and efficient. Before he came, there had been controversies and division of authority, but Printz was the unquestioned administrative and judicial head, and his position was recognized by the Crown, which paid him four times as much as anyone else. His duties, as he recognized, were too diverse for one man and he pleaded for an assistant who could handle his correspondence with neighboring colonies, conducted largely in Latin, or for one who could be put in charge of the administration of justice, where Printz found himself both the state prosecutor and the judge.

The first courts were held at Fort Christina, and important cases were heard by a number of men, with the governor apparently presiding. In 1653 twenty-two colonists signed a protest against Printz, accusing him of brutal and avaricious conduct and of carrying on trade with the Indians and the Dutch for his private benefit. Printz's reaction was swift and savage; he had the leader of the protesters speedily arrested, tried, condemned, and executed.

The arbitrary character of New Sweden's government was modified by the fact that Swedish law was in effect and that there was a higher authority than the governor. But this authority was overseas and from 1647 to 1653 not one word was heard from it. No ship, no person, no letter arrived in the colony from Sweden in all that time. One expedition left Sweden in those six years, but its single ship, bearing many colonists, foundered en route.

It is a tribute to the ability of Johan Printz, as well as to the quality of the colonists, that New Sweden lived on, forlorn if not entirely forgotten. Its few hundred Swedish colonists had successfully planted European culture in a valley that was to become one of the most prosperous and most densely populated parts of America. They had, in their weakness and their wisdom, initiated a policy of peaceful relations with the aboriginal inhabitants, the Indians, which would furnish a pattern of behavior for their successors. And they had set in motion the train of events which would account, more directly than the brief existence of a settlement at Swanendael, for the emergence in due time of a separate state of Delaware.

2

THE DUTCH CONQUEST

The survival of New Sweden depended on the maintenance of good relations between the colonists and their neighbors. In this respect, Governor Printz did very well. Surrounded by potential enemies—Indians, Dutch, and English—Printz managed to uphold Swedish pretensions and yet keep the peace.

Printz was not devoted to peace for its own sake but was rather a realist who recognized he was too weak to pursue any other policy. He would probably have preferred destroying the Indians to treating with them. "They are a lot of poor rogues," he wrote home, requesting "a couple of hundred soldiers" to be stationed in New Sweden until they would "break the necks" of all the Indians in the valley.

Instead of "a couple of hundred soldiers," Printz had less than three dozen, so he adopted a peaceful policy toward the Indians, as did his predecessors and successors. There were times when the policy was sorely tried. In 1643 and 1644, for instance, three Swedes and Finns were killed near Fort Christina; early in 1655 a woman was murdered in the same area and property was stolen. Yet unlike the English in Virginia or the Dutch in New York, the Swedes consistently avoided war with the Indians.

Despite continued good relations, the New Sweden Company did not profit from Indian trade as it had hoped to do. In the early years, large shipments of furs were sent to Europe, but as time went on and Swedish vessels no longer came to the colony, the supply of trade goods ran out, and the Swedes unhappily watched the Dutch reestablish their control of the fur trade.

* * *

The Dutch, and the English too, viewed the Swedes as trespassers. But European politics long protected New Sweden, for both the Netherlands and England were to some degree aligned with Sweden in the Thirty Years War. This conflict lasted from 1618 to 1648, and it suited neither Dutch nor English policy to provoke the Swedes in that time.

When Printz arrived in 1643 he found Dutch and English settlements in the Delaware valley, the Dutch upstream at Fort Nassau and the English downstream on the Salem River, both in what later became New Jersey. Weak as he was, Printz handled the situation very diplomatically, devoting his efforts to hindering and limiting Dutch and English incursions in the valley. He had greater success with the English than with the Dutch.

In 1643, for instance, at Fort Christina, Printz seized an English crew that had mutinied and deserted Sir Edmund Plowden; they were turned over to the English authorities and taken to Virginia for punishment. In the same year and at the same fort Printz seized and tried George Lamberton, one of the leaders of the Delaware Company of New Haven which had planted the English settlement on the Salem River. A charge that Lamberton was inciting the Indians to murder the Swedes was dropped, but Lamberton was expelled from the area after being fined for trading with the Indians almost in sight of Fort Christina.

Neither Printz nor his successors could stop New Haven merchants from entering the Delaware; indeed the Swedes became increasingly dependent on traders from New England, the Chesapeake colonies, and New Netherland, as a proper supply of goods never came from Sweden. But the Swedes and the Dutch together, though willing to trade with the English, so discouraged their settlement that even the toehold of the New Haven merchants on Salem River was abandoned in the late 1640s.

The English did not altogether renounce their ambitions here. In 1654 a Maryland settler appeared at Fort Christina, warning the Swedes that the English claimed this land. In the same year a governor of New Haven wrote the Swedes of the claims his colony had to the Delaware. And just one year later nine adventurers from New England showed up, led here by a rumor that the Swedes were dead or departed. They were heard by a Swedish court and quickly expelled, but they were portents of the doom that shadowed the colony.

The death blow to New Sweden came from the very people who had inspired its birth; Dutch it had been, and to the Dutch it was returned.

Peter Stuyvesant, who became governor of New Netherland in 1647, was annoyed by the Swedish presence on the Delaware. He was experienced in colonial affairs through service in the West Indies, where armed combats were frequent and islands passed back and forth between the European powers like pieces in a game. He had also become crippled in such service, losing a leg in battle with the French on the island of St. Martin.

In North America, however, Stuyvesant was hampered by orders that he must not attack the Swedes: he should insist on Dutch rights and resist Swedish attacks but not disturb New Sweden as it existed. We must "arm ourselves with some patience sooner than make use of force against them, provided they do [not] invade our jurisdiction insolently," ran his instructions.

It was a special irritation to Stuyvesant that the Dutch post on the Delaware, Fort Nassau, was located on the wrong side of the river for the fur trade and potentially cut off from the ocean by Swedish forts downstream. Several Dutch efforts to establish footholds on the west short of the Deleware, particularly along the Schuylkill, which offered a route to the Indian country and the fur trade, were blocked in one way or another by the Swedes, who, though minuscule in number, still had more able-bodied men on the Delaware than the Dutch.

Then in the summer of 1651 Stuyvesant suddenly took measures to rectify this situation. Without consulting authorities in Holland, Stuyvesant sent a fleet of eleven vessels to the Delaware and marched an army of 120 men across New Jersey to Fort Nassau to join the fleet. After overawing the Swedes by sailing his fleet up and down the river, Stuyvesant proceeded with the plan, which was to fortify a point on the west shore of the Delaware, downstream from New Sweden, so that he and not Printz would now be in a position to control the river traffic. Some Indians were persuaded to grant the Dutch land on the river shore between the Christina and the bay. The same land had been sold twice before (to Godyn and to the Swedes), but the show of legality still seemed desirable as a prelude to Stuyvesant's next step, which was to abandon Fort Nassau and move its cannon, its garrison, and its stores to the Sandhook, on the west bank, about seven miles below Fort Christina. Here a fort, called Fort Casimir, was quickly built, and around it some two dozen Dutch colonists were settled.

Printz was enraged at the audacity of the Dutch, but there was nothing he could do. Temporarily the Dutch had the greater strength on the river, and by the time winter came and the last Dutch vessel left, the new settlement was well established. Printz fumed and protested, but he was too wary to attack Fort Casimir lest he bring the Dutch in force into the river again. The best way to deal with Stuyvesant, Printz foresaw correctly, was to populate the river with Swedes and simply crowd the Dutch out of it. The West India Company did not want the expense of a war where no quick profit was to be made. What Stuyvesant did to place the Dutch in an advantageous position in the Delaware valley, he did on his own.

The construction of Fort Casimir at Sandhook in the summer of 1651 was the foundation of New Castle, the village that became the colonial capital of Delaware. But for the time being it was only a feeble Dutch outpost, a potential rather than an actual threat to the survival of New Sweden.

Nevertheless, this weak fort was the straw that broke Printz's patience. Far from populating the Delaware, the Swedish government and the New Sweden Company were not even supplying their handful of existing colonists. War and resultant budgetary difficulties, compounded by Queen Christina's frivolities once she had come of age, as well as by Chancellor Oxenstierna's preoccupation with other matters, explain the Swedish government's peculiar neglect of the colony. New Sweden was now, in essence, a state enterprise and in being the whole kingdom's concern it suffered from being no one's concern in particular.

After six years of complete neglect Printz became desperate; he first sent his son Gustaf back to Sweden and then went himself. It was not an easy journey. Gustaf Printz went as supercargo on a Virginia ship leased by his father to take tobacco to Sweden. There, Gustaf reported personally to a revived government agency, the Commercial College, which had charge of all trade and navigation and was now under the presidency of Eric Oxenstierna, the chancellor's son. The college wrote to Governor Printz, promising relief shortly, asking him to stay in New Sweden temporarily, and appointing its secretary, Johan Classon Rising, to be his counsellor and assistant.

The promise came too late. In the fall of 1653 Printz, his wife, four of his daughters, the New Sweden Company's business agent, Hendrick Huygen, who was Minuit's brother-in-law, and about twenty-five soldiers and settlers traveled to New Amsterdam to take a Dutch ship to

Europe. It must have been annoying to Printz to be forced to seek homeward passage from the Dutch, the very people who were threatening to strangle his colony. During the trip, moreover, Printz encountered problems that were worse than just annoying. His ship took almost three months to cross the Atlantic and then made port in La Rochelle, France, leaking from the battering of winds and waves. It took Printz two months more to get from France to Amsterdam, by a voyage that went west and north of the British Isles to avoid seizure. Before he completed the final leg of his trip, from Amsterdam to Sweden, Printz learned a Swedish expedition was at long last under way to the New World.

Printz never returned to America. The government found new administrative assignments for him, and eventually he had the pleasure of being governor of the district in which he was born.

Word was sent to Johan Rising, commanding the new expedition, that he should take over the government of New Sweden from Printz's son-in-law, Johan Papegoya, who had been left in charge. Rising was a scholar and a civil servant with no grasp of military realities. When his ship, the *Eagle (Örn),* arrived in the Delaware in May 1654, Rising discovered that Fort Casimir was all but abandoned, little more than a symbol of Dutch authority on the river and a nucleus for a small community of Dutch farmers. There were but nine soldiers in the fort, and though there were a dozen or more cannon, no powder was on hand to fire them. The *Eagle,* on the other hand, carried between thirty-four and forty cannon and a crew of eighty men and had started out with 350 colonists aboard, including soldiers, though some had died on the way.

At this time Stuyvesant and his advisers at New Amsterdam were debating whether to withdraw from their Delaware River post before the English could seize it. They decided against withdrawal, but had the Swedes bypassed Fort Casimir or settled peacefully around it they might gradually have crowded the Dutch out of the river, as Printz had proposed. Printz was willing to use force, but to do so he required not only a sufficient number of soldiers but two warships permanently stationed in the Delaware. Rising had men but no ships, for the *Eagle* was due to return to Sweden shortly. He was, moreover, under orders to pursue a peaceful policy: secure both banks of the river, his instructions said, but without hostilities. If the Dutch could not be removed by argument, they should be tolerated and a fort erected downstream from Casimir in place of the abandoned Swedish Fort Elfsborg on the Jersey shore.

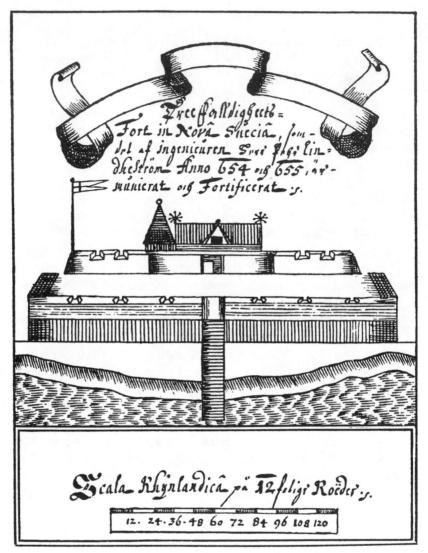

Fort Trinity, formerly Fort Casimir, at New Castle, 1655. A sketch by the Swedish engineer, Peter Lindeström, published in Amandus Johnson's edition of Lindeström, *Geographica Americae* (Philadelphia, 1925). Courtesy of the Eleutherian Mills Historical Library, Greenville.

Rising later argued that he captured Fort Casimir by peaceful means, but the argument seems specious. He demanded the fort's surrender and landed soldiers near it. While their commander, Sven Skute, negotiated with the Dutch commander, Swedish soldiers entered the open gates of the fort, disarmed the Dutch garrison, and raised the Swedish flag. Rising respected the land claims of all but two members of the Dutch farming community beside the fort, once they had taken an oath of allegiance to Sweden. But Casimir was a Swedish fort, and its name was changed to Fort Trinity, because it was captured on Trinity Sunday.

Following the capture of Fort Casimir, Rising's policies emphasized the Fort Christina area as the center of New Sweden. Most of the new colonists were settled between Fort Casimir and Fort Christina, where Rising himself resided, or up the Christina River beyond the fort and toward the Elk River, a tributary of the Chesapeake. Rising even purchased Indian lands along the Elk to give his colony a new western orientation. Behind Fort Christina, he divided the land into rectangular lots to form a village called Christinahamn.

Rising also proceeded to reinvigorate the government by holding courts and issuing ordinances regarding agriculture, forestry, livestock, and the like. Several times he assembled some representative men of the colony at Fort Christina to get their agreement to new ordinances, and apparently he won the support of both the Swedish and Finnish colonists, whose complaints against the absent Johan Printz were heard in Rising's court and forwarded to Sweden. But Rising's attempts to improve the position of New Sweden by diplomacy were a failure.

Rising asked the governor of Maryland to return colonists who had fled New Sweden to escape the harsh Printz regime, but the response was discouraging: a Maryland delegation at Fort Christina in June 1654 argued that this part of New Sweden belonged to them under Lord Baltimore's grant of 1632 and even cited Sir Edmund Plowden's grant to support English ownership of the entire valley. New Haven also pressed its claims to land on the Delaware when Rising sent delegates to this colony on Long Island Sound.

Fortunately for New Sweden, Anglo-Swedish relations in America were ameliorated by a treaty of April 11, 1654, between the two mother countries, providing for friendship between their colonies overseas. With the Dutch, however, Swedish relations were becoming worse. The end of the Thirty Years War in 1648 decreased Dutch need for a Swedish alliance and thereafter the Dutch began to side with Sweden's enemies, especially the Danes, in their jealousy of rising Swedish maritime strength in the Baltic. As for the colonies, when the Anglo-Dutch war ended in 1654 the Dutch West India Company felt free to encourage Stuyvesant not only to recapture Fort Casimir but to take all of New Sweden as well. In this same year, 1655, the Dutch began to seize a few posts the Swedes had established on the African coast.

By his seizure of Fort Casimir, Rising played into the hands of Stuyvesant, who appealed to Holland for permission to retaliate. When an emissary arrived from Rising with explanations and excuses, Stuyvesant put the worst interpretation possible on what had occurred and planned to make it an excuse to overthrow all Swedish authority on the Delaware and rid himself at last of this irritating presence.

While contemplating revenge, Stuyvesant had a stroke of good luck. The *Golden Shark (Gyllene Haj)* had set out from Sweden for America only two months after the *Eagle*. By accident or design on the part of the mate, a Dutchman, this ship, taking the usual southern route by the Antilles, sailed past the Delaware capes and into Raritan Bay, behind Staten Island. When the captain sent to New Amsterdam for a pilot, unaware of the recent trouble between Dutch and Swedes on the Delaware, he found he was not free to proceed. Ship and cargo were seized, and the immigrants aboard were persuaded to settle in the Manhattan area instead of New Sweden.

Rising could have used the colonists and supplies on the *Golden Shark* to strengthen his position. He had, of course, expected the assistance this ship would bring him, but as it happened he was destined never to receive any aid from Sweden. However, the New Sweden colony had already been greatly strengthened by the arrival of Rising and his party on the *Eagle*. The population, which had dwindled to less than a hundred by desertions, deaths, and the loss of the thirty or so colonists who had returned to Europe with Printz, was almost quadrupled by the new arrivals.

But still the Dutch were stronger. Approving Stuyvesant's capture of the *Golden Shark,* the West India Company sent him reenforcements in men and munitions, as well as a ship, the *Balance (Waag),* of thirty-six guns, with authorization to rent more ships for his expedition to the Delaware. Stuyvesant spent the winter and spring of 1655 in the Caribbean islands, which also lay under his jurisdiction, trying to improve the conditions of Dutch trade. He was ill when he returned to New Amsterdam in July 1655, but he soon had preparations under way for a military expedition to the Delaware. Drums were beaten daily to round up volunteers in the little Dutch capital on Manhattan Island, and every ship in the harbor was ordered to provide a few men for the expeditionary force. Though Stuyvesant tried to prevent news of his preparations from reaching the Swedes, Rising heard of them from Indian informers and sent scouts to spy on the Dutch from Staten Island.

Finally, late in August, a Dutch expedition of seven vessels, including the *Balance* and a hired French privateer, left New York Bay for the Delaware carrying 317 soldiers under Stuyvesant's personal command. The Swedes had strengthened Fort Casimir (Fort Trinity) and stocked it with arms, ammunition, and provisions. Sven Skute, who commanded the seventy-five man garrison, was ordered to challenge any ship coming up the river.

When the Dutch arrived on August 31, however, their fleet of seven vessels, the largest expedition ever seen in this valley, intimidated Skute, who withheld his fire. The Dutch sailed past the fort and landed troops to the north of it, cutting off the direct road to Fort Christina, where Rising had remained. Then Stuyvesant landed artillery, demanded Skute's surrender, and prepared to storm the fort when the Swedes tried to stall for time. Rising sent a small relief force from Fort Christina, but the Dutch surrounded it and captured all but two members who fled back across the river into the safety of the fort they had started from.

This skirmish on the Christina was the one armed conflict of the campaign. The only casualty at Fort Casimir was a Swedish soldier shot by one of his own officers for trying to desert by climbing the walls. The strength of the Dutch fleet, particularly the powerful flagship of thirty-six guns, and the size of the Dutch army, which was practically equal to the total adult male population of New Sweden, were overwhelming, particularly in view of the dispersion of Swedish strength over more than thirty miles of the valley. Rising was foolish in allowing a large portion of his fighting men and armaments to be cut off in Fort Casimir. If this fort could not command the river and keep the Dutch from sailing upstream, it should have been abandoned and the Swedish strength concentrated at Fort Christina, their main settlement.

Skute surrendered Fort Casimir on September 1, 1655, and his men were held as prisoners on the Dutch ships until they could be sent to New Amsterdam. After placing a garrison in the captured fort, the Dutch fleet moved into the Christina River to begin a siege of the Swedish

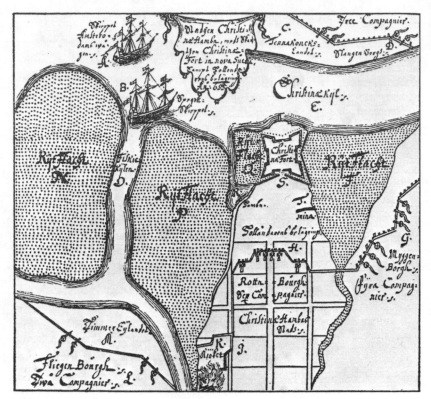

Siege of Fort Christina by the Dutch, 1655. The mouth of the Brandywine is to the left of the fort. Sketch by Peter Lindeström, published in his *Geographica Americae* (Philadelphia, 1925).

colonial capital. Dutch troops already stationed on the river bank opposite Fort Christina set up a battery and entrenched themselves. For a while Governor Rising hoped the Dutch were stopping there, limiting their claims to the land below the Christina and their former holdings around Fort Casimir.

He soon learned better. On September 5 the Dutch landed men in his rear, seizing all the fast land in the immediate vicinity and surrounding Fort Christina by land and by sea. As the Swedes labored to strengthen the fort's defenses the Dutch began firing regular volleys, apparently just to show their strength, for no damage was reported. An Indian carried a message from Stuyvesant to Rising demanding total surrender and removal of all Swedes from the Delaware valley unless they were willing to remain as subjects of the Dutch.

The situation of the rivals for control of the Delaware had become reversed. Rising had encouraged Dutch settlers to remain near Fort Casimir if they accepted Swedish rule, and now Stuyvesant offered similar terms to the Swedes. The outnumbered Swedes had only one round of ammunition on hand because so much had been sent to Fort Trinity. The walls of Fort Christina were not strong and with every passing day Swedish morale grew weaker as the soldiers saw or heard of Dutch depredations. The little village of Christinahamn, outside the walls, was burned. Up the Delaware the Dutch raided Swedish settlements and Indians looted Swedish farmhouses.

Rising spoke bravely of defying the Dutch and of resisting to the end, but he soon changed his mind. In two conferences with Stuyvesant, Rising argued that he would never have seized Fort Casimir had the Dutch offered any resistance, but such pleading did him no good. Terms of capitulation were worked out providing for free passage to Gothenburg of all settlers who wished it, respect of all private property, including that of the Swedish Crown and the New Sweden Company (except the claims of the company to the land), and continued residence and practice of their religion by the settlers who wished to stay in America. A special provision, apparently intended to be kept secret, provided that Rising and his commissary were to be taken to England or France and that Rising was to be advanced a sum of three hundred Flemish pounds against property of the New Sweden Company and the Swedish Crown.

At the very moment of victory, Stuyvesant was greatly embarrassed by news from New Amsterdam, where the Indians in the lower Hudson

valley had risen against the Dutch, weakened by the departure of most of
their soldiers. In three days 100 Dutch settlers were killed, 150 seized by
the Indians, and most Dutch farms abandoned as the residents fled to
New Amsterdam, which itself was in danger from Indians bands wandering over Manhattan Island outside the town.

Messages were sent at once to Stuyvesant, urging him to return to his
capital. If the Swedes had held out for one more week at Fort Christina,
Stuyvesant might have been compelled to abandon the siege. As it was,
the news he received from New Amsterdam led him to make a remarkable proposal: the return of Fort Christina and all the Swedish lands to the
northward to Swedish jurisdiction, with an offensive and defensive alliance between Swedes and Dutch, the latter retaining Fort Casimir and
the land to the south of the Christina. He offered, in essence, a return to
the state of affairs before Rising's arrival and seizure of the Dutch fort,
exactly the arrangement Rising suggested when he argued he would not
have taken Fort Casimir had he been compelled to use force.

Yet now Rising refused Stuyvesant's offer. After conferring with his
officers and some freemen, Rising declared he had no right to agree to an
alliance with Stuyvesant and that the losses suffered by Dutch and Indian
looting made it impossible to maintain New Sweden through the ap-
proaching winter. It was the officials who felt the weight of this last
argument; it meant nothing to the great majority of Swedish and Finnish
colonists, including the recent arrivals with Rising, for they stayed in
the colony and survived the winter very well. Rising and some of his
officers simply preferred to return to Sweden, complaining of Dutch
aggression, rather than maintain the colony as it was on their arrival and
before their aggressive action against Fort Casimir. Their selfishness
completed the fall of New Sweden.

On September 15, 1655, near Fort Christina, Stuyvesant and Rising
met to sign the capitulation, and at three o'clock on that afternoon the
Swedes marched out of the fort with drums beating, fifes playing, ban-
ners flying. In ensuing days Rising did his best to urge all Swedes to
return to their homeland, but he had little influence. In the end only
thirty-seven people comprised his party when he left New Amsterdam
for Europe on October 23.

As soon as he could, Stuyvesant sought to integrate the conquered province into New Netherland. By the end of the year 1655 a new regime
was established on the Delaware. The capital was moved from Swedish

Fort Christina to Dutch Fort Casimir and Jean Paul Jacquet, an official experienced in West India Company service in Brazil, was sent as vice-director under Stuyvesant. Two officials and two freemen served with Jacquet as an advisory council and court.

Beside Fort Casimir a town was developing that was soon called New Amstel, named for a town south of Amsterdam (now Amstelveen); it was to be for the next quarter century the economic and commercial center of the Delaware valley. Though only a small town and always of lesser importance than New Amsterdam, New Amstel gained significance because to reach the larger city, a voyage of several days or a difficult and often dangerous land transit through the unsettled backwoods of New Jersey was required.

Dutch rule increased the diversity of the population of the Delaware valley. Not only did Dutchmen settle beside the Swedes and Finns, but the Dutch, notorious slave traders, brought in Africans to satisfy the demands for labor. Also representatives of most of the people of western Europe came to Dutch America, generally from Amsterdam where they had first been drawn by the opportunities of that cosmopolitan center. Recent studies indicate that not more than 50 percent of even the white immigrants to New Netherland were Dutch by birth. Germans and Scandinavians made up a good part of the rest, with smaller elements of French, English, Scottish, and various other peoples.

The earliest inhabitants, the Swedes and Finns, prospered under Dutch rule, finding themselves less isolated than under neglectful Swedish control and now more easily able to acquire the goods they could not produce themselves. They even received an unexpected increment to their numbers in the spring of 1656, when the ship *Mercury (Mercurius)* arrived from Sweden, carrying over one hundred colonists (including thirty-one women and thirty-two children), mostly Finns, selected from double that number who came to Gothenburg in hope of a passage to America. Now, when it was too late, colonial life in America had gained popularity in Sweden.

When the *Mercury* left Gothenburg, the Dutch seizure of New Sweden had not yet been reported. Papegoya and Huygen, commanding the expedition, were astonished to find the Dutch in control of the Delaware. Their request to land the colonists till they could get further orders from Sweden was denied by Dutch authorities. However, local Swedes and Finns encouraged Indians to board the *Mercury* and then persuaded the master to run the ship upstream past Fort Casimir and unload his passengers. Jacquet, commanding the fort, was afraid to fire at the passing ship with Indians on its deck lest he precipitate at once a Swedish revolt and an Indian war. By the time Stuyvesant and his council on Manhattan Island learned what had happened, the deed was done. The colonists were allowed to remain on the Delaware, but the *Mercury* was required to bring its cargo to New Amsterdam and pay duty on it.

Decidedly outnumbered on the Delaware by Swedish and Finnish settlers, the Dutch were forced to be considerate of them. With English and Indian neighbors a constant threat to New Netherland, responsible officials did not wish to alienate a settled, modestly prosperous people who gave no trouble as long as they were left to themselves.

The Dutch did keep watch on the Swedes in the early years after the conquest, with the intention of expelling troublemakers or at least removing them to New Amsterdam. In 1658 Stuyvesant himself came to the Delaware to examine conditions there. He insisted that all the colonists swear allegiance to the Netherlands government but, at the request of the Swedes, he agreed to allow them to be exempt from taking sides in any conflict that might occur between Sweden and the Netherlands. This exemption bothered the Amsterdam directors of the West India Company, who wrote Stuyvesant that they preferred to see the Swedes disarmed and scattered among the Dutch settlers, so that they would have little chance to conspire together. The Amsterdam directors were even more disturbed at the idea that the Swedes should have their own officers.

In answer, Stuyvesant argued for a practical policy:

> We have good reason to believe . . . that neither the Swedes nor the English [on Long Island] who live under our jurisdiction . . . have a great affection for this State . . ., but how to . . . improve [this situation], Right Worshipful Gentlemen, *hoc opus hoc labor est*. We have thought the most suitable would be a lenient method of governing them and proceeding with them, to win their hearts and divert their thoughts from a hard and tyrannical form of government. [Therefore they are allowed their own officers] that in time of necessity, against the savages and other enemies, . . . they might keep order.

Colonial realities overcame European directives, and the Swedes were allowed to stay where they were. Gradually their numbers increased, both by natural increase and by immigration. Letters sent home encouraged more Swedes and Finns to come to America and, despite Dutch apprehensions, the need for colonists was so great that Dutch authorities allowed some reenforcement of the Scandinavian element on the Delaware. In 1663, for instance, thirty Swedes and thirty-two Finns emigrated to the Delaware.

Dutch settlement on the Delaware came largely through the efforts of the city of Amsterdam. In this city there were merchants, like Samuel Godyn a quarter century earlier, who believed that profit could be made from an American colony. They were also particularly concerned in 1656 with the warlike policy of Charles X of Sweden, who had attacked Poland, source of the Dutch grain trade. So on February 12, 1656, the Amsterdam city council appointed a committee "on the occasion of the present war in Poland" to inquire into the improvement of trade with New Netherland.

The committee's report was encouraging: ". . . the climate there is very mild and healthy, entirely agreeable to the constitutions of the inhabitants of this country [the Netherlands], also by nature adapted to the production of all kinds of products and crops which now have to come from the Baltic." All that the land required, the committee was told, was immigrants—people to reap the harvest of riches America could produce.

The West India Company had emphasized war and commerce, not settlement. Nor was it financially in any position to become a land developer; indeed, it was already in debt to the city of Amsterdam for assistance with the expedition to conquer New Sweden. A bargain was quickly struck and ratified by the States General in August 1656. For the sum of 700,000 guilders the company sold to the city of Amsterdam the land on the west shore of the Delaware from Bombay Hook, the head of Delaware Bay, to the Christina River, including Fort Casimir.

Two other tracts of land had been considered, one high up the Hudson and the other on the east bank of the Delaware. Amsterdam preferred a site on the Delaware, where "the soil is richest but the population smallest." Of the two Delaware River sites the one on the west shore was preferable because there was already a fort on the site.

Immediately the city set about peopling the new colony, convinced that all the Baltic products on which Amsterdam depended—"masts included"—could be procured from the Delaware valley. To attract immigrants the city council offered free land, with exemptions from taxation (except for the company's tariff) for ten years, timber for building, seed and clothing for one year, passage money (to be repaid later), supplies at reasonable prices, a smith, a wheelwright, a carpenter, a schoolmaster who will "read the Holy Scriptures and set the Psalms," and some popular participation in government at the local level, much as in Holland.

Settlers were found, but too often they were traders and artisans rather than the farmers who were most needed in America. Dutch farmers had good markets for their crops at home, and the farmer's son who was restless found greater attraction in the shops of Amsterdam or the newly reclaimed polders of North Holland than in the forests of America.

Not until the spring of 1657 did the city of Amsterdam take over control of its new colony, and meanwhile Vice-Director Jacquet established Dutch government on the Delaware. He met with his council of four men frequently, more than forty times in fifteen months. Their normal duties involved adjudicating quarrels over small debts, disciplining the soldiers, preventing the sale of liquor to Indians, and ensuring observation of the Sabbath.

Twice public meetings were held, the nearest approach to New England town meetings in colonial Delaware. The first, in November 1656, is remarkable as the forerunner of popular elections in this area. Two fence inspectors and four tobacco inspectors were nominated. As far as is known the choice of fence inspectors was final, but in the case of tobacco inspectors an electoral custom was introduced called "double nomination" that continued to be a feature of Delaware politics into the nineteenth century. This practice was a type of indirect election. The people nominated twice the number to be chosen; the vice-director chose from the nominees. In the eighteenth century, long before the practice was abandoned, it was, in effect, negated by the custom of choosing the man with a plurality of votes. In the Dutch period a more independent selection among the nominees was probably normal.

The choice of fence inspectors indicates the multiplication of livestock in the Delaware valley, for it was the straying of hogs and goats, in particular, that made ordinances requiring the fencing of farms and town lots necessary. Perhaps Jacquet also endeavored to have land claims bounded so that a tax of twelve stivers a morgen (slightly more than two acres) could be collected, both for revenue and to restrain "the immoderate desire for land." Tobacco inspectors were needed because the West India Company taxed tobacco imports and exports. It hoped, with good reason, that even if the Delaware area should not quickly fill with tobacco plantations as prosperous as those of the lower Chesapeake, it might become the center of a tobacco trade, with imports brought by land or by sloop from Maryland and exports sent directly to Amsterdam.

Jacquet used this first known public meeting on the Delaware not only for nominations but also to obtain community agreement and cooperation in the strengthening of Fort Casimir and in construction of a bridge over a small creek nearby. Early in the winter he called another public meeting. "The whole community" gathered with the vice-director and his council to agree on prices to be paid the Indians for furs and hides, lest the trade should be ruined by extravagant prices offered by rich men. Thirty-two men signed this agreement (eleven of them, being illiterate, by a mark), and two men are said to have dissented.

Dissatisfaction arose with Jacquet in the last months of his administration. High prices, trade restrictions, complaints from men hired to work for the company or Jacquet on shares, and dissastisfaction with his handling of damage claims were grounds for charges to Stuyvesant against the vice-director. Some settlers moved to Manhattan or across the peninsula to Maryland.

When the new colonists sent by the city of Amsterdam arrived at New Amstel in the spring of 1657 they found only twenty families, mostly Swedes, settled around the old Dutch fort. With the coming of this expedition, the settlements on the Delaware were divided into two colonies. Below the Christina River, centered on New Amstel (modern New Castle) was the colony administered by the city of Amsterdam, sometimes referred to by the name of its chief town. With the arrival of the 150 people of the city's first expedition, this "City Colony" became predominantly Dutch.

North of the Christina River lay a second colony, predominantly Swedish and Finnish in population, still administrated by the Dutch West India Company. Isolated from New Amsterdam by the unsettled wilderness of New Jersey, this "Company Colony" was administered by a deputy appointed by Stuyvesant who made old Fort Christina, now called Altena, his headquarters.

Because of complaints, Jean Paul Jacquet was relieved of all administrative responsibility when the new colonial administration was begun, though he lived out his life on a farm below the Christina. His successor at New Amstel was Jacob Alrichs, who had previous colonial experience in Brazil and soon set about making improvements and providing for the new settlers who came with him or arrived soon afterward on the Amsterdam ship, *Balance*. The fort was strengthened, public buildings were constructed, and plots of land were assigned by lot, with the stipulation that individuals should begin building on them within six months. After shelter and gardens were provided, fields were distributed, again by lot, in whatever quantity a man could use, with improvements to be under way in two years.

Greater provision for elections was made in the new government of the City Colony than had been known under Jacquet's administration. Three burgomasters were to be "appointed by the common burghers from the honestest, fittest and richest." Five or seven schepens or magistrates (roughtly equivalent to the English justices of the peace) were to be selected by the director from a double number nominated by the burghers. Finally, when the population of New Amstel amounted to two hundred families, twenty-one councilmen were to be elected for life. These councillors would thereafter form a sort of closed corporation, governing the colony with the burgomaster and schepens, filling vacancies in their own numbers caused by death, and annually choosing burgomasters and nominating a double number of schepens.

The council of twenty-one was never elected at New Amstel, probably because the population never reached two hundred families. But Alrichs did make use of a small executive council of officials, and in 1657 seven councilmen were elected and from them three schepens. In the contract drawn up to encourage settlement, the Amsterdam authorities specifically reserved to themselves the appointment of "the secretary, messenger, and other inferior persons," so it seems likely that minor appointments originated in Amsterdam or with Alrichs, acting for the Amsterdam authorities.

Alrichs's relationship with Stuyvesant was difficult because the City Colony was not entirely separate but held by the city of Amsterdam as a fief of the West India Company. The difference in the supervision of the two colonies in Holland was not very great. The city of Amsterdam was run by the merchants; they dominated the city council, which appointed two of its members to serve as commissioners supervising the colony. The West India Company gave control of New Netherland to its Amsterdam chamber, composed, like the city council, of Amsterdam merchants, and the chamber set up a committee to supervise the colony. Company Colony and City Colony were directed by the same sort of people, though not by exactly the same individuals. Neither colony yielded great profit.

In North America the relationship was more complex, because the City Colony was to some degree dependent upon the Company Colony. Not only was the City Colony inferior de facto because it had less real strength—fewer settlers, soldiers, supplies, ships—than the older colony; it was also legally inferior, because quarrels could, in serious cases, be appealed from the court at New Amstel to Stuyvesant and his council at New Amsterdam; it was fiscally inferior, because a duty to the West India Company had to be paid on imports and exports to New Amstel.

By 1658, when Alrichs had been at New Amstel for a year, Stuyvesant began to hear disquieting reports. There were now roughly six hundred people in the New Amstel colony, but their proper relationship to the West India Company was not being observed. The oaths required of new settlers contained no reference to the company or to its officials in America; appeals to Stuyvesant and his council were refused; removals to Altena and the Company Colony forbidden; and, worst of all in Stuyvesant's view, duties were not being paid on imports or on exports (such as furs).

Peter Stuyvesant was a vigorous man. He had already traveled over his colonial jurisdiction from Albany to Curaçao, so it was in character for him to visit the two colonies on the Delaware in the spring of 1658. In the Company Colony he met with leaders of the old colonists he had conquered and engaged to protect. Then at New Amstel, the capital he had founded, he interviewed Alrichs. "Many things there," he reported to the company after returning to New Amsterdam, were "not as they ought to be."

Stuyvesant decided to send a personal emissary to represent him on the Delaware and to function as vice-director of the Company Colony, residing at Altena, and also as customs collector for both colonies, with his customs office at New Amstel. William Beeckman, a schepen at New Amsterdam, received this assignment, a sensitive one since his responsibility stretched over both the City Colony and the Company Colony; he was the resident commander of the latter, but he had only limited authority in the former.

Alrichs had foreseen the underlying difficulty when he proposed, a year earlier, that the whole river valley be placed under one government. He was especially eager that Dutch settlers should take up all the good land available before English interlopers moved in, and he urged attention to the area called the Whorekill (spelled Hoeren-Kil and in other ways by the Dutch), site of the unfortunate Swanendael settlement, "a very fine and excellent country, . . . so good and fertile that the like is nowhere to be found."

In time his recommendation was accepted. But before it was, Dutch authorities had a fright when some Englishmen turned up at the Whorekill. Apparently they were fugitives from Virginia or Maryland who came in two small boats and were captured by the Indians. Alrichs paid a ransom and brought them to New Amstel, where they stayed for several months. As Alrichs observed, the English had "an eye to land lying on this side the Virginia river," meaning the Chesapeake. The Amsterdam commissioners responded quickly, and at their request Alexander D'Hinoyossa, an army officer representing Alrichs and the city, and Vice-Director Beeckman, representing Stuyvesant and the company, traveled to the Whorekill and found Indians who sold them the already much sold land from Bombay Hook to Cape Henlopen. Later in the same year, 1659, a small Dutch garrison was posted on what is now Lewes Creek. Swanendael lived again.

As Stuyvesant had noticed, many things in the New Amstel colony were not as they ought to be. Despite the successful efforts of the Amsterdam commissioners to send colonists, the colony did not prosper. To some extent the early years of the City Colony seem to repeat the early years of Jamestown, if not of Fort Christina and a dozen other footholds in the New World. The colonists were the wrong sort, ill-prepared for life in America and poorly led. Send farmers, wrote Alrichs again and again, industrious men, accustomed to the agricultural life. "We have no sawyers," he complained on one occasion; "[and our] brickmaker is dead."

The Amsterdam commissioners sent the colonists they could get, including children from the almshouse, but provisions were scarce and quickly exhausted. When artisans arrived, such as "weavers, tailors, shoemakers, buttonmakers," they found field labor too hard. "In consequence of laziness," wrote Alrichs, "they never prosper, and no payment is to be expected from them." To Alrichs the settlers' failure to pay their debts was a major problem for the colony. He tried to hold the settlers strictly to the conditions of their agreement with the city of Amsterdam: passage money was to be repaid, and all supplies after the first year.

With over five hundred settlers arriving in the first year, the colony's resources were bound to be hard-pressed. Inclement weather made the situation worse. When one hundred immigrants arrived in the fall of 1658, Alrichs complained of having so many mouths to feed. Winter began early that year and lasted long. Continuous rains prevented the gathering of fodder and did such damage to crops that even the veteran Swedish and Finnish farmers had little excess produce to sell.

Few if any Dutch settlers starved, but improper diet and shelter probably made them more susceptible to illness than they otherwise would have been. Agues and fevers spread through the colony, with the children particularly vulnerable. Alrichs's wife and one of his three councillors died. Among many others the miller also died, and there was a shortage of flour. The City Colony's vessel (a "galiot") was frozen in the ice and unable to bring provisions from New York. Another vessel bringing supplies from Virginia failed to arrive because the captain set off privateering.

Stuyvesant saw that Alrichs himself was at fault too. "Too great preciseness" was the way Stuyvesant spoke of the New Amstel director's weakness, by which he meant that Alrichs was too insistent on all the city's rights and privileges. Whether or not the director was indeed too rigid, his administration was clearly a failure. Death and desertion drained away New Amstel's population. Alrichs refused to permit his settlers to return to Holland or even move to Altena or Manhattan. His argument was that their removal meant the city lost the expense of their transportation, but he was accused of keeping even those who offered to pay their debts.

Nevertheless the settlers did flee. A population of six hundred in the City Colony in 1658 was reduced to one-third that number in a year. Settlers prevented from sailing to Manhattan (it was still very dangerous to go by land across New Jersey), could easily cross the peninsula into Maryland. Even the garrison of fifty soldiers which the city had supplied was halved by death and desertion, and despite the numbers of unemployed or underemployed colonists, Alrichs and his military commander, D'Hinoyossa, were not able to fill their ranks.

The flight of Dutch settlers to the Chesapeake called the attention of

Maryland authorities to the Delaware River. When Alrichs sent a letter to Maryland asking for the return of six Dutch soldiers who had fled from New Amstel, he stirred up a hornet's nest. It is a sign of the isolation of the Delaware settlers from those on the Chesapeake that Alrichs knew neither the name nor the address of the Maryland governor.

Alrichs sent his letter to Colonel Nathaniel Utie, a planter and Indian trader of significance, who was a member of the Maryland governor's council and resided on an island (Spesutie, or Utie's hope) at the mouth of the Susquehanna. The letter reminded Utie and Governor Josias Fendall that there were foreigners living on the edges of the Maryland patent, between 38° and 40°. Fendall, a restless, intriguing, ambitious man, ordered Utie to go to "the pretended Governor of a People seated in Delaware Bay" and demand he depart at once from this land on which the Dutch were mere trespassers. Further, he was to "insinuate unto the People there seated" that if they renounced Dutch rule and made a proper application to Fendall they would be protected "in theyr lives, libertys, and estates."

The mere news of Utie's coming weakened New Amstel, for fifty settlers had fled to Maryland or Virginia and at his arrival in September 1659, at the head of half a dozen men, barely thirty families and less than a score of soldiers remained. For several days Utie walked boldly around town, stirring up fright and dissension, before Alrichs, gathering his council and schepens and calling Beeckman down from Altena, invited the Marylander to a conference. There Alrichs and Beeckman attempted to justify the Dutch settlements, and when Utie swept their explanations aside, they asked time to confer with higher authorities. Utie granted them three weeks and departed, threatening to return with five hundred men.

Alrichs was frightened by his isolation, particularly when messengers he sent off across New Jersey were forced back by hostile Indians. "The citizens are few and disinclined to fight," he complained to Stuyvesant. "It is impossible to hold out here. . . . Please then not to let us come to grief. . . . We are living at their mercy." Beeckman was less nervous; nevertheless, since he had only fourteen soldiers at Altena he called on the Swedes upriver for assistance. They declined, answering that they were obliged to help only against Indians.

Stuyvesant sent sixty soldiers to New Amstel, along with a scolding to Alrichs for not arresting Utie for his insolence. Stuyvesant also sent two emissaries, Augustine Herrman and Resolved Waldron, to treat with the Maryland governor.

These men came to New Amstel and crossed the narrow peninsula (sixteen miles wide here) to the Elk River with the help of an Indian guide, for such was still the primitive state of settlement in the area. Aided by some Finnish refugees they found on the Sassafras River, they eventually crossed the Chesapeake to the western shore and were received by Governor Fendall on October 18, 1659. They explained the status of New Amstel as not a wholly separate but a subaltern colony, still part of New Netherland, which was responsible for its defense. On examining Lord Baltimore's patent they pointed to a flaw in it—something that was to be raised repeatedly through the next century—that though the outer limits of Maryland might seem to include most or all of the Dutch and Swedish settlements on the Delaware, these were specifically excluded because the grant was only to land uncultivated except by Indians. The Dutch, they told Fendall, were on the Delaware before the time of this grant. Though neither the Marylanders nor the Dutch emissaries had a very exact idea of the chronology of settlement, the Dutch claim was true.

There could be no agreement, because neither the English nor the Dutch had the power to yield any part of their claims, but the conversations were generally friendly. Herrman even had a chance for a private conversation with Philip Calvert, provincial secretary and brother of the proprietor, on the desirability of opening an easy land passage across the peninsula east of the Chesapeake. Before returning to New Amsterdam, Herrman, who was a Bohemian by birth, began working on a map of the Chesapeake Bay area (including Delaware) that eventually brought him fame and fortune. Philip Calvert, on succeeding to the governorship of Maryland, was so taken with Herrman's promise of a map that he gave the Czecho-Hollander a princely manor on the Eastern Shore. From this property, which he called Bohemia Manor, Herrman constructed a cart road via Appoquinimink Creek to the Delaware River. Herrman's road, known later as the Old Man's Road, helped the development of a close commercial connection between settlements on the Delaware and on the upper Chesapeake.

The immediate threat to the Dutch on the Delaware had evaporated. Utie never had five hundred men to lead against New Amstel, much as

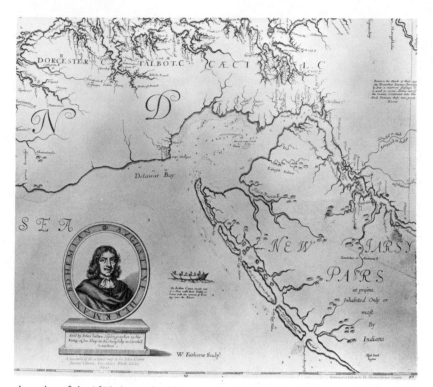

A section of the 1670 Augustine Herrman map of Virginia and Maryland showing the Delaware settlements and a self-portrait of Herrman. North is to the right of the map. The Maryland claim to lower Delaware is apparent. Photocopy from the Division of Historical and Cultural Affairs, Dover, based on a facsimile of a copy of the original edition in the John Carter Brown Library, Brown University, Providence, Rhode Island. Used by permission of the John Carter Brown Library, Brown University.

he might have enjoyed such a conquest, and Fendall lost his post as governor. Short-lived as the threat from Maryland was, New Amstel was all but ruined by it. Alrichs explained that agriculture was "thrown into a heap by the impending and all-destroying English War." He had a taste for the extravagant, as in writing "God Almighty has continually visited and punished the whole of New Netherland, but especially this Colony, since it was established. . . . This Colony has been oppressed and crushed . . . like a little willow in its beginning and sprouting."

What Alrichs saw as a divine malediction, other men blamed on his inactivity. The criticism seems fair, even though Alrichs had been ill intermittently for a year and finally succumbed to his illness on December 30, 1659. His chief assistants, perhaps excepting his relatives, were hard, selfish men who began before Alrichs was dead to complain behind his back to the commissioners in Amsterdam of his nepotism and inefficiency. Before Alrichs died, Alexander D'Hinoyossa, first councillor and commander of troops, was planning a trip to Amsterdam to inform the commissioners of the colony of Alrichs's incapacity. The trip was postponed when Alrichs's death gave D'Hinoyossa the opportunity that he coveted for sole command.

While Alrichs as director was petty and ineffective, his successor was harsh and domineering. Moving quickly to consolidate his authority at New Amstel, D'Hinoyossa dismissed many of Alrichs's officers, replacing them with men of his own choice. Very shortly a contest arose on the Delaware between D'Hinoyossa and the West India Company. The company's agent, Beeckman, was brushed aside by the new director of the City Colony. The cargoes of ships arriving at New Amstel were unloaded before Beeckman inspected them; his attempts to subpoena residents of New Amstel to his court at Altena were flatly repulsed.

Complaints mounted against D'Hinoyossa's haughty and insolent conduct. He was accused of seizing property from colonists without compensation, permitting the open sale of liquor to Indians, and refusing to prosecute his friends when they committed serious offenses. Religion, like morality, was at a low ebb in New Amstel, for after the Calvinist clergyman, Everardus Welius, died in December 1659, he was not replaced for a dozen years. A Dutch Lutheran minister who arrived in 1663 was apparently employed in the New Amstel area only as a catechist, or teacher, and did not conduct services.

Beeckman, in neighboring Altena, was shocked at D'Hinoyossa's disregard of the company by, for example, requiring ships passing New Amstel to lower their colors as though the city had jurisdiction over the river. D'Hinoyossa sought profit as well as power, selling everything he could lay his hands on, whether his own or not; he sold even the powder and musket balls from the fort to the Marylanders for tobacco. If Dutch authorities should treat him badly, he was said to have threatened that he would act "like one Minnewit [Minuit] . . . who, because he had not been treated well by the Company, had brought the Swedes here, adding, 'So I will go and fetch the English or them of Portugal, the Swede or the Dane, what the devil do I care whom I serve; I will get my revenge!' "

These reports come, of course, from D'Hinoyossa's enemies, but they were legion. Yet there must have been some positive achievements to this fierce soldier's credit since he managed to hold power for four and a half years. He did, indeed, as even his traducers attest, increase trade, particularly with Maryland. With the cart road between the two colonies under way, D'Hinoyossa took up land near its route along Appoquinimink Creek.

Apparently he also averted the shortages that had occurred under Alrichs; there is less oppressive talk of illness and death in the new regime. In 1660 Schout Gerrit Van Sweeringen (a schout combined most of the duties of an English sheriff and a prosecuting attorney) traveled to Amsterdam and persuaded that city's authorities to enlarge the powers of the New Amstel government, particularly in relation to New Amsterdam. Criminal cases hereafter were not to be appealed to Stuyvesant and his council, and in civil cases the final jurisdiction of the New Amstel schepens (before appeal to New Amsterdam) was enlarged. The city was also given additional rights in respect to direct trade with the colony and eventually was allowed to appoint its own customs collector, though he still had to take an oath of loyalty to the company.

The secret of D'Hinoyossa's success lay in his cultivation of good relations with the Amsterdam commissioners charged by the city council with adminstration of the colony. He held out before them the promise of a colony that would not only support itself but be a source of profit to Amsterdam. Gradually as the population and trade of New Amstel grew it offered an increasingly better market for European products and promised to realize its potential as a source of raw materials. The flow of immigrants also continued: in 1663, for example, when D'Hinoyossa himself went to Holland, he returned with one hundred and fifty new colonists, of diverse nationalities.

The most important result of D'Hinoyossa's voyage in 1663 was not the new immigration, however, but an agreement by the West India Company to cede the whole Delaware River valley to the city of Amsterdam. Despite bad reports on D'Hinoyossa that were forwarded by Stuyvesant, the Delaware River colony was a bothersome expense that the company was glad to be rid of, particularly if it could be disposed of without bringing the English closer to Manhattan. The city, on the other hand, saw that there could be economies in treating the whole valley as a unit. New Netherland was a costly colony; if the cost of a part of it, the Delaware valley, and especially its defense, could be turned over to the wealthy city of Amsterdam, the company would have a better chance of making a profit on the colony.

D'Hinoyossa's visit in Holland in June and July 1663 did not itself bring about the consolidation of the Delaware valley settlements into one colony; his visit was merely one contributing factor to a compaign he had initiated by correspondence long before he left America. For months previously the city and the West India Company had been reviewing the status and the relationship of their North American colonies. Early in February 1663, the company agreed to cede to the city both shores of the river from the ocean to its source, with the understanding that the city would replace the troops the company kept at Altena and would also provide at least four hundred new settlers each year.

A committee of the Amsterdam city council reported enthusiastically on the potentialities of the colony, "it being beyond contradiction the finest country in the world," their report declared, "where everything can be produced that is grown in France or the Baltic, and which can in course of time be as great as both these kingdoms together." An abundance of colonists was the only need, and they were available in the refugees thronging to Holland because of hard times in Germany and Norway or from religious persecution in France and Savoy. "Trade will come," they were sure, "not only from the city's colony but from the English who offer, if we will trade with them, to make a little slit in the door, whereby we can reach them overland" in case the English navigation laws put an end to trade by sea.

The city of Amsterdam, company directors explained to Stuyvesant, shows zeal and vigor, will populate the land quickly, and will help bring pressure on the Dutch government to arrange a boundary settlement with the English. The latter hope was a vain one, but the city's zeal in sending out colonists is undeniable.

One group of colonists whom the city assisted was a group of Mennonites, followers of an idealist named, as written in English, Peter Cornelisson Plockhoy, who planned a utopian, pacifist community on the Delaware. When Plockhoy, speaking for twenty-four families, petitioned the city of Amsterdam for assistance in establishing them on the Delaware, the city council agreed to lend one hundred guilders per family, plus free transportation for the women and children, free land, and exemption from taxes for twenty years. Forty-one Mennonites, including Plockhoy, were brought to America in 1663 on the ship *St. Jacob* and were landed in July at the Whorekill on Delaware Bay.

The same ship that brought the Mennonite colonists landed fifty farm laborers and twelve young women at New Amstel. And the same Amsterdam commissioners who aided Plockhoy's antislavery, egalitarian colonists, made arrangements to increase the number of black slaves on the Delaware. The Dutch West India Company, which profited most in these years from its West African commerce, had a thriving slave trade, centered on the island of Curaçao, where cargoes from Africa were forwarded to the best market. In 1664 the Amsterdam commissioners contracted for a shipment of at least sixty black farm hands, or one-fourth of the cargo of the *Gideon,* which arrived at New Amsterdam on August 15. The fourth part turned out to be thirty-eight men and thirty-four women, who were delivered to Peter Alrichs, nephew of Jacob Alrichs and commissary of West Indian cargoes for the City Colony. Alrichs was also empowered to buy oxen, cows, and horses in Manhattan.

There were, by 1663, 2,000 cows and oxen, 20 horses, 80 sheep, and several thousand swine on the 110 plantations in the Delaware valley, whether kept by Swedes, Finns, or Dutch. The land could produce all kinds of grain and many types of fruit. Two or three breweries were operating, with the brew much in demand in Maryland. One thousand tubs of tobacco could be purchased each year from Maryland and about ten thousand furs from the Indians. So D'Hinoyossa reported when he visited Holland and aroused new enthusiasm there for the City Colony.

When he arrived back in America in the fall of 1663, prospects for the City Colony in general and for its director in particular seemed very good. The Amsterdam commissioners reported to the burgomasters that finally, after great expense, the colony exhibited a favorable appearance, with the capability "of producing all sorts of Baltic commodities and other foreign productions. About 7,500 bushels of wheat were to be expected here from thence within two years, after which it will increase and improve more and more every year, and therefore will realize an annual profit of several thousands."

Even in relations with Maryland, all seemed serene. At the restoration of the Stuarts the Baltimore patent had been confirmed and representations had been made with the West India Company in Holland against trespassing on the Maryland grant. But the company stood up for its rights: no one was exactly sure where the proper boundaries should be; and the need for a common Indian policy and the attractions of trade led to a series of visits back and forth between the upper Chesapeake and New Amstel. D'Hinoyossa had helped the Marylanders reach peaceful agreement with the Delaware Indians, and they had shown great eagerness for the "Dutch trade, [it] being," as the Maryland council declared, "the Darling of the People of Virginia as well as this Province." There were rumors to the effect that the Marylanders were interested in a peaceful boundary settlement, rumors probably spread abroad by D'Hinoyossa, and quite possibly true. Stuyvesant was irked that he knew nothing of D'Hinoyossa's negotiations. Boundary settlement or not, it was incontrovertible that a Maryland delegation of three men, including the provincial secretary, visited New Amstel and Altena in September 1661, and the new governor of Maryland, Charles Calvert, son and heir of Cecilius, Lord Baltimore, visited New Amstel and Altena in August 1663 with an entourage of twenty-seven men.

In both cases the visit to Altena was merely incidental; New Amstel and the City Colony dominated the Delaware valley. On December 22, 1663, a deed was executed at New Amsterdam formally conveying all the land on both shores of the Delaware "from the sea upwards to as far as the river reaches, . . . especially also Fort Altena," to the City Colony. Beeckman was transferred to a post on the Hudson.

On the Delaware D'Hinoyossa was now in unchallenged control. What great possibilities may he have foreseen for his colony under stern, vigorous leadership, with the support of the wisdom and riches of the first commercial city in Europe? Yet within a year all of these prospects were ruined.

3

THE DUKE OF YORK'S COLONY

James, Duke of York and Albany, heir to the English throne, was annoyed with the Dutch on several counts. First, when in exile from England he had resided for a time in Holland but had been made so uncomfortable there that he was forced to continue his travels. Second, and more recently, as governor of the African Company he had found the Dutch to be annoying and even militant competitors for the trade of the West African coast, especially the trade in slaves.

He was therefore quite happy when his royal brother, Charles II, determined to grant him a large area of the American coast, consisting of two major sections, one from the St. Croix to Pemaquid (much of what was to become the state of Maine) and another from the west side of the Connecticut to the east side of the Delaware, along with a number of offshore islands, including Nantucket, Martha's Vineyard, and Long Island.

The exact dimensions of the grant are a puzzling business on a number of counts. For instance, the grant from the Connecticut to the Delaware, together with Long Island, was obviously intended to take care of New Netherland. Yet the English did indeed already occupy the west bank of the Connecticut and some distance beyond it (for example, the New Haven Colony), and the king had recently recognized this by a charter given to Connecticut. The Dutch domains, furthermore, did not halt at the Delaware but continued on to its western side.

Geographic confusions, purposeful or not, did not deter His Royal Highness. As Lord High Admiral he was in a position to act quickly upon the grant of March 12, 1664. Four ships were assigned to the duke's service, and on them 450 soldiers embarked under command of Colonel

Richard Nicolls, a faithful companion of the duke in his exile, a tested soldier, and now an officer of the duke's household. With Nicolls went three other gentlemen as a commission of four to investigate conditions in New England, where the propensity to commonwealth government disturbed true royalists.

Rumors of this fleet's departure came early to Stuyvesant, who began calling for troops and supplies from outlying posts, such as New Amstel. From Amsterdam, however, came the comforting but erroneous advice that the rumors were untrue and that the English were concerned with New England alone. Stuyvesant abandoned his preparations, which were probably insufficient anyway, and he was consequently surprised by the arrival of the English, with a demand for his surrender, in August 1664. New Amsterdam was then practically defenseless and its residents unwilling to sacrifice themselves for a lost cause, particularly when they learned that Nicolls, who was reenforced by militia from New England and from the English towns of Long Island, offered them protection as well as peace.

Thus circumstanced, Stuyvesant surrendered on Monday, August 29. Sly King Charles rejoiced when told of English victories in America and also on the African coast over the Dutch, with whom England was officially at peace. "Fresh news comes of our beating the Dutch at Guinny quite out of their castles almost, which will make them quite mad here at home sure," noted Navy Secretary Samuel Pepys in his diary on September 29, 1664. "And Sir G. Carteret did tell me, that the King do joy mightily at it; but asked him laughing, 'But,' say he, 'how shall I do to answer this to the Embassador when he comes?' Nay they say that we have beat them out of the New Netherlands too; so that we have been doing them mischief for a great while in several parts of the world, without publique knowledge or reason."

The duke's contest with the Dutch was also a contest between London merchants, whom the duke represented, and Amsterdam merchants, whom they wished to expel from the Atlantic seaboard. This meant expulsion not only from the colony directed by the Amsterdam chamber of the West India Company but also from the colony on the Delaware directly controlled by the Amsterdam city council and the loss with these two colonies of that illicit Anglo-Dutch trade which was "the Darling of the People of Virginia" and its English neighbors.

Very shortly after New Amsterdam had surrendered, its conqueror,

Colonel Nicolls, dispatched expeditions to its two chief satellites on the North American continent, Fort Orange (renamed Albany when captured) and New Amstel. Sir Robert Carr, a colleague of Nicolls in the royal commission of four to investigate New England affairs, was placed in charge of ships and soldiers sent to the Delaware. Two of Nicolls's four ships were assigned to this expedition, the *Guinea,* of thirty-six guns, his most powerful, and the *William and Nicholas,* of ten guns, and with them went all the soldiers not in the fort at New York or on the way to Albany, probably somewhat less than two hundred men.

The voyage from Manhattan to the Delaware was "long and troublesom," prolonged by the ignorance of the pilots and the "sholeness of the water," according to Carr. He left New York soon after September 3, 1664, and did not arrive at New Amstel until September 30. When Carr reached the Dutch capital on the Delaware he passed right by it, going upstream first to establish relations with the Swedes, whom he was especially instructed to placate with assurance of King Charles's "good inclination" to their nation and congratulationf on a "happy return under a Monarchicall government."

The Swedes, in Carr's words, "were soone our frinds," and three days of conversations satisfied most colonists with the terms Carr offered, which were recognition of their property rights with the same privileges as under the city of Amsterdam, liberty of conscience in religion, freedom of trade as allowed Englishmen under the acts of Parliament, and government through their own local magistrates for at least six months, all on condition of peaceful submission.

But D'Hinoyossa would not submit. At the beginning of the negotiation he was hopeful that his diplomatic skills and his good relations with the English of Maryland would win him special consideration, perhaps even a position of some authority. He ordered four chickens roasted and a ham boiled and had a nine-gun salute fired when the English came ashore to parley. But his attentions to the English were wasted. In Sir Robert Carr, D'Hinoyossa was dealing with a man who had extravagant ambitions of his own. There was no room on the Delaware for both of them.

The parley failing, 130 English soldiers were landed above New Amstel under John Carr, a relative of Robert, and sent around to the rear of the fort, where its defenses were weakest. The two ships then dropped downstream sufficiently to fire two broadsides, and at the fire the English soldiers stormed the fort, climbing over its palisades. The

Dutch soldiers in the fort, to the number of about thirty, made no attempt to fire their cannon at the ships (perhaps because D'Hinoyossa had sold so much of their powder to Maryland), but they did exchange some fire with the troops climbing into their fort. However, the defenders did no damage and were quickly overwhelmed. There were no English casualties, but three Dutch soldiers were killed and ten were wounded.

There is some mystery as to why the Dutch would fight against such odds, thirty men against one hundred and thirty, fourteen cannon in the fort, poorly supplied, against forty-six, well supplied, on the English ships. The fort itself, as Carr testified after the surrender, was "not tenable . . . without a great charge." On the other hand, a muster before the English ships appeared had turned out ninety civilians, a number that would have made the ranks more nearly equal had they joined the soldiers in defending New Amstel. Possibly D'Hinoyossa counted on these men coming to his aid and on being joined by more citizen soldiers from up the river. Or, more likely, he was moved to fight by the stubborn intransigence he had already exhibited as governor.

"Your first care," Colonel Nicolls instructed Sir Robert Carr, "is to protect the inhabitants from injuries as well as violence of the soldiers." The resistance of D'Hinoyossa, however, subjected New Amstel to some plundering. Once the English soldiers had stormed the fort they could not be stopped when they found its storehouses full of trade goods: cloth, wine, brandy, stockings, shoes, shirts, etc. The sailors soon joined them, and for a time, as Carr admitted, commands could not or would not be heard. What the soldiers and sailors did not seize, Carr took for himself, for his officers, or for the Crown. All together, according to an official of the City Colony, Carr and his men in the New Amstel neighborhood seized £4,000 sterling, 100 sheep, 30 to 40 horses, 50 to 60 cows and oxen, 60 to 70 African slaves, the year's farm produce, such as hay and corn, all sorts of tools for artisans and farmers, a brewhouse and a still-house, a sawmill ready to be set up, besides 9 sea buoys with iron chains, cannon, arms, powder, and shot. The Dutch soldiers themselves were taken on a merchantman to the Chesapeake Bay and there sold as indentured servants.

The estates of D'Hinoyossa and two other officials, Van Sweeringen and Peter Alrichs, were confiscated by Sir Robert and parceled out— D'Hinoyossa's estate going to Carr himself. The possessions of the independent farmers and craftsmen who had capitulated to the English, whether at New Amstel (if outside the fort) or farther up the river, were apparently undisturbed, but the company fort at the Whorekill near Cape Henlopen and the Mennonite colony of Plockhoy were looted "to a very naile."

Nicolls was disturbed by the tales he heard of plunder and greed on the Delaware, and especially by Carr's presumption in disposing of confiscated property as he pleased. Besides grants to military leaders, Carr had bestowed a manor upon the captains of the two ships in his little fleet, entitling himself the "sole and cheife commander & disposer of the affayres . . . of His Majesty . . . of Delaware Bay and Delaware River with all the lands thereunto belonging." As Nicolls noted, Carr had no right to such a grand title.

Nicolls and his two remaining colleagues in the royal commission summoned Carr on October 24, 1664, to join them at New York so they could proceed to their inspection of the New England colonies, but Carr did not come. Nicolls himself had to go to the Delaware before Carr could be pried loose from his conquest. And when Carr finally did join two of the other commissioners in Boston on February 4, Captain John Carr was left in command on the Delaware, though Nicolls had intended to appoint someone else.

The difficulty which almost caused a serious disruption in the English command was that the Dutch colony on the Delaware (still wholly on the west shore) was not included in the Duke of York's grant. Nicolls had been appointed deputy governor by the duke, but there was doubt that this gave him power in the Delaware colony. Therefore when Carr was sent to the Delaware, his powers came from the royal commissioners, not simply from Nicolls. Carr's orders made it clear he was to act on behalf of His Majesty the King and made no reference whatever to His Royal Highness the Duke.

When Carr had successfully reduced the Dutch colony and had begun making grants of confiscated property, he made them in the king's name, without reference to the duke, the grants being all on the west bank of the Delaware. Later, in December 1665, after his grants had been canceled, he wrote the king's secretary of state, requesting a proprietorship of his own or at least a governorship and mentioning that he had the king's promise of something of this sort. "The King spoke to you, for me," he told the secretary, "in your owne house, at a private musicke." And he advised that "if His Majesty have not disposed of Delaware and if he please to keep it in his owne hands, it will make a very convenient place of tradeing."

Though Nicolls had spent much effort in removing Sir Robert and establishing the hegemony of his government at New York over the Delaware settlements, he was willing, under certain circumstances, to cede them away. The duke's grant of New Jersey to Lord John Berkeley and Sir George Carteret, made soon after Nicolls's fleet had left England for New York in the spring of 1664, seemed to Nicolls a serious mistake. To him it was the best part of the duke's patent, able to support twenty times as many people as Long Island. (Most of what became New York State was then Indian country and seemed likely to remain so.) Nicolls proposed that instead of New Jersey, Berkeley and Carteret should be granted the land taken from the Dutch on the Delaware River. "Now seated with Sweeds, Finns, and Dutch, [it] is so crush'd," he wrote, "between the Lord Baltimore's Patent on the West side, and the Lord Berkeley's indenture on the East, that the present inhabitants cannot possibly subsist in so narrow a compasse."

On the other hand, Nicolls was resolutely opposed to yielding Delaware to the pretensions of Lord Baltimore. In sending Carr to the Delaware in September 1664, Nicolls had instructed him to call on the governor of Maryland for assistance if necessary, with a warning that Governor Calvert might claim the Dutch colony. In that case, Carr was to avoid any argument and merely to explain that his expedition was sent at the king's expense "to reduce all fforeigners in these parts to his Majesties obedience" and that therefore he must hold Delaware in the King's name until ordered otherwise. Since the English in Maryland, bribed by the high prices the Dutch gave for tobacco, had been carrying on a trade with the Dutch that was illegal by act of Parliament, they deserved, in Nicolls's opinion, to forfeit any claim they had to the Delaware region.

Nicolls thought the Dutch, if treated right, would make good subjects of the duke and the king. They were less contentious to the mind of this cavalier than the Puritans of New England, with their assemblies and general courts and commonwealth mindedness. But one Dutchman he would not make a place for was Alexander D'Hinoyossa.

That gentleman had been shipped off to the Chesapeake by the English after they had captured his fort, confiscated his estate, and sold his slaves. When Nicolls indicated his disapproval of the confiscation,

D'Hinoyossa quickly offered to resume his labors, and his lands, on the Delaware. Though the estate was not restored to him, he was not left without resources. Before the conquest he had sent large amounts of clothing, cloth, wines, and brandy to Maryland for the best quality tobacco to be delivered at the proper season. In due time he collected what was coming to him and shipped his tobacco, as well as a variety of furs, his family, his secretary, and himself off to London. When the English continued to reject his services, he entered the Dutch army again and is reported eventually to have been executed for desertion or treason.

Schout Van Sweeringen lived at St. Mary's, the old capital of Maryland, for many years after losing his Delaware lands. But Councillor Peter Alrichs, the third official who lost property, returned to Delaware after a brief sojourn in New York and quickly rebuilt his fortunes. Colonel Nicolls gave him a patent to two islands in the river and a special permit to trade with the Indians on Delaware Bay, and finally made him a member of a council to assist Captain Carr.

Finding a place for Alrichs was in keeping with the policy of the English authorities toward the Delaware settlements, for during the years that immediately followed the conquest the English hand lay light on this colony, and local customs and local officials—Swedish or Dutch—were left as they had been found in 1664. The English governor, Colonel Nicolls, was apparently given a few instructions for ruling this colony, though it lay outside his grants. "Tis pitty that place should be neglected," he wrote to his superior in England in 1665, "for the trade will be quite lost, and all the planters upon the river will goe naked if not supplyed."

Part of the problem was that the Anglo-Dutch war which had broken out in 1664 (nominally not until after the English seizure of New Netherland) continued to 1667. Only then, with the signing of a peace treaty at Breda, was the English seizure recognized by both nations. In the course of the war the Dutch had taken from England the area called Surinam, on the Guiana coast of South America, and the promise of this country seemed such that the Dutch agreed to both sides keeping their war conquests. Thus New Netherland was, in effect, exchanged for Dutch Guiana.

Gradually, as permanent possession seemed assured, English institutions were established on the Delaware. A council of five settlers—three Swedes and two Dutchmen—was appointed by Governor Nicolls in

April 1668 to advise Captain John Carr, along with the schout, on local problems. They were orderd to take an oath of submission to the Duke of York and directed to allow appeal of all important questions to the governor and council on Manhattan Island. The Duke of York's laws, drawn up in 1665 to govern the English settlements on Long Island, were gradually to be introduced on the Delaware, but in fact no copy of these laws was even seen there for many years.

In August 1668, a new governor, Colonel Francis Lovelace, replaced Richard Nicolls, who had long been eager to return to England. For the next five years the Delaware colony continued under Lovelace the very slow process of anglicization. Settlement gradually spread as old land titles were confirmed and new grants were surveyed and patented. An attempt was made to realize some profit from the land by collection of a modest quitrent. Fees charged for confirmation of patents were apparently very small, and lands were taken up in an irregular pattern, though some effort was made to see that grants were occupied. Swedes, Finns, and Dutch from the Christina valley and New Castle moved west and south, while English settlers, including some from Maryland, moved to the west bank of the Delaware in small but increasing numbers. Often they brought slaves with them.

There was also growth in the area of the Whorekill settlement, near the mouth of the bay. In 1670 Governor Lovelace appointed a schout and three commissaries at the Whorekill; probably this was the first local court in the area and therefore the foundation of the judicial district that came eventually to be called Sussex County. The commissions were in Dutch, suggesting the nature of the Whorekill settlement, and in a few years the Dutch custom of double nomination was established there when Governor Lovelace asked that the inhabitants send him the names of twice the number of officials to be chosen when the old commissions expired.

Upriver, the council was still using Dutch in its letters to Governor Lovelace in 1670, but another step in the anglicization process was taken in the following year, when Lovelace ordered that constables be appointed as in the rest of the Duke of York's dominions. The king's arms were to be placed on staves and were also to be set up in all courts on the Delaware. A new fort and a local militia were to provide for the defense of New Castle. Its economic well-being was encouraged by ordinances forbidding direct trade with settlers higher up the river, establishing inspectors of grain and meat, and ordering construction of a road halfway

Log house built by a Swedish family during the eighteenth century after the period of Swedish rule in Delaware. This structure was given to the State of Delaware by the Harvey Fenimore family; it has been moved from its original location at Price's Corner to The Rocks, Wilmington. Courtesy of the Division of Historical and Cultural Affairs, Dover.

across the peninsula toward Bohemia Manor, to meet the road being built from Augustine Herrman's plantation.

Lovelace visited the Delaware in March 1672 and incorporated New Castle as a bailiwick, to be governed by a bailiff and six assistants appointed by the governor. The office of schout was transformed to that of a high sheriff, who was to have jurisdiction over all settlements on the Delaware, and English laws were to be introduced "according to the Desire of the inhabitants." John Carr remained commander of military forces on the river, but appointment of Edmund Cantwell as high sheriff was a step in the separation of civil government from military authority.

Not all the inhabitants were eager for English institutions. In 1669 the colony was thrown into a mild panic by rumors of a plot among the Swedes and Finns to restore Swedish rule. The central figure was one Marcus Jacobson, called the Long Finn, who spread fanciful tales of Swedish warships being on their way to the Delaware. Seized by the authorities, the Long Finn was tried in New Castle in December 1669 by a jury of twelve men. After trial the Long Finn was whipped, branded, and transported to Barbados to be sold as a servant, while his accomplices, largely "simple & ignorant People" (but including a Swedish pastor), were fined various sums, ranging from the confiscation of all or parts of the estates of the chief offenders to as little as fifty guilders for the less guilty.

A more serious threat to the established government under the Duke of York came from the English in Maryland, who in 1669 began pressing their claim to the Delaware once again. The surveyor general of Maryland came up the Delaware River in this year to ascertain the proper bounds of his province. He reasoned that the entire western shore of the river to a point well north of New Castle lay within Lord Baltimore's proper domain. For the comparatively well settled New Castle area the Marylanders were content merely to state their claim, but near Cape Henlopen, where settlement was sparse, they sought to establish control.

Commissioners sent from Maryland in 1669 withdrew after being rejected by residents near the cape. But the Maryland authorities had created a county, first called Durham and later Worcester, on the west side of the Delaware, and they were not easily turned from their purpose of integrating this land into their government. When Maryland surveyors were repulsed by the inhabitants in 1672, an armed band led by Thomas Jones invaded the Whorekill region with power to seize "all

Indyan goods or skins." Captain Edmund Cantwell, the high sheriff, was sent to St. Mary's City to protest, but the Maryland authorities insisted the Whorekill was properly theirs. However, it is likely that they were a bit abashed by the instructions the council at New York sent to its officers at the Whorekill, bidding them accept orders from the New York government and none other "untill his Majesties or his Royall Highness Pleasure be signifyed to the contrary." It was a bold Englishman who dared dispute the rights of the king and his brother and heir.

The Swedish ships of which the Long Finn spoke were wholly chimerical, but relief of a conquered people by a Dutch fleet became a reality. War broke out again between England and the Netherlands in 1672, the third war between these two nations within a quarter century. In the summer of 1673, a Dutch fleet suddenly appeared at New York and called on the English to surrender. The visit was not part of any planned reconquest of New Netherland. A flotilla from Zeeland, commanded by Cornelis Evertsen, Jr., and operating against the English in the West Indies, had joined there with a smaller force from Amsterdam under Jacob Binckes. Together the two admirals proceeded to raid the Virginia coast. Learning from a captured merchantman late in July that New York was poorly defended, they sailed there immediately.

In the spring of 1673, a false alarm of a Dutch threat had caused Governor Lovelace to call soldiers to Manhattan from outlying settlements, such as Albany and New Castle, but when Evertsen and Binckes really did arrive in New York Bay, Lovelace was off in Connecticut and less than a hundred men manned the New York defenses. After an exchange of fire and an attempt to bargain, New York surrendered on July 30 to Captain Anthony Colve, who commanded a Dutch landing party that was prepared to assault the fort.

With the fall of New York in 1673, the events that followed its conquest in 1664 were almost duplicated. Captain Colve was made governor, and the admirals and their ships sailed off, but not before the outlying towns on Long Island, up the Hudson, in New Jersey, and on the Delaware had acknowledged the Dutch administration.

Indeed, in 1673 the transfer of authority seemed to take place more easily than in 1664. Many of the inhabitants were Dutch after all and cheered the new regime, while on the Delaware many were Swedes and Finns to whom the change of rulers made little difference. This time, unlike the situation in 1664, no military action was necessary for the conquest of the Delaware.

Although the settlers on the river submitted quietly to the new conquerors, there was one scene of violence that interrupted the peaceful surrender of the valley. When the Dutch seized the Delaware settlements in 1673, the Maryland authorities had an opportunity to renew their claims without directly defying their king or the Duke of York. Maryland Governor Charles Calvert commissioned Captain Thomas Howell, of Baltimore County, to raise forty men and lead them in a surprise attack on the Whorekill, which Howell was to seize and hold against all persons. Howell and his men occupied Whorekill Town (modern Lewes) in December 1673. After residing there two or three weeks they ordered all the residents of the area to report to town and turn in their arms. When the arms were secured as well as all the vessels in the creek, Howell put the town to the torch and also burned houses as far as eight miles away. Then he and his men cruelly left the defenseless inhabitants to get through the winter as well as they could.

Fortunately one barn was spared, and here the women, children, and some of the men took refuge, while others sought to get help from the Dutch authorities in New York or on the river. (Two men seeking to walk to New Castle were killed by Indians on the way.) A war was on, of course, but the brutal tactics of Thomas Howell were not a normal part of the contests fought over the Delaware. English settlers at the Whorekill were treated as badly as were the Dutch, probably on the excuse that they had surrendered to the enemy. The aim of the Marylanders was obviously to destroy the Whorekill settlement, and Howell declared he was under strict orders to burn every building. He allowed one to stand only because he felt it was the will of God after the barn had resisted three attempts at burning.

The Whorekill settlement was soon strengthened by the Dutch; they recognized its court and gave it jurisdiction over settlers on both sides of Cape Henlopen and northward to Bombay Hook (approximately the head of Delaware Bay). They also set boundaries to the jurisdictions of the courts at New Amstel and Upland (modern Chester, Pennsylvania) and thereby provided a shape for the eventual development of English counties on the Delaware. The New Amstel court (New Castle had resumed its Dutch name) was given jurisdiction over settlers on both sides of the Christina River and southward to Bombay Hook. The Upland court also took jurisdiction over both sides of the Christina, as well as over all settlers northward on the river. The overlapping authority of two courts in the valley of the Christina may have meant that the Upland court was intended to serve the Swedes and Finns, while the New Amstel court would take care of the Dutch and English, just as the Dutch had left Swedish officials in charge up the river in early days while Dutch officials controlled affairs at New Amstel.

At any rate, in setting boundaries to the jurisdiction of the Whorekill, New Amstel, and Upland courts, the Dutch were providing for the future counties of Sussex, New Castle, and Chester.* All the residents of this area were guaranteed their houses, lands, and personal property but were to take an oath of allegiance to the Dutch government. Elections by double nomination were also reinstituted, for in each district the inhabitants were asked to nominate eight candidates, from whom the governor in New York would choose one half to be schepens or magistrates. The bailiwick government of New Castle was apparently abandoned, but Peter Alrichs, who had become bailiff, was made schout and commander of the Delaware settlements.

Before further hostilites could involve New Netherland, political developments in England brought this Anglo-Dutch war to an end. The war had thrown England into an unpopular alliance with France, and the government yielded to public opinion in February 1674 by concluding the Peace of Westminster. One of its terms was the restitution of all conquests, and thus the Dutch once again freely gave up their claim to New Netherland.

Months passed, however, before the Dutch colony was actually surrendered. On the theory that the Dutch conquest might have voided the Duke of York's rights to the province, a new patent was given him by Charles II on June 29, 1674, in almost the same terms as the earlier patent, once again making no reference whatever to the land on the west side of the Delaware.

Governor Lovelace was in disgrace because of the surrender of the province in 1673, and Governor Nicolls was dead, killed in a naval battle with the Dutch, so a new governor, Major Edmund Andros, was chosen.

---

* Modern Chester County, Pennsylvania, does not lie on the Delaware River because its eastern portion was separated in 1789 and given the name of Delaware County.

He, too, was a proven adherent of the Stuarts and, like many English soldiers of his time, had the advantage of having learned Dutch during military service in the Netherlands.

Andros came to America in the fall of 1674 and on October 30 received the surrender of New Netherland from Captain Colve. English officials who had been in office in 1673 resumed their places on the Delaware and on the Hudson with two major exceptions. John Carr, former military commander on the Delaware, had been in New York when it surrendered in 1673 and had fled to Maryland, where he found it safer to remain, lest charges be brought against him. Peter Alrichs, former bailiff and schout, lost all favor because he had offered his services to the Dutch too eagerly. But Edmund Cantwell, who had become high sheriff on the Delaware in 1672, was restored to his place as chief civil officer, and Walter Wharton, who had been surveyor before and during the Dutch conquest, remained in his office.

Under Major Andros, who became Sir Edmund after he returned to England and was knighted in January 1678, the process of anglicization of the Swedish, Finnish, and Dutch settlements on the Delaware was resumed. "By all possible means satisfy ye inhabitants," his instructions read, "as well Natives as Straungers as English that your intention is not to disturb them in their possessions, but on the contrary that your coming is for their protection and benefitt."

In May 1675, the first spring after his arrival in America, Andros crossed New Jersey to the Delaware and attended a high or general court held at New Castle by not only the local justices of the peace but also those from Upland and from the Whorekill. Besides hearing a number of cases, this court issued orders for the building or upkeep of churches, roads, bridges and ferries, and the distilling and sale of liquor. Another such general court, including all the New Castle and Upland justices and two from the Whorekill, but without the governor's attendance, met at New Castle in May 1676. This turned out to be the last "high court" for the whole river valley, though the New Castle justices asked Andros to call such a court into session again in 1677, particularly to raise revenue for local needs by a poll tax. Andros responded that each court could set rates as it pleased.

By that time Andros had apparently adapted the administrative structure of the Delaware colony to suit its needs as he saw them. Twice the New Castle settlement had been upset in these early years. First, in

Portrait of Reverend Erik Björk, Lutheran pastor of the Delaware congregation and supervisor of the construction of Old Swedes Church in 1698. Artist unknown. Courtesy of the Eleutherian Mills Historical Library, Greenville. Used by permission of the Holy Trinity Church.

Recent photograph of Old Swedes (Holy Trinity) Church, Wilmington. The south porch and the tower are additions, the former in about 1750, the latter in 1802. Courtesy of the Division of Historical and Cultural Affairs, Dover.

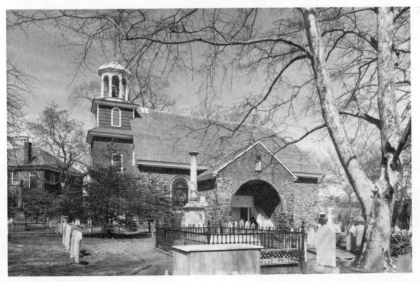

the summer of 1675 there had been a near riot involving the Lutheran minister, Jacob Fabritius, when the magistrates tried to force the inhabitants to labor on the footroads—partly through private land—crossing a marsh north of New Castle. Later, in 1676, Sheriff Cantwell had "three great guns" fired and called up armed men all along the river at rumors, which proved faulty, of an Indian attack. In the one case, Fabritius and an English planter, John Ogle, were called before the governor's council in New York and Pastor Fabritius was suspended from ministerial functions for a time.

Possibly as a result of the second affair—the false Indian scare of 1676—Andros changed the nature of Cantwell's appointment and decreased his authority. Thereafter Cantwell was to serve as a sheriff after the English fashion, as an arm of the court, and was not to sit as a judge like a Dutch schout. Furthermore, his military command was given to a Captain John Collier, who was not only to be commander of the river settlements but also collector of customs and of quitrents.

By these actions in 1676 Andros apparently intended to complete the extension of English institutions to the Delaware, but he was not entirely successful. For instance, Andros declared the Duke of York's laws, nominally introduced by Lovelace, to be now completely in effect on the Delaware, with the exception of a few details such as constables' courts and other provisions intended for Long Island. But it was still two years before a manuscript copy of these laws reached the magistrates at New Castle and there is no evidence that the justices of the other courts ever did receive a copy.

Nor was the new organization of the government successful. After one year Collier was found unsatisfactory and replaced by Captain Christopher Billop. The New Castle court soon complained of Billop's assumption of unauthorized powers, and he was summoned to New York by Andros and dismissed. Despite such difficulty the Delaware settlements grew and, though most accounts continued to be kept in guilders, the colony became increasingly English.

In the distribution of land to settlers, an attempt was made to attract English immigrants by grants as generous as those available in the New England colonies or in Maryland. Tracts of approximately fifty acres went to each member of a family, but the actual surveys seem to have varied from less than two hundred to over one thousand acres. Surveys were apparently made almost anywhere a planter chose, though warrants had to be secured from the governor and one surveyed plot normally bordered another. Surveyors were ordered to make their fees reasonable, not higher than in Maryland or Virginia.

The ducal government sought to collect quitrents, normally set at one bushel of wheat per hundred acres. Custom duties were the same as on the Hudson and were collected at New Castle and, at least some of the time, at the Whorekill. Vessels from outside the river were not permited above New Castle, except with special permission. The courts were empowered, with the permission of the governor and his council, to levy taxes for local needs, such as care of the poor and upkeep of a prison, courthouse, or roads. There were complaints that a property tax was unfair, because farms were too far apart to be properly assessed; a capitation or poll tax was also employed, and the settlers were sometimes called out to labor on public works as well as for "watch and ward."

When Andros was in England in 1678 he testified that the chief produce of his colony was provisions of all sorts, especially wheat, Indian corn, peas, beef, pork, and fish, tobacco, furs, especially beaver, timber, and various wood products such as planks and pipestaves, horses, and some pitch and tar. With the exception of the last three items, it is likely that his testimony applied to the Delaware as well as to the Hudson. The main imports, he added, were English manufactures, including blankets, duffels and the like for the Indian trade. The chief obstruction to the prosperity of planters and traders, in his mind, was the duty charged on the products of different colonies, as though they were foreign lands. A merchant worth £500 or £1,000 was accounted substantial, and a planter with half of that in movables was considered rich. There were few slaves, though some brought from Barbados sold from £30 to £35. He could give no accounting of births, marriages, or deaths.

On Andros's return from England in 1678 he was met by a series of requests from the New Castle magistrates, ranging from their desire for what they called "an Orthodox minister" (meaning a Dutch Calvinist), to "Liberty of traede" with their Maryland neighbors (whose supply of "negros, Servants and utensils" was vital) and freedom to send their vessels to England, Barbados, and other places, without touching at New York, but observing the navigation laws. A Dutch domine was soon sent to New Castle, after ordination at New York, and Andros promised the settlers on the Delaware every favor that was in his power in relation to their trade, as long as the laws of Parliament "and ordinances there-upon" were not infringed and "due Regard" was paid to the customs house at New York. Just how much freedom of trade this permitted is not clear, but it is likely that at least with Maryland the settlers could carry on almost any trade they pleased.

Settlements were spreading to such a degree that the New Castle court asked to have its southern boundary extended beyond Bombay Hook to the St. Jones River. Settlers on the St. Jones, however, who were under the jurisdiction of the Whorekill court, requested a court of their own because of the "Hazards and perills both by land and water" that they had to undergo in attending Whorekill court.

Attendance at court was not only necessary to settle land disputes, which were legion, and to register deeds and probate wills, but the justices were the source of most local government, setting prices of many commodities, performing marriages (there were not ministers of any denomination on the Delaware south of New Castle), binding out orphan children, licensing taverns, providing public scales and measures. The St. Jones settlers, amounting, they said, to about one hundred tithables, midway between the Whorekill and New Castle, had a justified complaint that was recognized by Andros in May 1680, when he granted their request by appointing justices for a new court. The St. Jones court was given jurisdiction so far south that a rectification of the boundary was requested by the Whorekill justices, who also asked for a new and more dignified name. Whether the boundary was settled to their satisfaction is uncertain, but their county town and court were both renamed Deal, or New Deal, both terms appearing in the records. The boundary between the Upland and New Castle courts, once set vaguely at the Christina, had been fixed by mutual agreement in 1678 at Quarryville Creek, almost four miles south of Naaman's Creek, which was itself south of where the boundary finally was settled.

Andros had discouraged establishment of an annual general court for the whole river valley, arguing that the individual courts could take care of most needs in local government. Similarly the Duke of York discouraged any thought of an elected assembly for his province, despite the example offered in the New England colonies to the north and in Maryland and Virginia to the south. On his initial appointment as governor, Andros had been ordered to choose a council of not over ten "of the most prudent persons" to serve at the duke's pleasure and to be consulted upon all extraordinary occasions. According to the duke, the governor and council, together with the annual meeting of the justices in a court of assizes, should be able to take care of all the needs of the inhabitants. An assembly would probably assume privileges destructive to the peace of the community; besides, the men who would be elected to the assembly were probably the very ones who would sit in the council or the assize court. The duke was willing to reconsider if Andros felt strongly about the matter; eventually he did reconsider, but by that time Delaware was no longer a part of the duke's domains. Meanwhile no Delaware residents ever served on the council or sat in the court of assizes.

Perhaps this was because of the weakness in the duke's title to the west side of the Delaware, of which he was well aware. Early in 1676 his secretary asked Andros to send details about the proper boundaries so they could be included in a new patent. Counsel advised the duke, however, to let the matter rest until there was some occasion to renew or alter his other patent, which would be a good time "to insert Delaware into the same graunt"; after all, the duke was already possessed of Delaware "as an appendix to New York," and why muddy still water? Yet, the duke's secretary concluded, "I must confesse I should be glad [Delaware] were confirmed in the Dukes possession by a better title than this, which indeed to an ordinary person would not be very secure."

The duke, of course, was not an ordinary person, but his situation was still somewhat uneasy and affairs of state had to take precedence over comparatively minor problems, such as the boundaries of his American domains. A virulent wave of anti-Catholicism swept England in the late 1670s, impelling the duke, a practicing and admitted Catholic, to leave London and spend most of his time in Scotland in order to be out of the public eye until the storm of mass hysteria was spent. There was a real fear among his adherents that his rights to the throne might be lost if he did not maintain low visibility for the time being.

As Richard Nicolls had thought he might, the duke had come to regret the great generosity he had displayed in giving away New Jersey in 1664, even before he had obtained his American lands from the Dutch. The part of New Jersey bordering on the Delaware had remained largely unsettled following the failure of the early New Haven colonists on Salem River and the abandonment of early Swedish and Dutch posts at Fort Nassau and Fort Elfsborg. A very few Swedish and Dutch settlers did move across the river, including one of the early New Castle justices with the intriguing name of Fop Outhout, but their plantations were for all practical purposes considered within the jurisdiction of the county governments of Upland and New Castle. In 1675, however, a company of English Quakers, led by John Fenwick, founded a settlement called New Salem (soon just Salem) on the river to which they gave the same name.

Fenwick insisted that he was an independent proprietor by virtue of purchase of the rights of John, Lord Berkeley, one of the two recipients of the Duke of York's now regretted largesse of 1664. The 1664 grant was to the soil, with no reference to rights of government; therefore Andros ordered authorities at New Castle, the closest of the Delaware courts to Salem, to treat Fenwick and his colonists civilly but to insist they were subject to the duke's government. When Fenwick, who was a veteran soldier before he became a convinced Friend, insisted on his independence and refused a first summons to a hearing in New York, Captain John Collier, then military commander on the river, seized him in December 1676 and sent him as a prisoner to the court of assizes, which held him in custody for several months. After another shipload of English Quakers arrived, Andros released Fenwick but insisted on naming magistrates for the settlements in New Jersey and on subordinating the authority of the local officials at Salem to the court at New Castle. This arrangement continued until 1680, when the Duke of York signed away his rights to govern New Jersey.

In the confrontation with Maryland, however, there was no yielding. In 1677 the Maryland claims to the Whorekill were revived when lots of five hundred to one thousand acres were offered in that vicinity from a tract of eight thousand acres. Seven years were allowed for payment, except for a quitrent of two shillings a year for every hundred acres. But despite this challenge to his authority and later fears for the security of plantations in the St. Jones area as well as near Cape Henlopen, the Duke of York retained control of the west side of the Delaware until 1682.

4

A QUAKER PROPRIETOR

In 1682 Delaware came into the hands of William Penn. This most unusual of English colonial proprietors—whose father was an admiral and his mother the daughter of a Dutch merchant residing in Ireland—had been educated at Christ Church, Oxford, at Lincoln's Inn, London, and at the Huguenot school at Saumur, France. To his father's chagrin he had, about 1667, become a convert to the plain sect known as the Society of Friends, which was growing rapidly among the middle classes of England but was not considered respectable in the society of gentry and courtiers, where William Penn belonged by reason of his father's prominence.

As a member of Parliament, the elder William Penn had gone to Holland in 1660 to bring Charles II back from exile and restore him to his throne. On the return trip he was knighted by the king, who also befriended him by many subsequent appointments, including that of commissioner of the navy. In this post Sir William worked on intimate terms with the Duke of York, who was Lord High Admiral and whose flagship Penn commanded in the Second Dutch War.

King Charles was not as generous with his money as with his honors, and when the admiral died in 1670 the Crown owed him a considerable sum. Ten years later, the debt being still unpaid, young Penn, the admiral's heir, petitioned the king for a grant of land in America as part or full satisfaction. The request was inspired not only by the persecution Quakers suffered in England, in common with other radical dissenters, but by Penn's own experience with the Quaker settlements in New Jersey.

Partly because of the quarrelsome nature of John Fenwick, disputes had arisen over West Jersey among various claimants, mostly Quakers.

In 1677 Penn was made an arbitrator of these disputes, and arbitration led to the establishment of a trusteeship of three men, one of them being Penn.

His responsibilities in New Jersey, added to broad interests in American colonies as a Quaker refuge from persecution, led him to become sufficiently acquainted with America to realize there was a vast unappropriated area west of the Delaware and north of Maryland. In the spring of 1680, therefore, he petitioned the king for a grant of this area. The Lords of Trade and Plantations, an advisory council to whom the petition was forwarded, sent copies of it to the agents of the Duke of York and Lord Baltimore, the proprietors whose lands bordered the tract Penn sought.

Lord Baltimore's agents asked that the grant, if made, be so written as to apply only to land north of "Susquehanna Fort" and a horizontal line based there and running east all the way to the Delaware River. Though the point was not specifically made, these agents were thereby repeating Lord Baltimore's claim to all the lower settlements on the Delaware.

The Duke of York's secretary, Sir John Werden, was at first unfriendly to Penn's pretensions which, he wrote, seemed to apply almost exactly to the area "by the name of Delaware Colony, or more particularly Newcastle Colony," a plantation held ever since 1664 "as an Appendix or Part of the Government of New York." Its proper boundaries, he confessed, were uncertain and it might "not prove to be strictly within the Limits of the Duke's Patent." Though he did not admit it, Werden knew very well it was not within these limits; in any case, the Lords of Trade should not encourage Penn's pretensions to this area because the duke's right to it was at least "preferable to all others (under his Majesty's Good-liking)." If there were other unsettled and unpatented lands in those parts, the duke would have no objection to their being given to Penn.

Penn agreed to the Susquehanna Fort as his boundary with Maryland. He relied upon his close personal friendship with the Duke of York to overcome objections from this quarter to his petition. After Penn had seen the duke, the latter's secretary addressed the Lords of Trade again, in October 1680, to declare the duke's approval of a grant to Penn beginning "on the North of Newcastle Colony (Part of Delaware) [at] about the Latitude of 40 Degrees."

The way was thus cleared for the grant of the colony that became Pennsylvania. When a draft was sent to Sir John Werden, he suggested that the location of lines of latitude in America was very uncertain and the duke's intentions would therefore be best served by bounding Penn's grant on the east side by the Delaware River and on the south at twenty or thirty miles north of New Castle, this distance being enough, Werden supposed, to reach "the Beginning of the 40th Degree of Latitude." Penn quickly complained to Werden that such a southern boundary might leave him too little of the navigable section of the Delaware for the proper commercial development of his huge, inland colony; Werden agreed to reducing the distance of the boundary from New Castle to twelve miles, it being the duke's intent merely "to keep some convenient Distance from Newcastle northwards" for the boundary. The exact number of miles, "in a Country of which we know so little," was unimportant, whereas it was certainly intended that Penn have as much opportunity to develop his colony as other proprietors enjoyed.

When the charter of Pennsylvania, as the king named the new colony, was completed on March 4, 1681, the Delaware Colony finally took shape as a separate entity. To this point it had been part of New Sweden, New Netherland, and New York. In 1681 the Delaware Colony still remained an administrative appendage of New York, but geographically it was separated from the duke's province by New Jersey and constitutionally it was distinct by the failure of the duke's patents, both of 1664 and of 1674, to include the west side of the Delaware. The geographical and legal separation from New York had existed for several years, but only in 1681 was a line established twelve miles north of New Castle separating the lower counties on the Delaware from the Pennsylvania counties.* The boundary with Maryland was still to be fixed, but the settlements on the Delaware had actually always been distinct from those on the Chesapeake.

William Penn did not long rest content with the new division of the settlements on the west side of the Delaware. Almost before his cousin William Markham, sent as his deputy, had reached Pennsylvania, Penn was addressing his friend the Duke of York with a request that all the latter's claims on the west side of the Delaware be yielded. Possibly Penn

---

* The City Colony of New Amstel had a certain degree of independence from the rest of New Netherland from 1656 to 1663, but the boundary of the City Colony was then at the Christina, and Wilmington (Altena) was not part of the City Colony except when, in 1663–64, this colony was briefly extended to include all the Delaware River settlements.

had hoped for such a cession all along but hesitated to risk the larger grant of Pennsylvania by begging for the smaller grant of the duke's dependencies, particularly since the duke's title to them was not clear.

Penn saw the advantage of controlling the entire Delaware valley, and the problems the Quakers in West Jersey had experienced with the Duke of York's agents in America taught him that he should avoid a repetition of these troubles if he could. He was also determined that his province should not be landlocked, and only by possessing the river and bay shore could he be sure the trade of his colony might flow unimpeded to the ocean.

By June 30, 1681, Penn had sent two letters to the duke, requesting cession of his claims to Delaware. The duke was slow in responding. If he listened to his colonial officials (and Andros was back in England), he might have been told that the prosperity of New York depended on Delaware. As a later governor explained, the tobacco trade from the Delaware had contributed a large share of the customs revenue in New York and had also furnished an article of exchange for beaver and other furs with the Indians up the Hudson River. Quitrents, too, were said to have derived in "the greatest part" from the Delaware River settlements in Andros's day, since many New York grants had not mentioned them.

Penn's zeal for Delaware was stimulated by the news he received from America, where Markham, his deputy, was having trouble coming to any satisfactory boundary agreement with Lord Baltimore. Penn had hoped to establish his southern boundary low enough for a port on the headwaters of the Chesapeake as well as on the Delaware, but his charter spoke of a boundary at the 40th degree, and observations made in America indicated clearly that the line marking this degree lay far up the Delaware and completely beyond the navigable waters of the Chesapeake. Penn argued for other ways of locating his boundary as, for instance, that it should begin at the 39° line, since there the 40th degree began, if considered as a measurement rather than a point, but he could not help being disturbed to find that Lord Baltimore claimed all land south of the Schuylkill, including, of course, all of Delaware.

The Duke of York's friendship for Penn, as the son of his loyal companion in war and peace, was sufficient to bring a favorable answer to his petition. Perhaps the duke was put in a good frame of mind early in 1682 when the king welcomed him back to England and recognized him openly as his heir. Then too, reports came from New York of such troubles that the duke may have despaired of the future of his province. Andros had been recalled and a special investigator, John Lewin, sent out in 1680 to look into conditions on the Hudson and the Delaware; an acting governor, Anthony Brockholls, proved to be unable to collect the customary revenue or even to keep the colony in good order. Having already abandoned his remaining claims to East and West Jersey, the Duke of York on August 21 gave Penn a quitclaim to all his interests in that part of the west side of the Delaware that lay within the new province of Pennsylvania. Then on August 24, he added to Penn's domains by two grants, one of New Castle and the land within a twelve-mile circle around it, the second of the lands beside the Delaware from twelve miles below New Castle south to "the Whorekills otherwise called Cape Henlopen." For the former, Penn was to pay ten shillings outright and five shillings yearly; for the latter ten shillings outright and a rose annually at the Feast of St. Michael, if demanded, plus one half of all "rents, issues and profits" from this area.

There were actually four legal documents involved in these grants, an absolute deed (called a "deed of feoffment") and a lease for ten thousand years for New Castle and the circle around it, and another deed and a similar lease for the land from twelve miles south of New Castle to Cape Henlopen. Why both a deed and a lease had to be granted is not apparent, nor is it clear why the Delaware settlements were split into two parcels instead of being granted to Penn in one piece. Probably the division is explained by the duke's desire to get some revenue from these territories (in fact, however, nothing was ever paid to him thereafter) but not to interfere with Penn's use of New Castle or with his revenues from it, since it was considered likely to become the major port of entry for Pennsylvania. Perhaps both deed and lease were used because of the uncertainty of the duke's legal rights to Delaware. The duke did later refer to Penn as his "lessee" for Delaware. Possibly the lawyers advised that though there might be a question of the duke's right to deed Delaware away, there was less doubt of his ability to transfer to Penn in a lease his rights in this land, which the ultimate authority, the Crown, was unquestionably allowing the duke to treat as his own. If this is so, it may have been felt that the lease might be the effective document for the moment, until the duke's title to this land was proved in law. Because of the uncertainties regarding the title, a clause was inserted in each of the deeds to the effect that the duke agreed, at the request and at the expense of William Penn, to make any further conveyances needed, in the opinion of Penn's legal counsel, to assure Penn's rights to this property.

On October 27, 1682, William Penn arrived at New Castle aboard the *Welcome*, accompanied by approximately seventy colonists, survivors of a smallpox epidemic during the crossing. In his deeds for the Delaware counties, the Duke of York had named two residents of New Castle, John Moll and Ephraim Herman,* to act as his attorneys in formally delivering possession of the land. But when the *Welcome* arrived, Herman was away, so the ceremony of possession was put off one day until he could return.

Then on October 28, in a ceremony called "livery of seisin," Penn formally took possession of New Castle and the territory within twelve miles about it, except on the east side of the Delaware. After the deeds from the Duke of York were read, Penn took the key to the New Castle fort, entered and locked himself in alone, then came out and received a piece of turf with a twig upon it and a porringer with river water and soil as symbols of his new possession.

On the next day Penn proceeded to Upland, which he renamed Chester, and ten days later, on November 7, Markham in Penn's name took possession of the lands below New Castle, in a ceremony at Edmund Cantwell's house on the south side of Appoquinimink Creek, "about twelve miles distance," in John Moll's words, "from the Town of New Castle."

After taking possession of Pennsylvania, Penn returned to New Castle, where he had called the justices from all three of the Lower Counties to meet with him on November 2. Since he had not allowed enough time for notification of the St. Jones and Deal magistrates, only the New Castle justices met him. To them, however, he made an important announcement. The inhabitants of the three Delaware counties were to enjoy, fully and equally, the same privileges as the people of the Province of Pennsylvania; for the time being they should abide by the Duke of York's laws, but in the future their laws would be such as they themselves would consent to by representatives in an assembly.

A few days later, Penn issued writs of election to the sheriffs of each of his six counties, three in his province (including Philadelphia, which

---

* The son of Augustine Herrman, Ephraim spelled his last name with only one "r."

Markham had established as Penn's capital) and the three downstream that Pennsylvanians began to call "the territories" or "the Lower Counties." Each sheriff was to convene the freeholders in his county to meet on November 20 "and elect, out of themselves, seven persons of most note for wisdom, sobriety and integrity," as their delegates at an assembly to convene in Chester on December 4.

Before the assembly met, Penn hurried to New York as a courtesy to the duke's government and to register his deeds with Acting Governor Brockholls, who had not yet received these documents from England. Brockholls issued notice of the change of title to all the justices, magistrates, and other officers of the duke's government in the Lower Counties "to Prevent any Doubt or Trouble that might Arrise," as well as to thank them for their services. Privately Brockholls told the duke's secretary he did not know how the province of New York, thus reduced, could survive.

At Upland, or Chester, on December 4 the first delegates elected from the Delaware counties to a representative assembly met and approved what their new proprietor and governor hoped was a permanent act of union with Pennsylvania.

Very little is known about the first legislative election in Delaware. Presumably the freeholders met together at the county seat or a place selected by the sheriff and there in some way, probably not in writing, voted for seven delegates. The sheriff presided at the election and submitted to the governor or assembly the names of the delegates selected. As soon as the first assembly was organized, the returns submitted by the New Castle sheriff were criticized for containing the name of one Abraham Mann. The objection raised against Mann was that he and his supporters "had made some illegal Procedure the Day of Election at Newcastle." After witnesses had been heard on both sides the assembly voted unanimously to expel Mann and to seat John Moll in his place. No other details of the contest are known, but it must have taken a rather clear case of skulduggery at the elections for the assembly to expel Mann by an overwhelming vote, especially when this apparently meant rejecting the returns submitted by Sheriff Cantwell.

After adoption of rules, the assembly considered a petition signed by nineteen freeholders of the Lower Counties asking for the formal incorporation of their area with the province of Pennsylvania. Since the nineteen

Colonial court house, New Castle. Courtesy of the Historical Society of Delaware, Wilmington.

freeholders seem to have all been delegates to the assembly, it is likely that Penn or his agents encouraged them to present this petition after they arrived at Chester. At any rate, the Act of Union they requested was quickly passed and taken to the governor for his signature.

By this action the Delaware and Pennsylvania counties were merged as far as they could be by action taken in America. Probably it was Penn's aim in this union to make his control of the Lower Counties so firm that any efforts Lord Baltimore should make to annex them—as, for example, by sending in settlers from Maryland, or by winning over the present inhabitants—would be doomed to failure. For this purpose the statute carefully detailed the history of this territory granted by the Duke of York to Penn, relating that the Dutch had bought this land from the Indians and surrendered it, first to "the king's lieutenant governor, Colonel Nicholls" (thus the statute tried to establish a royal and not just a ducal approval of the government of the Lower Counties) and then, after Dutch reoccupation, "to Sir Edmund Andross, lieutenant-governor to the said duke," who has "quietly possessed and enjoyed" it.

Another petition, this one from the Swedes, Finns, and Dutch, led to the preparation, apparently by the governor with the approval of the assembly, of a statute providing for the easy naturalization of all foreign landholders in the province and the Lower Counties. All they needed to do was to record in their county court their promise of allegiance to the king and "lawfull obedience" to the proprietor to enjoy the same privileges as other freemen. The privileges were very real, for before leaving England Penn had prepared a "frame of the government" as a constitution for his colony and also a document he called a "Great Law" that was a series of by-laws forming an idealistic code of government which the assembly adopted hastily, but with some alterations, in seventy-one articles. In this fashion the government was quickly established, though not till 1683 was Penn's frame to be put into effect with the election of a council, which he meant to join with the governor in preparing legislation, and a larger assembly, which was to approve or reject the bills presented to it.

The government did not work out as Penn had planned it. The assembly, for instance, gradually gained the initiative and became a unicameral legislature, while the council shrank into the status of an appointive advisory body. The idealism of the Great Law which provided for a mild, humane, tolerant government was somewhat tarnished in the years to come as less idealistic men than William Penn wrote the laws and administered the government of this colony. But the spirit of Penn, who was determined, as he wrote in the preamble to his Great Law, to establish a government where "true Christian and Civil Liberty" would be preserved and wherein "God may have his due, Caesar his due, and the people their due," was largely retained in the Lower Counties as in Pennsylvania.

Penn's virtues were not readily perceived by authorities in Maryland. Before he came to America Penn irritated Charles, the third Lord Baltimore, by a letter sent to Augustine Herrman and some other residents of northeastern Maryland in September 1681, advising them to cease paying taxes to Maryland because a boundary adjustment would probably determine their lands to be in Pennsylvania. Early in the summer of 1682 Lord Baltimore sent representatives to New Castle to find its latitude. Their observations suggested that the northern boundary of Maryland, if at the 40th parallel, lay at least twenty or thirty miles north of New Castle, well above the twelve-mile circle. On receiving this report, Lord Baltimore crossed the peninsula himself with more than a score of armed men. When Markham, the acting governor, would not come to New Castle to meet Baltimore, the latter went on to Markham's headquarters and made further astronomical observations there that confirmed the earlier findings. Before retiring, Baltimore publicly declared his right to all of Delaware as well as to the land in the Chester area. This was a right he had always claimed, but when his antagonist was the Duke of York, heir to the throne, Baltimore showed a discretion in pressing it that was not so necessary when the duke's claim fell to a Quaker, even though the Quaker was a member of the gentry.

Because of this controversy, Penn traveled to Maryland a few days after his first assembly adjourned, "a longe Journey," in his words, "in a cold and unpleasant Season." But when he met with Lord Baltimore on December 12 and 13, 1682, Penn refused to discuss his Delaware grant. What he wished was, as he put it, "a back door" to his province, a port on the Chesapeake, and if the Pennsylvania boundaries did not entitle him to such a port, he wanted to make some adjustment of them. He wanted water, not land, and water was something Lord Baltimore abounded in.

But Baltimore was adamant, insisting on a northern boundary at the 40th parallel, unwilling to yield on his patent rights, and to strengthen his case in any future litigation he had a report taken down of all that was said. "I found it uneasy with him," declared Penn, who finally broke off the conference on the excuse of attending a Quaker meeting.

The two antagonists came together again in May 1683, at New Castle, but again there was no meeting of minds. This time Lord Baltimore wanted a private conference and Penn insisted their negotiations should all be in writing. When they could not agree, Penn decided that he had no choice but to appeal to England.

Meanwhile Lord Baltimore had been taking steps to press his claims to the Lower Counties. In March of 1683 he ordered his cousin Captain George Talbot to do his best to settle land along the seaboard up to the 40th parallel, and especially "those parts at the Whore Kills," where bargain prices were offered (up to five hundred acres per settler at fifty pounds of tobacco per fifty acres, plus one shilling per fifty acres annual quitrent). "Persons of Brittish or Irish descent" were specified, probably in distinction to the mixture of Dutch, Swedes, and Finns who had long dwelled on the Delaware.

Talbot was also instructed to settle as near as possible to the 40th parallel and to lay out one thousand acres around Christiana Bridge (now in Delaware, though Lord Baltimore, of course, claimed this as part of Cecil County, Maryland). A fiery, headstrong man, Talbot took control of the upper Christina River watershed in what is now western New Castle County, erecting a small log fort near Christiana on the land of the Widow Ogle, whom he threatened to oust if she did not acknowledge the authority of Lord Baltimore and pay him a quitrent. When the sheriff of New Castle County came to inquire about this small fort, which was garrisoned with four men, Talbot threatened him, as he did a settler named Joseph Bowles near Iron Hill. In June 1684, Talbot rode up to his house, Bowles claimed, and said, "Dam you, you Dogg, whom doe you Seat under here, you dogg! you Seat under noe body; you have noe Warr[an]t from Penn, no my lord; therefore, get you gon, or Else Ile sent you to St. Mury's. . . . You Brazen faced, Impudent Confident Dogg, Ile Sharten Penn's Territories by & by." Other Maryland agents approached settlers in St. Jones and Deal counties, which Penn had officially re-named Kent and Sussex in December 1682, when he had also given the name Lewes (county seat of Sussex in England) to the old town at the Whorekill.

Though opposed to violence, Penn had no intention of giving Delaware up. "Finding this place necessary to my Province," he wrote in July 1683, "I endeavoured to gett it, & have it, & will keep it if I can."

To make good his claims, he sought to settle the land, to enforce the law, and to appeal to higher authority. On his arrival he had urged settlers to present their claims for confirmation, had commissioned his magistrates to authorize surveys of up to three hundred acres for heads of families and one hundred for single persons at a penny an acre quitrent, in money or produce, and had ordered that lands previously granted but not settled in a reasonable time should be declared vacant and available to the first claimant.

When told that a Captain Murphy and other agents of Baltimore were subverting settlers in one of the Lower Counties, Penn directed his magistrates to seize quietly one at a time all those who had cooperated with Baltimore and try to get a jury verdict against them. "Be assured that one judgement of ye jury of that county were worth two of any jury of this Province, "he declared. Four members of his council were especially commissioned to go to Kent County and inquire into the degree and nature of disaffection being raised by Baltimore's agents "and in your conversations refute them." Penn sent two agents to Thomas Dongan, the new governor of New York, looking on him as the closest representative of the Duke of York, from whom Penn's authority in Delaware derived, and Dongan responded by asking Baltimore, and Penn too, to give up any forts or other buildings newly established on lands in dispute and to leave things as they were before the construction of Talbot's fort near Christiana Bridge.

Lord Baltimore and his government disregarded Dongan's peaceful message. The fort near Christiana continued to be occupied by the Marylanders until 1687 or later. It was not finally abandoned until the handful of soldiers stationed there got drunk one winter night, abandoned their posts, and were found by their neighbors lying frostbitten in the snow. Meanwhile the negotiations over the boundary had shifted to England.

In England, at Penn's expense, efforts had continued to bolster his title to the Delaware counties by formal recognition of the suzerainty over them that the Duke of York had been exercising. On March 22, 1683, the king formally granted the Lower Counties to the duke, specifying boundaries extending from twelve miles north of New Castle to "Cape Lopen" and including the right to govern this area. Probably because Penn had paid the legal costs of this transaction, he was given the document (though when is not clear) by the agents of the duke.

For some reason this grant apparently did not satisfy Penn or those acting for him while he was in America. On April 13, 1683, the attorney general approved a new grant to replace the letters patent of March 22. It seems likely that someone in America suggested the specific provisions of this new grant, for it included all the land on the Delaware (including part of Pennsylvania) that was in dispute between Penn and Lord Baltimore.

At the northern extremity of this area all reference to the twelve-mile circle was dropped and the northern boundary was set at the Schuylkill. Probably this provision was a defensive maneuver in reaction to Lord Baltimore's claim to lands that were more than twelve miles north of New Castle. The southern boundary was described as "Cape Henlopen now called Cape James being the South part of Asia Warmet Inlett." By specifying "Asia Warmet" or Assawoman Inlet, Penn was making sure that not only Lewes, but a large hinterland below it, would be his. To this end his agents introduced into the negotiations a Dutch map of Nicholas Visscher, which showed Cape Henlopen at modern Fenwick Island, the place that was named Cape Henlopen originally. If his southern boundary had been the cape at the mouth of Delaware Bay, to which the name Henlopen had moved, Lewes itself would have been barely within Penn's domains, for the cape was almost directly eastward of the town.

Had this grant been finally legalized, the less extensive March 22 patent would have been surrendered gladly, and the next step would have been a deed from the Duke of York to Penn, repeating the grant the duke made in 1682 when he had no title himself. In this case, much trouble about the status of the Lower Counties could have been saved, and Penn's ownership would have been beyond question.

But apparently Penn had overreached himself. Before the extensive grant of April 1683 received final approval, Lord Baltimore interceded, asking that action on it be postponed till he could return to England to plead his case. When Lord Baltimore returned to England in 1684, Penn felt he had to follow. As the Lords of Trade, who would advise the Crown on this matter, waited, first for Lord Baltimore and then for William

Penn, who left America on August 18, settlement of the controversy was postponed through 1684 and into 1685, when, on February 6, Charles II suddenly died and William Penn's friend the Duke of York became King James II.

The situation was now much more favorable to Penn than to Lord Baltimore. In October 1685, the Lords of Trade, impressed by the evidence Penn presented of early Dutch colonization on the Delaware, decided that the Delaware counties, previously settled by a Christian nation, were excluded from the Maryland grant. In November the lords decreed that the boundary between the Lower Counties and Maryland should run up the middle of the peninsula between the Delaware and the Chesapeake from a horizontal line in the latitude of Cape Henlopen on the south to the 40th degree at the north. All to the west belonged to Lord Baltimore; all to the east to King James II.

James II, of course, as Duke of York, had already ceded his rights to the Delaware counties to Penn, but when the cession was made he had no title to them; furthermore Penn had never paid the half of all revenue from the lands beliow the twelve-mile circle that he had been directed to pay annually to the duke. James could now complete the grant by repeating it and waiving the payments if he wished to do so. Probably he did so wish, but his reign was a troubled one. Only when his situation seemed most difficult did he at last attempt to complete his obligation to Penn.

This was in December 1688, when James had a document drafted by which he granted what he called the province of Lower Pennsylvania to William Penn, declaring it to be the territory assigned to the king in November 1685: that is, the land east of a north-south line dividing the peninsula approximately in half from the latitude of Cape Henlopen to the 40th degree. He freed Penn of all obligations, past or future, to share the revenues and declared him true and absolute proprietor of this province, leaving him free to merge it with Pennsylvania in one government under one set of laws if he chose.

Unfortunately for the security of Penn's title, the king had delayed too long. Before final legal authorization had been given this document, James II had to flee England to escape capture in what came to be called the Glorious Revolution. Penn's situation was also difficult, because he was known as a close friend of the departed king. The one comfort he had was that Lord Baltimore's claim to Delaware had been rejected. Whether

Penn could hold the Delaware counties was uncertain in January 1689, when the reign of William III and Mary II began.

Despite James's failure to complete his grant of 1688 to William Penn, his earlier actions, in 1682, had given Penn a claim that courts eventually upheld. The grant in March 1683 to the Duke of York of lands he had previously deeded to William Penn created an "estoppel," a bar to any further alienation of this territory by the duke, who could be considered, according to Lord Chancellor Hardwicke in 1750, to be, as far as the Lower Counties were concerned, merely a trustee for Penn.*

Through these years steady economic progress was taking place in the Delaware colonies despite almost constant political turmoil. While the government went through innumerable crises, including adoption of four different constitutions or charters, a sound economy was being developed, with agriculture as its basis. By distributing his lands quickly Penn hoped not only to acquire some immediate income but also to gain additional profits in the long run by the increased value of the lands remaining in his possession. Quitrents of a penny an acre were considered a valuable supplement to the income from the sale of land, but in practice these expectations were never realized. Once settlers obtained a title in fee simple they refused to recognize any debt to a proprietor they never saw and did not need, and the amounts to be collected on the average property were so small as to discourage collectors.

Penn bought up what Indian claims still existed in Delaware; there were few Indians left here when he came because they had earlier moved up the Delaware valley, away from the settlements, or west into the interior of the peninsula and then north up the Chesapeake Bay and the Susquehanna. Penn's peaceful relations with the Indians of Pennsylvania had their effect on Delaware inasmuch as the settlers in the Lower Counties were long undisturbed by any need to help their neighbors in Indian wars.

Though Philadelphia quickly became the preeminent city on the Delaware, New Castle, the port where ships customarily cleared, shared the increased prosperity. Lying immediately beside the river, it was the

---

* As late as 1934, the United States Supreme Court through Justice Benjamin Cardozo, in the *New Jersey* v. *Delaware* boundary case, declared that the Duke of York's title to the Lower Counties "inured by estoppel" to Penn.

natural place for incoming ships to stop for fresh water and supplies and, similarly, the most convenient place for last-minute purchases or boardings upon departure. A weekly market, approved by Penn in 1682, improved the attractions of the town to its settlers.

Tobacco, grown in the Delaware counties below New Castle or rolled overland from the Maryland plantations on the Chesapeake, remained, as it was before Penn's arrival, the most profitable local crop and the chief export commodity to England. Debts and other obligations in Kent and Sussex counties were frequently stated in amounts of tobacco. Corn and wheat had a more modest beginning in subsistence agriculture, but as trade developed between the Delaware valley and the West Indies they became the staples of the upper valley and in the next century replaced tobacco in importance.

Surviving rent rolls indicate that in 1689 landholdings were larger in Kent and Sussex than in counties to the north. For example, 55 percent of the landowners in Kent and Sussex owned five hundred acres or more, as against 17 percent and 18 percent in two Pennsylvania counties, Chester and Philadelphia. (No comparable statistics are available for New Castle County.*)

It seems likely that tobacco farming plus the proximity to Maryland produced a larger concentration of Negro slaves in the lower Delaware counties than in New Castle or in Pennsylvania, but statistics to demonstrate this for the seventeenth century are hard to find. On the other hand white indentured servants were probably more numerous in New Castle County than in Kent and Sussex because the ships bringing them to America customarily landed in New Castle.

The concentration of wealth in Kent and Sussex is indicated by the number and the proportion of landowners rated as worth over £200 in 1693. The following table, in which political divisions are listed from north to south down the Delaware (and into tobacco country), shows more wealthy persons in Philadelphia City and in New Castle County, but since Philadelphia and New Castle were the chief ports this is to be expected.†

---

* Only one landholder in Kent or Sussex had over 5,000 acres; two more landholders had over 3,000 acres; six had between 2,001 and 3,000 acres; and five between 1,501 and 2,000 acres. On the other hand, seventy-nine landholders in these two counties owned between 251 and 500 acres.

† The statistics are adapted from Gary B. Nash, *Quakers and Politics: Pennsylvania, 1681–1726* (Princeton, 1968).

Taxpayers with Property Worth over £200

	Number	Percentage
Bucks County	2	1.4
Philadelphia County	6	1.8
Philadelphia City	43	11.2
Chester County	2	.7
New Castle County	20	7.5
Kent County	18	11.5
Sussex County	19	10.0

It is possible that some taxpayers in the Lower Counties were absentee landholders, resident in Philadelphia. It is also worth noting that the richest man in the Lower Counties was rated only at £750. In all of the Lower Counties, only two taxpayers, both in Kent, were rated at over £500; twelve Pennsylvanians, all in Philadelphia, were rated this high.

The comparative wealth of the counties on the Delaware is also indicated by the sums raised for the support of the government in 1693 by a tax of a penny on each pound of private wealth.*

Tax Collected, 1693

	£	s	d
Bucks County	48	4	1
Philadelphia County	314	11	11
Chester County	65	0	7
New Castle County	143	15	0
Kent County	88	2	10
Sussex County	101	1	9

Although it is possible that the tax was collected more efficiently in one county than in another, no complaints on this score are recorded. The farms of Sussex and Kent were probably valued higher than those of Chester and Bucks because the first pair of counties produced tobacco and the latter pair did not.

---

* These figures are taken from Robert Proud, *The History of Pennsylvania* (Philadelphia, 1797), I, 393n., and are also found in *Pennsylvania Archives*, 8th ser., I (1931), 169.

* * *

The first assembly called by Penn, which met in Chester in December 1682, was a special convention to deal with particularly pressing matters, such as giving statutory blessing to Penn's acquisition of the Lower Counties by providing for their union with Pennsylvania. The second assembly, which met in Philadelphia in March 1683, was the first with two houses, as called for in the frame of government Penn had prepared for his colonists. By this document the upper house, or legislative council, should have consisted of seventy-two members, and the lower house, at this first constitutional meeting, of all freemen, and thereafter of not more than two hundred delegates.

Collecting all of the freemen in one assembly was a preposterous notion, as became clear when Penn arrived in America and saw the distances involved. He issued writs for the election of seventy-two representatives (twelve to a county) as the frame called for, but by an agreement apparently entered into with the sheriffs conducting the election in each county three representatives in each delegation were specifically chosen to sit in the council and the other nine in the House of Assembly.

Other provisions in the original frame of government seemed similarly in need of alteration, so the General Assembly* set up a committee, with members from both houses and every county, that worked out with the governor an acceptable second frame of government. Though this was obviously a matter of great importance, some of the representatives elected from the Lower Counties did not regard it so. Two of them, both Dutchmen from New Castle, were fined for not attending at all; two other delegates from the Lower Counties were fined for missing some sessions.

Perhaps to counter such incipient particularism, the proprietor with some members of his council journeyed in May 1683 to Lewes. If the trip was intended to bolster Penn's support in the southernmost counties, it was a failure. When the assembly met in Philadelphia in the fall of 1683, the Kent and Sussex members did not appear. There was fear in government circles that leading men in the Lower Counties were receptive to Lord Baltimore's enticements, or at least were waiting to see which way the wind would blow in the contest between the two proprietors for control of the river and bay shore south of Philadephia.

---

* The term General Assembly is used hereafter, as is customary in Delaware (and Pennsylvania), to refer to the entire legislature, whether consisting of one or two houses.

Among the Delaware members there were specific complaints, such as one to the effect that Penn had broken his promise to require all vessels to stop and clear at New Castle on entering or leaving the Delaware River. There was also a more general suspicion of the proprietor and his entourage of Quakers, newcomers all. In his turn, Penn was concerned about the development of antiproprietary and anti-Quaker feeling in the Lower Counties, where the Quaker immigration was hardly felt and the freemen, when not Dutch or Swedes, were largely Church of England in background and prejudices, if not in practice. "Should they outnumber us, we are gone," wrote Penn in relation to these non-Quakers from the Lower Counties, and he sought, in vain, to have special representation given to Philadelphia City, so that the Lower County delegates would not be able to stifle all legislation by their equal vote in the assembly.

Fortunately for Penn, he did have some friendly supporters in the Lower Counties who kept this area from operating as a solid bloc against his bills in the assembly or council. To win support in the Lower Counties, the council sent a delegation there to talk with influential people, and in May 1684, as a further gesture of friendliness, the General Assembly met in New Castle. Furthermore, when Penn was making out the commissions for judges of the provincial court he prepared two separate commissions, one for Pennsylvania and one for the Delaware counties. The names were the same on both commissions, but on one a Pennsylvanian was listed first as the president, while on the second the order was changed and a man from the Lower Counties was listed as president of the court.

It was, Penn clearly felt, worth doing all he could to pacify and content the people of New Castle, Kent, and Sussex before he left America in August 1684 to defend his right to these counties before the Privy Council.

In Penn's absence executive power in his colony was left to his council, presided over by a proud and stubborn Welsh Quaker, Thomas Lloyd. The council seldom met; therefore to provide a more permanent executive Penn in 1687 appointed a commission of five men, including Lloyd. On the whole, the Lower Counties may have enjoyed the absence of a strong executive, but they resented judicial neglect. A provincial judge was impeached and removed from office, because, among other reasons, he had refused to go on circuit in the southernmost counties. By 1687 Penn's custom of preparing two commissions for the provincial judges had been abandoned; in this year the assembly protested that none of the provincial judges came from the Lower Counties.

Enforcement of navigation laws was so weak that pirates were said to land at midday in New Castle with assurance of their freedom from arrest. After reports of such conditions reached the Lords of Trade and Plantations in London this committee of the Privy Council asked the Crown for legal proceedings against the proprietary government of the Lower Counties, as well as of several other of the colonies that were not directly under royal control.

In 1688 Penn decided to appoint a single executive as deputy governor and, after Lloyd rejected the appointment, he turned to an acquaintance who happened to be in Boston, a veteran of Cromwell's army named John Blackwell. It was not likely that a soldier from outside the colony would suit the pacifist but contentious Quaker leaders of Pennsylvania. The Lower Counties, on the other hand, were generally sympathetic to Blackwell. War broke out with France and Spain in 1689, and Blackwell sought to establish a militia and erect defenses on the Delaware. The Lower Counties, open to attack by any marauding fleet, were angry at the refusal of the Quaker leadership to support military measures. The Dutch in the Lower Counties seem to have been especially unhappy that the Quaker leaders in Philadelphia were slow to recognize the new Dutch king of England.

The accession of William of Orange, stadholder of the Netherlands, and his wife (and cousin) Mary as the joint monarchs of England in 1689 seriously reversed William Penn's standing at the English court. All friends of the old king were suspect, Penn among them. Arrested in the very month in which James II fled, Penn was quickly released on bail, but he was arrested twice more in the next two years and might have been jailed in 1691 had he not gone into retirement for almost three years. At the end of that time some of his friends gained such influence at the court of William and Mary that he was relieved from fear of further prosecution.

While Penn's influence in America as well as in England was in eclipse, the Lower Counties virtually seceded from Pennsylvania. For the next three and a half years the people of Pennsylvania and the Lower Counties in effect ruled themselves. Governor Blackwell resigned his powers early in 1690 to the council, which continued to annoy the Lower

Counties by its pacifist policy. Becoming defiant, they organized a voluntary militia, successfully demanded a meeting of the assembly at New Castle in May of 1690, and attempted to name their own slate of provincial judges.

Relations between Pennsylvania and the Lower Counties became still worse in 1691 when Thomas Lloyd became deputy governor. Penn had offered a choice of type of government to the council, and seven of the nine Delaware councillors walked out when Lloyd was chosen. The Delaware delegates refused to attend a meeting of the assembly in May, and an attempt to elect new delegates from Delaware was "tumultuously" prevented. When the council met in August 1691, with seven of the nine Delaware councillors still absent, a bill was drawn up providing that the Pennsylvania members of the council and assembly might form a government by themselves, passing laws and accomplishing other business of the General Assembly without fear of the lack of a quorum through the recalcitrance of the Lower Counties.

Penn, hearing of the schism among his colonists, was displeased and sought to solve it in a way of his own. He blamed Lloyd for accepting the deputy governorship when it meant a break with the Lower Counties, and though hesitating to remove Lloyd, probably because he was powerless to do so, Penn still retained sufficient influence in 1691 to diminish Lloyd's power by giving the Lower Counties a governor of their own. This was William Markham, who had sympathized with the seceding Delaware councillors and followed them out of the council, of which he had been secretary.

With two executives, Thomas Lloyd for Pennsylvania and William Markham for the Lower Counties, the councillors and assemblymen agreed to work together once again, and for approximately one year there was a legislative union but an executive division between the province and the territories. In council the members from both sections pledged Penn their support of his division of the executive power and assured him of "the happy Union and Understanding that now is and is likely to continue between his people here." When the new assembly met in May 1693, William Clark, of Sussex County, who had been one of the seceding councillors, was chosen speaker, probably as a compromise gesture to the Lower Counties.

In England the Lords of Trade had recommended in October 1691 that Penn's colony should be placed under royal government and be united with New York or with Maryland, which had been recently transferred from the Calvert family to the Crown. Time passed before any action on this recommendation was taken, but eventually Benjamin Fletcher, already governor of New York, was given an additional commission as royal governor of Pennsylvania and the Lower Counties.

Arriving in the Delaware valley in April 1693, Fletcher carried instructions that superseded Penn's charter and the frame of government that was dependent on it, and he wasted little time in reorganizing the government. Most of Thomas Lloyd's party was swept out of office, to the delight of the Lower Counties. Markham was appointed lieutenant governor, to be chief executive when Fletcher returned to New York. The elective council was replaced by an appointive body, as in other royal colonies, and to it were named some men from the Lower Counties, including William Clark and John Cann, another of the councillors who had seceded in 1691. Clark and Cann were also named to a new provincial court. The assembly was reorganized, with a new apportionment of seats, three for each county except the two most prosperous, Philadelphia and New Castle, each of them being assigned four seats. The new apportionment, like the old, kept a parity between the representation of the Lower Counties and Pennsylvania.

Fletcher, like Markham, was a member of the Church of England, as were most of the English inhabitants of the Lower Counties, who welcomed him in the hope that he, in contrast to his Quaker predecessors in power, might do something about their defenseless and exposed shoreline. When he met his recast council and assembly, Fletcher demanded that they vote money that he could use on the frontier near Albany, where the French threatened. The assembly tried to bargain with him, but when he threatened to leave in disgust and stated there was no answer but to join this government to New York, they gave in and voted a tax of a penny a pound on assessed property and six shillings a head on all freemen not housekeepers and without assessed property.

Ten of the twenty assemblymen signed a protest against Fletcher's procedure in demanding funds before he redressed their grievances but only one of them (Samuel Preston, a Quaker in the Sussex delegation) was a representative of the Lower Counties. The other delegates from Delaware apparently were either satisfied with Fletcher's procedures or were unwilling to be listed in opposition in company with the Pennsylvania delegates.

Fletcher soon returned to New York, leaving Pennsylvania and the Lower Counties to be governed by the justices and other officials he had appointed, including Markham as his deputy. The antagonism between these two areas was muted for the time being, mainly because the Quaker party in Pennsylvania was out of power. Its strength was merely dormant, however, as was indicated when an assembly was elected in 1694. Fletcher came to Philadelphia to meet it and to ask their assistance "to feed the hungry and cloath the naked" on the frontier: that is, to supply friendly Indians with the necessities of life so they would not be tempted to join the French. But the Quakers in the assembly insisted on granting funds only on their own terms and soon reached an impasse with the governor. Angered, he dissolved the assembly on June 9, 1694, and returned to New York emptyhanded.

The episode might have led to serious trouble for the colonists except that in this year events in England turned in William Penn's favor. His friends regained positions of influence in the government, and when Penn, in July 1694, petitioned the Privy Council for the return of his rights to government (his rights to the soil had not been suspended), his petition was granted, and on certain stated conditions Penn was restored to full power.

5

A BRITTLE CONNECTION

The English government exacted certain promises from William Penn before restoring his provinces to him. First, Penn had to recognize the statutes enacted during the administration of the royal governor, Benjamin Fletcher. Second, Penn agreed that until he could come to America himself Fletcher's lieutenant governor, William Markham, would remain in control. Finally, Penn had to pledge fidelity to the new monarchs.

None of these requirements was very difficult for Penn. Markham, after all, was his own cousin; the death of Markham's chief antagonist and rival, Thomas Lloyd, in September 1694, one month after the Crown restored Penn's rights, eased Markham's continuance in office. The Lower Counties were probably distinctly pleased that Markham remained their acting governor, as he had been even before Fletcher's arrival in 1693. They looked upon him as a buffer against the political power of the Quakers, as one who could maintain the brittle connection with Pennsylvania to the satisfaction of the Lower Counties.

Markham's authority, however, was weakened by the appointment of two assistants, and he was obliged to get the advice and consent of at least one of them before taking any action. Since both of these men were Quakers and followers of Thomas Lloyd, it is likely that through them Penn sought to reconcile the Lloyd faction to Markham. Still, the major obstructions to Markham's authority came not from the assistants but from the rise to power in the assembly of David Lloyd, a young lawyer who had come to America in 1686 as Penn's attorney general, had become a Quaker after his arrival, and recently had replaced his kinsman, Thomas Lloyd, as the leader of the Quaker faction in Pennsylvania politics.

Under David Lloyd's leadership a newly elected council and assembly blocked Markham's efforts to raise money for defense, though a watch of two men was established at Cape Henlopen. Most of the politically conscious element in Delaware recognized that they resided on an exposed coast and agreed with Markham in wanting appropriations for defense. However, a few delegates from the Lower Counties were Quakers (for instance, two of the nine councillors elected in 1695) and their support gave the Lloyd faction control of the General Assembly.

Since he was accomplishing little under the terms of the 1683 frame of government, Markham decided in 1696 to act under the authority he could claim from the royal approval of his appointment. He replaced the elected council with an appointed body and called for election of an assembly with the apportionment set by Fletcher: four delegates representing Philadelphia County and the same number from New Castle County; three from every other county.

Probably Markham was feeling hard-pressed by enemies of proprietary government and their attacks on the colony. For example, Francis Nicholson, governor of Maryland, now a royal colony, complained that residents of Pennsylvania and the Lower Counties were smuggling tobacco out of the Delaware counties to foreign countries in defiance of the navigation laws and with a loss of revenue for England, where these laws required the tobacco to be sent. "They cunningly convey their tobacco in casks," he wrote, "with flour or bread at each end." Nicholson and other English agents charged that Maryland tobacco, as well as the produce of Kent and Sussex, was thus being illegally exported from New Castle and Philadelphia, and that if ever a cargo was seized for violation of the law, the local judges and juries refused to convict the smugglers.

Because his adoption of the forms of royal government had not enabled him to meet this criticism, Markham capitulated to his assembly in the fall of 1696 and offered them a new, revised frame of government such as they had been seeking. Though the revision decreased the size of the provincial council to twelve (two per county) and of the assembly to twenty-four (four per county), the Lower Counties retained the equality with Pennsylvania in representation that they had always enjoyed. The number needed for a quorum remained two-thirds of each body; therefore the Delaware delegates could bring all legislation to a halt if a substantial portion of them absented themselves.

The franchise requirement was possession of fifty acres of land, of

which ten acres were "seated and cleared," or other property of the value
of £50. A previous requirement of election by ballot was dropped, possibly in deference to the wishes of the Lower Counties, where elections are
said to have been determined by the use of white and black beans. The
governor's consent and that of six-sevenths of the councilmen and assemblymen were required in amending this frame of government, but
the proprietor, by a signed statement, could invalidate the entire document at any time.*

Though the new frame of government did not please Penn, he took no
action to invalidate it. Probably he appreciated the *quid pro quo* Markham extracted from his assembly in 1696 after presenting them with the
new frame, for they had then passed a bill Markham and Penn wanted: a
property tax of a penny a pound and a capitation tax of six shillings on
freemen worth less than seventy-two pounds. This tax was to provide
some funds for the assistance of the government, though the assemblymen were careful to make no reference in the law to military needs. By its
passage the charges of enemies of proprietary government, such as Governor Nicholson who thought Pennsylvania and the Lower Counties
should be placed under royal rule, were temporarily blunted.

The Lower Counties had reservations about government under the
new frame of 1696, though it is not clear whether their objections were to
the new frame itself or were merely an expression of their distrust of any
unified government with Pennsylvania. Griffith Jones, an elected councillor from Kent, clearly was objecting to the new frame in 1697 when he
refused to qualify himself under it for membership in the council, declaring that he recognized the validity only of the old frame of 1683. Other
delegates from the Lower Counties, however, raised no such objections,
and the representatives from Sussex were probably gratified that their
request for reestablishment of a watch for enemy vessels at Cape Henlopen was accepted and that its expense was made a public charge.

---

* Terms of councilmen were reduced to one year, matching the terms of assemblymen.
A voter was required to be at least twenty-one and a resident for two years or more before
the election, a provision designed to protect the old inhabitants from a swarm of immigrants. The assembly was strengthened by being given equal authority with the council
to introduce legislation, as well as to judge the qualifications of its members and to
adjourn to what time it chose until finally dismissed by the governor and council, upon
whose summons it could be reconvened.

In 1698 two of the twelve members of the assembly from the Lower Counties refused to attend, without offering any excuse, and in 1699 the county of New Castle neglected to elect any representatives to either the council or the assembly. Though Markham ordered a new election in New Castle on May 1 and a considerable number of the voters gathered in the town on that day, they "utterlie refused" to choose representatives. To make things worse, three of the eight representatives from Kent and Sussex elected to the assembly in 1699 refused to attend, though one of them, who happened to be Governor Markham's son-in-law, absented himself on the very personal grounds that he was accused of being a pirate and was afraid of being arrested if he appeared to take his seat.

The legislature, angry at the poor attendance, passed a law levying a fine of £100 on any county neglecting to elect representatives to the council and assembly under the terms of the 1696 frame of government, as well as a fine of £50 on any sheriff neglecting his duty in elections and of twenty shillings a day on elected members willfully absenting themselves from either chamber. A final provision in the law allowed the council and assembly to proceed with important business even if a quorum was lacking because of the failure of some counties to elect delegates or of some elected delegates to attend.

A clue to the behavior of the voters and the absenting delegates from the Lower Counties may be found in a petition from twenty-five residents of the town of New Castle that was presented to the governor and council in August of 1699. A year earlier, at the end of August 1698, according to this petition, a company of pirates, numbering about eighty, had raided Lewes. After plundering the town, carrying away whatever they pleased, they planned to sail upstream and attack New Castle but were diverted by the chance appearance of a Dutch immigrant ship from which they seized all the necessities they wanted. More recently, on June 20, 1699, a six-gun brigantine, richly laden and lying in the river before New Castle, was taken over by a mutinous crew who put a few honest sailors ashore and then, without interference, sailed the vessel out of the river and bay on a piratical voyage.

It was against such actions as these that the New Castle petitioners protested, "having neither fort, castle nor breastworke, to Comand anie ship or vessell; no militia, arms or ammunition to make use of." Even though they lived almost one hundred miles upstream from the ocean, their lives and their estates were at the mercy of pirates at any time of day or night, for they were utterly "defenceless & void of protection." The fault, they intimated, lay with their Quaker-dominated government.

This intimation was supported by the answer given the petitioners, that since forts and arms and ammunition had not eliminated raids by pirates on such strong colonies as Virginia and Maryland, they would not be sufficient to protect the Delaware counties, where the people were not capable of maintaining strong points if they were built. And as to a militia, New Castle should have sent delegates to the General Assembly to raise this question in the proper place. Content with the logic of this reply, the council dropped the matter, doing nothing for the defense of the Delaware.

There had, indeed, been a law against pirates passed at the spring 1699 meeting of the General Assembly, but it was too weak to be very effective. In reaction to what they regarded as their abandonment, the residents of New Castle County made no effort to collect the new penny-in-the-pound tax voted by this General Assembly.

Meanwhile, the laxity of the Pennsylvania government was producing a reaction in England more formidable than any that could develop out of the growing dissatisfaction in the Lower Counties. Piracy had become prevalent in American waters after the close of King William's War (called the War of the League of Augsburg in Europe) in 1697, when sailors, grown accustomed to the profits of wartime privateering, continued their raids on merchant vessels under any flag.

Edward Randolph, Surveyor General of the Customs in North America, complained, like Governor Nicholson of Maryland, of the toleration of pirates and of illegal trade in Penn's colonies, particularly of the export of Maryland tobacco through Delaware to Scotland (not united to England until 1707). Nicholson was also distressed because numerous sailors were deserting the Chesapeake Bay tobacco fleet for attractive terms offered by ship captains at Philadelphia and New Castle, who were hiring men, he suspected, for illegal voyages, probably involving piracy. When stationing rangers at the head of Eastern Shore rivers to intercept deserters proved ineffective, Nicholson dispatched an expedition of sixty men overland from the Elk River to New Castle in October 1696 to seize the brigantine of a Captain James Day, who had been recruiting sailors. It was a strange invasion. Sixty armed men marched into New Castle with colors flying and drums beating, terrifying the residents and taking possession of Day's vessel. Apparently the Marylanders also invaded the New Castle taverns, for before the day was over they were helplessly drunk and their commanders were forced to surrender to local authorities. When the Maryland invaders were allowed to march away the next day, eight of their number deserted.

The complaints of Nicholson and Randolph encouraged an inquiry by the House of Lords into Penn's right to govern the Lower Counties. Randolph told a committee of the Lords that Penn held these counties only by lease from the Duke of York, but Penn countered by claiming that his deeds gave him the same power of appointing a governor that the duke had enjoyed.

Markham, Penn's governor, was directly attacked for harboring pirates. Specifically he was charged with sheltering some of the crew of the notorious Captain John Avery,* with winking at the piratical connections of his own son-in-law, James Brown (sometime assemblyman from Kent), and with failure to support his vice admiralty judge, Robert Quary, when Quary tried to capture another notorious pirate, Captain William Kidd, at Cape Henlopen. In July 1699 the Board of Trade called for the dismissal of Governor Markham, and in September the Privy Council ordered Penn to remove both Markham and Attorney General David Lloyd from office and led him to believe he must go to his colonies personally if he wished to retain his full powers. He was instructed to enforce the acts of trade, prevent piracy, and report to the king on the state of affairs as he found them. He was also urged to establish a militia. Most important of all, his return was expected to restore order and the laws of England in a colony so loosely managed that a neighboring governor referred to it savagely as "that no-government."

The return of William Penn to America in December 1699 brought a temporary resumption of orderly relations, if not of genuine good feelings, between Pennsylvania and the Delaware counties. Acting vigorously, Penn dismissed some of his old officials, as he had promised to do, and called the assembly back into session to enact legislation needed to satisfy his obligations to the Crown. Since New Castle County had chosen no delegates to the assembly, Penn ordered a special election there. The New Castle authorities cooperated; they were apparently impressed

---

* Avery had added to his crew from a Lewes vessel he met with in the Indian Ocean. On his return to the American coast, several of these men left his ship to return to their homes in New Jersey or the Delaware counties. When apprehended, they claimed Avery's piratical acts had all predated their joining him.

by the fact that Penn had, at least temporarily, suspended the power of David Lloyd and his Quaker coterie by installing new officials.

Early in February 1700 the General Assembly passed bills against piracy and illegal trade, after some trouble with Kent County, which at this time surpassed Sussex County in the production of tobacco. The assembly expelled one member of the Kent delegation—James Brown, Markham's controversial son-in-law—and ordered a customs agent stationed at the Dover (or St. Jones) River, the center of an illegal trade with Scotland.

A report on the revenue collected from the penny-in-the-pound tax of 1699 showed that New Castle County, which had sent no delegation to the assembly in that year, had also been recalcitrant in taking any steps toward collection of the tax. Yet it was to Penn that New Castle residents and other aggrieved elements in his colonies looked for solution of their ills. To satisfy their complaints, Penn set aside Markham's charter of 1696 and despite the protest of some assemblymen called for the election in March 1700 of three councilmen and six assemblymen in each county, as provided for by the charter of 1683. New Castle and the other Lower Counties chose new delegates as requested, but those chosen in Kent County were apparently miffed by the new trade law or by Brown's expulsion (and his later imprisonment), for they were slow to report for their new duties; consequently no Kent members were in council on April 1 when Penn urged his new councilmen to change any details in the charter that they did not like.

He hoped to confine their dissatisfaction to details, avoiding clashes on major issues of government. "Friends," he pleaded, "away with all parties." But the assemblymen were not satisfied to confine their attention to minor details in a government in which the proprietor and the council, according to Penn's idea, should prepare the laws, and the assembly merely vote its consent to them. From the time of Penn's first assembly, in December 1682, the members had sought an initiative for themselves in law-making, and now they again forced Penn's hand, rejecting the old charter and demanding a new one.

A major difficulty, however, was the problem of reconciling the demands of the Pennsylvania delegates with those of their colleagues from the Lower Counties. Pennsylvania, with a greater population, wanted more delegates, but the Lower Counties refused to accept a minority status in the legislature. The one thing both province and territories could agree upon was the surrender of the old charter; they did so for-

mally on June 6, 1700, when two councilmen, one from Pennsylvania
and one from the Lower Counties, and two assemblymen, also representing the two sections, delivered the charter into the hands of the proprietor, who made a little speech to the effect that he would govern by
royal authority and the Act of Union until a new charter could be
adopted.

By the willful action of the General Assembly, Pennsylvania and the
Lower Counties were now reduced to a government without a charter,
much as they had been in the days when Penn's powers were suspended
and Benjamin Fletcher had come from New York as their governor under
Crown authority. In a new council Penn appointed on June 25, 1700, to
replace the elected council, only two of eight members—John Moll, of
New Castle, and William Clark, who had frequently represented Sussex
in the assembly—came from the Lower Counties.

To carry on with the work of revising the charter and the laws Penn
had to call a new assembly into session in the fall of 1700, when the
harvest was over and planters had the freedom to attend to political
duties. As part of his desire to heal the split between his Lower Counties
and his province, Penn decided that this meeting should be held in New
Castle, where the assembly had previously met only twice in twenty
years. A new election was necessary because the last assembly had dissolved itself along with abandoning the charter under which it was chosen, and in calling the election Penn reverted to the practice of Markham, asking each county to choose four delegates.

The assembly that met at New Castle in the fall of 1700 was the
longest and the busiest in the legislative history of Penn's colonies to
date. Taking seriously their mandate to revise the laws, the members
passed a total of 104 statutes, many repetitious of old laws and the whole
forming in effect a new codification of the statutes. Yet one major task
remained unfinished, for despite protracted efforts the General Assembly
failed to produce an acceptable new frame of government.

It was not only the desire to revise old laws and the normal need for
new legislation that led the assembly to enact so many statutes at New
Castle; some of the legislators, at least, were motivated by a belief that
laws previously passed were placed in jeopardy by abandonment of the
charter. Delaware delegates expressed doubt that the Act of Union remained in force, but they conceded that the royal commission to Governor Fletcher and the restoration of Penn to the government gave full
legal power to the assembly to legislate for the Lower Counties.

The validity of the Act of Union was questioned by the Delaware delegates because they were determined to block efforts to grant increased representation to Pennsylvania, which was already more populous and, with vastly more space to be filled, was growing much more rapidly than the Lower Counties. The provincial delegates (that is, those from Pennsylvania) and the territorial delegates (those from the Lower Counties) could agree that one-third of future assembly sessions should be held in New Castle or elsewhere in Delaware, but no agreement was reached on representation. The Lower Counties insisted on equality, whereas the Pennsylvania delegates were eager to change a system that allowed a mere appendage of the province an equal vote, meaning, in effect, a right to block any legislative measure. To make peace, Penn proposed requiring a two-thirds vote of the Delaware delegates, plus a majority vote of the Pennsylvania delegation, on any matters in which the Lower Counties were "particularly concerned, in Interest or Privilege, distinct from the Province." He added the phrase "& e converso," meaning, presumably, that matters particularly concerning the province of Pennsylvania would similarly require a vote of two-thirds of the provincial delegates and only a majority of those from the Lower Counties.

But this would not do, and when the assembly closed its long session on November 27 there was still no agreement on a new frame of government. However, one subject of disagreement between the provincial and the territorial delegates was settled when a new tax levy for support of the government was agreed upon. The territorial delegates objected to as high a tax as the Pennsylvania members wanted, probably because the Lower Counties would benefit less than the province from the sums raised. The compromise agreed upon was to raise a total of £2,000, clear of all expenses of collection, allocating responsibility for the tax to each county, as follows:

	£
Bucks County	225
Philadelphia County	1,025
Chester County	325
New Castle County	180
Kent County	139
Sussex County	106

The proportions for the Lower Counties, where the total obligation was only £425, were obviously different from those employed in the upper counties, an apparent recognition that the proceeds were expected ˌto benefit the province more than the territories. After eighteen years of union, the connection, whether of law, or of interest, or of affection, was a brittle one.

Isaac Norris, a Pennsylvania delegate, felt comfortable about the outcome of this session of the assembly. "I am," he wrote, on December 8, 1700, "at length got home from wearisome New Castle, after near seven weeks' session, much teasing, and sometimes almost off the hinges, for they would creak loudly; then we used to sit and reduce ourselves to good order again. Some turbulent spirits would often endeavor to drive it to a pitched battle betwixt upper counties and lower, Quakers and Churchmen; but, in short, we at length brought it to a pretty good conclusion."

Norris's satisfaction with the proceedings at New Castle and his sense of well-being could not last long. The animosity he noted between "upper counties and lower, Quakers and Churchmen," grew to a point where, in the 1701 assembly, the union fell "off the hinges" and never could be set right again.

Provincial and territorial rivalries were evident in a special assembly session held in August 1701. Only an emergency justified calling an assembly in this season, Penn admitted, but a royal command created an emergency for the proprietor. The command was for a contribution toward the heavy expense of fortifying the New York frontier against hostile Indians and the French. However much he deprecated warfare, Penn wanted the funds voted to the Crown, for royal disapproval could seriously endanger his property rights in America.

But the assembly majority was uncooperative. They had various excuses: "the infancy of the colony," the cost of settlement, the burden of taxes already assessed, the inaction of adjacent provinces. They gave Penn nothing but sweet words with which to assuage the disappointment of the king.

A minority of the assemblymen, however, had a special grievance. This minority consisted of seven Delaware delegates who, though no more eager than their colleagues to vote funds for New York's defenses, embarrassed Penn by complaining of their own defenseless state, exposed without cannon, without forts, without even a militia along a coast frequented by hostile ships. They asked the proprietor to explain their situation to King William so he would not expect these counties that lacked forts themselves to raise money for forts elsewhere.

It was a plea not only of Penn's territories against his province that would vote no money for defense; it was also a plea of Churchmen against Quakers who had religious scruples against military preparations. But from Penn's point of view this plea was most worrisome because of the trouble it could raise for him in his relations with authorities in England—possibly trouble enough to cost him all his American claims.

In England Penn's position was already insecure. A bill reuniting all private colonies to the Crown, the result of Edward Randolph's constant pressure against the chartered and proprietary colonies, had been introduced in the House of Lords. The Treasury was demanding that Penn pay the long-forgotten moiety of all revenue from Kent and Sussex, a sum claimed for the Duke of York in the 1682 deed of feoffment to Penn for the lands below the twelve-mile circle. Penn excused himself, weakly, for never paying a penny on the basis that the bounds of this territory had never been determined, but inasmuch as the duke had become king the claim had been inherited by the Crown, and the Treasury figured the debt to amount to £6,000. Still more seriously, the very origin of Penn's government of the Lower Counties was being challenged, for Edward Randolph argued that Penn had usurped this government on an imaginary title "grounded upon a sham law of his own contriving [the Act of Union] made at Chester by wheedling the credulous inhabitants to entreat him to take them under his protection."

Shortly after the close of the unproductive special assembly session in August 1701, Penn received such troubling reports from friends in England that he decided he must return to defend his rights and prevent the annulment of his charter. Consequently he called for elections to a new assembly which convened in Philadelphia on September 15. "Review again your laws," he told the assemblymen when they were met; "propose new ones that may better your circumstances, and what you do, do it quickly, remembering that parliament sits the end of next month; and that the sooner I am there, the safer, I hope, we shall be here."

The assembly did more and sat longer than Penn wished. He had hoped they would vote the £350 requested by the king for the New York frontier; such an evidence of willingness to support imperial needs would have helped him face his critics in England. But his petulant assembly-men preferred to present Penn within five days with a list of twenty-one requests, largely relating to property. Six of these requests particularly applied to the Lower Counties, including provisions for commons at New Castle and in the marsh lands along the bay and an assurance that the price of lands not yet disposed of would not be raised but would remain at the old rate of a bushel of wheat for each hundred acres.

Penn agreed to establish a New Castle commons, which he had previously promised, but regarded any attempt to prevent his sale of the bay marshes or to limit the price charged for land as an impertinence. He found the assemblymen hard to satisfy, possibly because of a widespread belief that he would soon lose his powers and be supplanted by a royal governor. A friendly Philadelphia assemblyman, commenting on the contentiousness of many of his colleagues, wrote, "They are now worse than ever, believing themselves cock-sure of the government change. Their endeavors are (I mean the lower county members and our malcontents here) to leave us, if possible, without laws, or liberties—oppose anything that we offer for our settlement."

The "lower county members" were particularly difficult on October 10 when a bill was read confirming the 104 statutes adopted at New Castle in the preceding fall. In Pennsylvania some question had been raised regarding the legality of acts passed outside the province proper, particularly in view of the current challenge to Penn's right to govern the Lower Counties and the possiblity that the 1682 Act of Union was illegal from the beginning or that it had expired upon the renunciation of the frame of government in 1700. Protesting that if laws passed at New Castle could be considered illegal in Pennsylvania, then laws passed in the province might be equally questionable in the Lower Counties, nine members from the Lower Counties, including the entire New Castle and Kent delegations, walked out of the assembly. (The close commercial connection between Philadelphia and Lewes, home of the river pilots, apparently produced more sympathy for the province in Sussex than in the other Delaware counties.)

The nine members who walked out of the assembly called on Penn on October 14 to submit their objections in writing. Penn conferred with the assembly, which proceeded to debate the matter in the presence of the seceders, but no solution could be found that would satisfy everyone. The nine dissenters offered to rejoin the assembly if they could record their objections to the bill confirming the laws and if nothing would be carried over their heads by outvoting them. This second proviso was considered preposterous and refused, and so the nine members once again withdrew.

Penn pleaded with them to "yield in Circumstantials to preserve Essentials" and begged them, "Make me not sad now I am going to leave you." His plea had some success. The Delaware delegates returned to the assembly and continued there, though attending irregularly, through the remaining two weeks of the fall session of 1701. To gain this much cooperation, Penn promised these delegates they could break away if they wished. On October 27, the next-to-last day of the session, he sent a new charter to be read in the assembly, the fourth and last charter or frame of government that his colonists were to live by. After the reading the assemblymen dispatched William Rodeney and a Pennsylvania delegate to ask Penn to keep his promise by adding some provision for an end to the union of the province and the Lower Counties. Reluctantly Penn provided a codicil as a postscript to the charter, permitting the division he did not wish.*

If within the next three years, the codicil read, the majority of the elected members of assembly from either the province or the territories should inform Penn that they no longer wished to meet in a joint assembly, he would permit them to meet separately. In that case each Pennsylvania county might elect at least eight assemblymen and the city of Philadelphia two. The Lower Counties might choose to their "distinct Assembly" as many delegates as they wished.

For Penn, this clause was a surrender, an abandonment of his desire to bulwark his claims to the Lower Counties by a tight union between these counties and Pennsylvania. Immediate necessities, however, forced this surrender. The entire proprietorship was in danger from those who, like Randolph and Nicholson, would convert all private colonies into royal territories, directly subject to the English government. The dissenting territorial delegates were largely members of the Church of England and friends or adherents of a Church faction forming in the Delaware valley

---

* At this time Penn also ordered a survey of the northern boundary of the Delaware counties, the twelve-mile circle that separated New Castle from Pennsylvania. Isaac Taylor and Thomas Pierson marked this line between November 26 and December 4, 1701, cutting three notches on each side of the trees along their way.

that sought to weaken or destroy the hegemony of both the Quaker and the proprietary interests. Any sign of discontent could be used against Penn in England.

The charter of 1701, conferring a large measure of autonomy on his colonists and permitting their division into two colonies, was the price Penn reluctantly paid for putting his house in order before he sailed for England on November 1, 1701. With the likelihood before him of losing his American possessions, it was not a time for petty quarrels over the terms of their government.

Despite Penn's best efforts over the next three years he was unable to prevent the permanent legislative separation of the Lower Counties from Pennsylvania. Differences of opinion over military defenses increased in the regime of Andrew Hamilton, whom Penn appointed as deputy governor in November 1701. Hamilton, who was already governor of New Jersey, tried to establish a militia, but he could not enlist enough men to make a good showing; not only did the Quakers oppose him on the grounds of religious principle, but the antiproprietary party, hoping to bring down the whole structure of Penn's government, dissuaded non-Quakers from cooperating with Hamilton both in Philadelphia and in the Lower Counties. One leader of this party, Judge Robert Quary of the Admiralty Court, took a petition to England from eight of the seceding Delaware assemblymen, complaining bitterly of their defenseless state and permitting Quary to appeal on their behalf for a change of government that would make the Lower Counties the direct responsibility of the Crown.

Despite such efforts to weaken or destroy proprietary government, Penn's influence with the new monarch, Queen Anne (who succeeded her brother-in-law William III in January 1702), was sufficient to gain royal approval of his appointment of Andrew Hamilton. By the influence of the Board of Trade, however, the approval was for one year only and was accompanied by a declaration that it did not diminish the rights of the Crown to the Lower Counties. Thus, the challenge to Penn's rights in the Lower Counties was kept alive, but the proprietorship escaped a frontal assault when a bill to convert Pennsylvania into a royal colony was allowed to lapse without passage.

The Board of Trade sent Quary home in the fall with a message of encouragement to the Delaware petitioners; their professed interest in military defenses naturally endeared them to those charged with over-seeing the problems of a far-flung empire. The board's response did little to put these Lower County politicians in a mood to cooperate with Andrew Hamilton.

Therefore early in October 1702, when the new charter called for elections to the assembly, the Lower Counties ignored the matter completely, explaining that they had never accepted the charter. The speaker of the assembly had approved the new charter by signing it, they admitted, but he had done so after the Lower Counties had ceased to be fully represented in the assembly. With no delegates present from the Lower Counties the majority needed for a quorum was lacking and the Pennsylvania assemblymen could pass no legislation. Under the leadership of David Lloyd and his father-in-law, Joseph Growdon, they asked Hamilton to put into effect that proviso of the new charter which enlarged the provincial representation and allowed them to act separately if the territorial delegates withdrew permanently.

Hamilton sought to delay a final schism. There could be no new election under the terms of the charter, he explained, until October 1703. To break the tie with the Lower Counties meant a risk of losing the chief export crop, tobacco, which originated there, for leaving the Lower Counties out of the assembly would strengthen the movement to make a separate royal colony of them. The Pennsylvania assemblymen agreed to adjourn for a month, and Hamilton rushed off writs of election to New Castle, Dover, and Lewes.

When the Assembly reconvened in Philadelphia in November 1702, newly elected representatives from the Lower Counties were in the city. But they would not meet with the Pennsylvanians. The Lower County delegates insisted they were elected under writs issued by the deputy governor; if they met with Pennsylvanians, elected under the charter, they might seem to be approving the charter, and this they were resolved not to do.

This specious reasoning pleased some Pennsylvanians, notably David Lloyd, who looked upon the Lower Counties as a hindrance to Quaker control of legislation, but most of the provincial delegates, eager to free themselves of blame for the separation, were more cooperative than Lloyd and consented to meet with the Delawareans. The latter, however, would not cooperate. They had accepted election and come to Philadelphia—probably only by accepting election could the antiproprietary leaders be sure of maintaining control of the delegation—but eight of them, including the ringleaders from New Castle (the other four territorial delegates were absent because of illness), refused to sit in a joint assembly. As Jasper Yeates, a New Castle delegate, explained frankly, they chose to wait to see what happened in England since affairs relating to them were on the anvil.

To the delight of David Lloyd, the recalcitrance of these eight men made it impossible for the assembly to enact legislation on two matters that Governor Hamilton regarded as pressing: aid for the New York frontier against the French and Indians, and defense of the Delaware by establishment of an effective militia. Both measures were disagreeable to the Quakers, who were glad to shift blame for inaction to the representatives of the Lower Counties.

Andrew Hamilton died in April 1703, before he could make a further effort to reunite the two parts of Penn's domains. The council temporarily acted as the executive and, in the absence of any strong single deputy governor who might represent the proprietor's policies, political leaders in Pennsylvania ran the fall elections as they pleased, doubling the number of representatives from each county and adding two from Philadelphia so as to create a new and complete provincial assembly according to the terms of the codicil to the charter. To their delight, they could at once free themselves of the encumbrance of the Lower Counties representation and yet blame the state of affairs upon these same counties. The council, however, refused to accept the Pennsylvania returns, and the Lower Counties held no elections because they still argued that the charter was inoperative.

While decisions in America were thus delayed, Penn's position in England was growing stronger. With friends in positions of power at the court of Queen Anne, he was able to repel the antiproprietary measures of the Board of Trade and of such colonial agents as Quary, Randolph, and Nicholson. Pressed by debts, particularly those in which he was entangled by his own steward, Philip Ford, Penn offered to sell a part of his proprietary rights, the right to the government, while retaining his rights to the soil and asked for a patent to the Lower Counties that would complete the "grant begun by the late King James."

In this very year of 1702 just such a transfer of governmental power as Penn had in mind was under way, as Penn well knew, in the neighboring colonies of East and West Jersey; there the two boards of proprietors ceded all their troublesome governmental rights and responsibilities in return for the maintenance of a firm title to the soil. The details of the bargain Penn sought would have been, for him, very good indeed: £30,000 to give up the cares of government in return for a firmer title than he had ever before held to the soil of the Lower Counties, as well as retention of his magnificent domains in Pennsylvania and some other perquisites. With much reason, the Board of Trade, otherwise eager to end all political proprietorships, recommended against acceptance of Penn's terms which, including as they did some special political concessions, seemed likely to weaken the Crown's authority rather than to strengthen it.

To replace Hamilton as his deputy, Penn chose a young Welshman, John Evans, who arrived in America early in February 1704, having been properly approved by the Crown after Penn agreed, once again, to concede that in regard to the Lower Counties the royal approval of Evans did not diminish in any manner any rights of the Crown. The new governor quickly sought to heal the schism on the Delaware. To encourage support in the Lower Counties, Evans made new appointments from them to his council, where it was agreed there should be at least one member from each county. His pleas strengthened by popular knowledge that Quary's efforts to remove the Lower Counties from Penn's jurisdiction had failed, Evans persuaded them to elect delegates to an assembly he scheduled to meet at Philadelphia in April 1704.

When the new representatives went to Philadelphia, however, they found that the Pennsylvania representatives, elected according to a new apportionment in the previous October, claimed to be a complete assembly in themselves. It was the delegates of the Lower Counties who now played suitor and the Pennsylvanians who rejected them. Governor Evans tried his best to bring about a reconciliation, but David Lloyd and the Quaker faction in Pennsylvania presented the new governor with a *fait accompli*. They had their new assembly of eight delegates per county and two from Philadelphia City, and they had no intention of decreasing their numbers or, and here was the rub, of admitting the Lower Counties to equal status, which would mean an opportunity to obstruct all legislation. As Penn had argued, one Pennsylvania county alone (Philadelphia County) had more taxable wealth than all three Lower Counties. This being the case, no popular political faction in Pennsylvania could possibly assent to revival of a situation in which the tail could wag the dog.

The only recourse left to the Lower Counties was to go their own way, as they had been threatening to do. After a conference with his chief justice, Governor Evans decided there must be a special election before a separate assembly could be held in the Lower Counties. Although writs were first issued for the election of representatives on May 12, 1704, to attend an assembly on May 22, the election was apparently postponed until October 25, with the first Delaware assembly, consisting of four representatives from each county, meeting in New Castle in November 1704. Governor Evans and at least some of his councillors traveled to the old riverside town and there approved the first two laws enacted for the Delaware colony by its own separate assembly: one confirming all the laws previously enacted by the joint assembly and another increasing the number of representatives from each county to six and providing that they should be elected at the time given in the 1701 charter.

William Rodeney (as he spelled his name), of Kent County, is believed to have been the speaker of this assembly; by coincidence his grandson, Caesar Rodney, presided over the last colonial assembly of the Lower Counties. Governor Evans, who had established a militia in May, wanted the assembly to pass a militia law, but they postponed this matter, exhibiting in this first session some degree of the independence that they apparently felt. Possibly there was some difference of opinion in the assembly about Quakers being exempt from militia duty. Governor Evans had restricted his militia proclamation in Pennsylvania to those inhabitants who had no religious compunctions against taking up arms in their own defense; in the Lower Counties he made no exceptions to his call, arguing that few of the people were Quakers.

Another difference of opinion may have emerged at this first assembly that was to be a characteristic of Delaware politics for years to come—a difference in attitude between New Castle and the rest of this small colony. In this assembly, according to James Logan, the provincial secretary, a New Castle junto sought to make the separation from Pennsylvania complete so that New Castle would replace Philadelphia as the center of trade of all the Lower Counties. Others saw no advantage in such an arrangement and sought to retain some connection with Pennsylvania, even at the price of accepting the 1701 charter.

In the long run, there was a compromise. The political separation from Pennsylvania, so far as it went, was permanent. An assembly continued to meet at New Castle and the laws it enacted, though they still required the governor's approval, gradually added to the differences, heretofore largely geographic and cultural, between the Lower Counties and Pennsylvania. Some political unity remained, in the person of the governor and other elements of proprietary authority (for example, the council, as an advisory body of ever diminishing responsibility, and the land office). Moreover, the economic and intellectual suzerainty of Philadelphia over the Lower Counties grew rather than abated. New Castle simply could not provide sufficient competition. As a mart of trade, it remained only a station (though the most important station) on the river route between Philadelphia and the sea. Periodically, when the Lower County assemblymen gathered at New Castle and the governor and his small retinue came from Philadelphia to meet them, this small port and county town had a moment of grandeur. But it lacked the waterfalls that might have made it the center of a milling industry and it lacked an easy water route to the hinterland which some stream tributary to the Delaware might have afforded. In time Wilmington, "an upstart village on a neighboring creek," gained significance as an economic satellite to Philadelphia and replaced the old river town as the economic center of New Castle County.

6

THE REWARDS OF OBSCURITY

Six assemblymen were chosen in May 1705 from each of the three Lower Counties in a special election called by Governor Evans. He was rewarded by prompt passage of a militia act, despite the opposition of four Quaker assemblymen, including Speaker William Clark of Lewes, who died "of a surfeit of cherries" soon after the assembly adjourned. By fall, Penn's American secretary was happy to report that the Lower Counties, though "miserably poor," had the best militia for their number of any place on the continent. "They appear very well affected and easy," he wrote, happy that for the first time in four years they had taxed themselves for the support of the government.

The assembly that gave James Logan so much satisfaction in the fall of 1705 was elected according to the terms of the charter of 1701, which the Lower Counties now acknowledged as the basis of their government. "By this Charter," the Pennsylvania assemblymen had assured them, while rejecting union in 1704, "you . . . have the Opportunity of forming yourselves into a distinct Assembly and enjoying the Privileges thereof as well as the Province." In 1705, at last, the Lower Counties accepted their new status, and in the fall of 1706 they capitalized upon it by passing seventy-nine laws, some new, but many of them mere reenactments of statutes passed in the old joint assembly that had represented both province and territories until the schism of 1701.

There was one truly remarkable feature connected with the legislation of the New Castle assembly. Unlike the acts of the old joint assembly, unlike the acts of the newly separate Pennsylvania assembly, the acts of the assembly at New Castle were never subject to review in England. They did, of course, need the approval of the governor, and he was, by his commission, a representative of the Crown as well as of the proprietor in his role in the Lower Counties. But even after receiving the governor's approval, all Pennsylvania statutes, by a provision of Penn's royal grant of the province, had to be submitted within five years to the king in council, and disapproval of a statute at this step nullified it absolutely.

The royal grant, however, was for the province, not the territories, which had gained a share in legislation only when Penn invited them to join the delegates from Pennsylvania in an assembly in 1682. Subsequently, passage of an act of union and then, when the union was splintered in 1701, provisions in the codicil to Penn's last frame of government for an assembly in the Lower Counties had seemed to establish permanently the right to legislate. It was, after all, a right that colonial Englishmen expected by the eighteenth century. Still, both Penn and his secretary questioned whether the Lower Counties had any power to make laws, let alone the large number they did make in 1706. Penn seemed to assume that these laws would need to be confirmed in England, but his governors never forwarded any of the laws made at New Castle.

Probably both Penn and Logan were tempted to question the authority of the New Castle assembly because there was a strong antiproprietary spirit in the Lower Counties. Uncertainty about the status of the government, whether it would remain under Penn after the separation or become a royal colony, like neighboring New Jersey, led landholders to withhold the payment of quitrents. Even payments from new settlers were hard to collect, especially when the land they took up lay anywhere near the disputed Maryland boundaries. At New Castle, James Logan reported to Penn, "they use the same language [in relation to Pennsylvania] as the Scots do in relation to England," even demanding "that all their officers shall live among themselves, even the Councils and Attorney General."

Hope arose of close cooperation between Pennsylvania and the Lower Counties after the young governor, John Evans, bought a plantation in the vicinity of New Castle. In that hope, some of the leading men in New Castle joined the governor in an elaborate hoax intended to demonstrate to Philadelphians the danger of their defenseless position in time of war. On the morning of May 16, 1706, John French, sheriff of New Castle, accompanied by the clerk of the peace, rode pell-mell into Philadelphia, bringing dire tidings. Lewes was plundered and burned, he said, and showed a letter from Sussex to that effect; worse yet, six French brigantines had passed New Castle moving upstream at 2 A.M. and had unleashed a cannonade against the town from forty or fifty guns.

The news spread quickly, as Governor Evans galloped through the streets on horseback with drawn sword, urging able-bodied men to hurry with arms to a rendezvous on Society Hill. Three hundred men gathered there, but others hid in their homes or fled up the Delaware; in the excitement silver and other household valuables that marauders might steal were thrown down wells or outhouses.

The bulk of the Quakers remained calm, their leaders reported, despite the mutterings against them. Gradually, Philadelphians began to suspect they were being trifled with. Secretary Logan persuaded four oarsmen to row him down the Delaware till they met a shallop coming upstream and learned there were no enemy ships in the river. By evening Philadelphia was seething with anger at the governor and his New Castle confederates. A local rimester summed up the excitement:

> Wise men wonder, good men grieve,
> Knaves invent, and fools believe.

Governor John Evans was young, imprudent, and possibly foolish, but not knavish. His feud with Philadelphia that began with the hoax of May 1706 almost turned into warfare in 1707—if, that is, there could be a war where one side would not bear arms. Disregarding the advice of the governor's council, which was granted no share in legislation, the assembly of the Lower Counties decided in the fall of 1706 to erect a fort at New Castle for protection of the river and to levy a charge of one-half pound of gunpowder per ton on all passing ships on the Delaware except naval vessels and those belonging to a river port, whether in Pennsylvania, Jersey, or the Lower Counties.

Councilmen protested, without success, that Penn's grant to Pennsylvania guaranteed free access to the ocean. To the consternation of his Pennsylvania advisers, Governor Evans hurried the project along by journeying to New York and bringing back a Captain Rednap, a royal engineer, to supervise the fort's construction, and in the spring of 1707 Evans ordered the collection of powder money to begin.

A merchant named Richard Hill, son-in-law of Thomas Lloyd and a member of council, determining to test the law, took personal command of a new sloop, the *Philadelphia*, of which he was part owner, on her initial voyage to Barbados. As a ship based on the Delaware, the *Philadelphia* was not obliged to pay duty, but Governor Evans became angry at Hill for declaring that his sloop would not even stop at New Castle to show her papers. The *Philadelphia* did drop anchor north of the fort, and two councilmen, Isaac Norris and Samuel Preston, Quakers and possibly part-owners, went ashore to ask Evans to permit the ship, already cleared for this voyage in Philadelphia, to pass without inspection. Evans refused, whereupon Hill sailed by the fort without suffering any damage from its guns except for one shot through the mainsail.

However, New Castle sheriff John French, commander of the fort under Evans, pursued the *Philadelphia* in an armed boat and boarded her. Once French was aboard, the line to his boat was cut and he found himself a prisoner. Out-distancing pursuit, Hill brought his sloop into the Salem River in New Jersey and turned Sheriff French over to Edward Hyde, Lord Cornbury, governor of both New Jersey and New York, who happened to be there. Cornbury, of course, was as angry as the Pennsylvanians at the attempt of the New Castle assembly to tax vessels using the river and he reprimanded French coarsely, extracting promises before releasing him. Apparently attempts to collect powder money were thereafter abandoned, probably in response to Cornbury's warnings as well as to a petition signed by over 220 Pennsylvanians who insisted that the New Castle assembly could control only such vessels as were bound to ports in the Lower Counties.

Perhaps Lord Cornbury's logic was compelling. It was ridiculous, he argued, for the Lower Counties to dare think they could interfere with trade between New York and Burlington. If they persisted he would put guns at the point where the Swedes once had a fort at the mouth of Salem River and would charge vessels going to or from New Castle three times as much as Governor Evans sought to collect.

The reports of Evans's actions, including tales of his descending beneath the dignity of his station "in midnight revels and low frolics of youthful folly," had meanwhile reached Penn, along with demands that Evans be replaced. In choosing a successor to Evans, Penn again looked to the military, perhaps because the nation was at war and the choice of a soldier as his deputy might deflate some criticism of Quaker government. The new choice was Charles Gookin, a professional soldier who was older than Evans and thought to be more mature. Gookin's appointment was approved by the Queen in July 1708, but only, as far as the Lower Counties were concerned, at the Queen's pleasure (for Pennsylvania the term of appointment was at Penn's pleasure) and only after Penn once again acknowledged that this approval should not be construed in any way to diminish the Queen's claim to the Lower Counties. Penn remonstrated against this implied challenge to his rights to the Lower Counties, suggesting that only his right to govern them (as distinct from land ownership) was in question, but the government rejected his protest.

A serious challenge to Penn's title was raised in October 1708 in New Castle, where some assemblymen hoped to enlist the retiring governor as their ally in challenging proprietary claims. Evans was about to marry the daughter of John Moore, the customs collector at Philadelphia, a member of the antiproprietary faction, and bring her to his plantation at Swanhook, outside New Castle. Hoping Evans might want to remain among them, these assemblymen planned to seek his reappointment as a royal governor.

As an entering wedge to a full-scale attack on the proprietorship, the assemblymen asked Evans for a vindication of his powers of government. This was no attack on Evans himself, for everyone knew a new governor was on the way; it was an attempt to probe the weakness of Penn's title. Evans refused to cooperate. He had published his commission on his arrival, he said, and once the proprietor's charter was accepted he had cooperated with the assembly, even though they passed many more laws than he thought necessary for any colony. It was not necessary now to vindicate an authority he was about to give up.

Failing to win Evans's cooperation, nine of the seventeen members of the assembly of the Lower Counties (one seat was vacant) prepared an address to the Board of Trade in England to be delivered personally by Speaker James Coutts. They were defenseless, they said; they lacked power to enact laws; they had had no provincial courts for about seven years, or since their legislative separation from Pennsylvania. These and other complaints were due to their proprietary government, and particularly to the influence of Penn himself and of the Quakers. And all these problems might be cured by a change to a direct royal government either as a separate colony or in connection with an existing royal colony.

This address had no support at all among the Sussex delegates, who were apparently satisfied with their relation to the proprietorship and to Philadelphia and no wish to exchange their Philadelphia connection for an entire dependency on New Castle. It might have been expected from their proximity to the ocean that the inhabitants of Sussex County would have had the most to say about the defenselessness of the colony against maritime raids. Possibly this was of more concern to the merchants of New Castle than to the farmers of Sussex, for the six Sussex County delegates, joined by one ally from Kent and another from New Castle (the latter a Quaker), and with the approval of Governor Evans, withdrew from the assembly and returned to their homes. Their withdrawal necessarily adjourned the assembly, for the remaining nine members were one short of the majority needed for a quorum. At their request Evans issued a writ for a special election to fill the vacancy in the New Castle County delegation, but fear of upsetting the established order on the Delaware apparently turned voters against the antiproprietary faction, and they lost the election by a very decided margin. Nevertheless, Coutts carried the address to the Board of Trade in England, protesting the existing government, but the force of the address was weakened by the fact that it was only an unofficial statement by nine members of the assembly.

Relations between the new governor, Charles Gookin, and the Lower Counties were initially very good. Penn instructed Gookin to unite the Lower Counties to Pennsylvania, but this was patently impossible and Gookin wasted little time in the effort. The assembly of the Lower Counties did quickly vote Gookin £200 for the support of the government, about as much as they had voted Evans in his entire term. This act of generosity was most likely motivated by the continuing threat of a French attack.

The French had attacked Lewes on May 7, 1709, landing several dozen men who roamed through the town seizing whatever they wanted and holding four citizens for a ransom of Indian corn and sheep. Gookin called on the Pennsylvania assembly to aid the defense of the Lower Counties. "You are not now *falsely alarmed*," he warned, referring to Evans's hoax; "if they perish, in all probability your destruction will not be far off."

On July 6 and 7 the French returned to Lewes and attempted a landing, probably again seeking provisions for their ships that were standing off the American coast to raid British commerce. This time, however, Governor Gookin was in Lewes, commanding defense forces—probably the local militia—and drove off the French.

Meanwhile Penn, encouraged by his agents in America and impelled to action by the financial morass he was in, was making serious efforts to sell the Crown his claims to the government of both Pennsylvania and the Lower Counties. In 1712 an agreement was reached, with the sum to be paid Penn for the two governments set at £12,000. The price, though less than Penn had first sought, seems reasonable in view of an estimate made by ex-Governor Evans of the annual income to the Crown. Evans thought Penn's two colonies brought in roughly £10,000 a year, mainly from the sale of tobacco grown in the Lower Counties but also derived from the tobacco duty, liquor and tavern licenses, fines and forfeitures (including the Crown's third of seizures for unlawful trade), ship registrations and clearances, and the proceeds of property and capitation taxes voted by the assemblies. Nothing was said of land sales because the soil and the government were considered separately. In return for sale of the government, Penn hoped to be able to make good his title to the soil of the Lower Counties, as well as of Pennsylvania.

The English government had paid Penn a substantial installment on the purchase price when suddenly he suffered a stroke that made him unable to consummate the sale. After his major attack, which occurred in October 1712, Penn never recovered sufficiently to attend to business. He was able to get about, to talk with friends and, with guidance, to sign his name to documents, but for the six final years of his life, from 1712 to 1718, it was his wife, Hannah Penn, who gave direction to proprietary affairs. The question of title to the Lower Counties, which might have been settled by the sale of Penn's claim in 1712, was kept alive by the accident of his illness to 1718, and then other problems arose to prevent a conclusive settlement.

One old problem declined in importance, for the Peace of Utrecht in 1713 ended what the colonists called Queen Anne's War and freed the Lower Counties from concern about their defenses against possible French naval attacks. To Governor Gookin the peace brought problems that were more difficult to meet than military assault. Increasingly he spent his days at a farm he had bought near New Castle, but residence in the Lower Counties did not noticeably enlarge his sympathy for the assemblymen who represented these counties. Perhaps some mental illness troubled him, for his political actions became very erratic, "the wildest of any thing that has ever been known this way," according to James Logan. In 1714 Gookin voided the commissions of all the justices of the peace in New Castle County and left the county without any courts for a month. He is said to have sold the office of clerk in Kent to the highest bidder and to have refused to recognize the 1715 election in New Castle when it returned John French, whom he disliked, as sheriff. When the assembly met, it ordered French to take possession of the jail, whereupon Gookin and some associates tried to break down the jail door and forcibly remove French.

Startled assemblymen watched the wild scene until the distraught governor gave up and left town, refusing to sign any bills and offering the assembly, in their words, only "Contemptuous Usage and il Language." The assembly complained to William Penn then and again the next year, when Gookin once more refused to cooperate with them in any way, stifling any hopes of new legislation.

The proprietor's friends warned him (which meant in reality warning Hannah Penn, for her husband was beyond such cares) that Gookin undervalued proprietary rights in the Lower Counties and must be replaced before he secured direct royal authorization to govern. They were glad to be able to recommend a replacement, one William Keith, soon to be Sir William and a Scottish baronet, a young man of vigor and understanding who was temporarily unemployed and almost permanently impoverished. He had briefly served as surveyor of customs in the southern colonies, but had been dismissed and was returning to England when he passed through New Castle and heard of the problems that the Lower Counties, and Pennsylvania too, were having with their governor. In a very short time he succeeded in promoting the idea that he would be a logical replacement for Gookin, and he returned to England with the endorsement of such leading colonial figures as James Logan.

Like Logan, Hannah Penn was favorably impressed by Keith and had her husband sign a commission, as well as the necessary waiver promising that royal approval of the appointment would not diminish the Crown's rights to the Lower Counties. Haste in making the appointment was obviously in order, not only because of Gookin's erratic actions in America but also because Parliament was considering a bill to abolish all colonial proprietorships. It was to the advantage of the Penns to bring good order to their colonies before colonial complaints against Gookin forced Parliament to consider the status of Pennsylvania and the Lower Counties. Apparently Hannah Penn did not take the time to look into the complaints of "unjustifyable proceedings" in Jamaica that had led in less than two years to Keith's dismissal from his last post.

It was probably very fortunate for the Penns, as far as their control of the Lower Counties was concerned, that they had moved quickly on the appointment of Keith, who was finally approved as governor by the Prince of Wales, acting as regent, on December 17, 1717. At this very time a new claimant to the Lower Counties had gained the ear of King George I, who had returned to his German domain, the electorate of Hanover, where he had been seated before the death of Queen Anne had propelled him to the throne of England.

The new claimant was a Scottish nobleman, John Gordon, the sixteenth Earl of Sutherland. As far as is known he had never seen the Lower Counties nor any part of America, in that respect being like William Penn when he sought an American province. Just as it was the interest of fellow Quakers that won Penn's attention to America, so it was the interest of fellow Scots in the Delaware valley that led Sutherland to petition King George for a grant to the three Lower Counties on the Delaware.

A kinsman named Kenneth Gordon, of whom little is known, and a well-remembered Anglican missionary of Scottish birth, the Reverend George Ross, rector of Immanuel Church in New Castle, are said to have brought the uncertain status of the Lower Counties to Sutherland's attention. Arrears of over £120,000 were due him from the Crown for his loyalty to the Hanoverian succession in 1715. He cited "his great zeal and activity for the Protestant Succession" in requesting a grant of the Lower Counties which, his petition read, "he is ready to prove do belong to the Crown."

On December 18, 1717, exactly one day after the Prince of Wales approved William Keith's appointment as lieutenant governor of Pennsylvania and the Lower Counties, the king's secretary forwarded Sutherland's petition from Hanover to the Board of Trade with a notation that the king was "inclined to favour his Lordship's request."

News of Sutherland's petition quite naturally upset the Penn interests. They pointed to the development that in thirty-five years had made the lands along the Delaware prosper. Naval stores, iron, and grain were resources that could be produced plentifully in the Penn colonies. The West Indies were already being supplied from there with flour and provision; grain was being sent to Portugal and other parts of Europe. A good market existed for clothing and other English manufactured goods. The production of hemp had begun in the Lower Counties, but Sutherland's petition put a full stop to development. Many of the settlers who had come to enjoy liberty of conscience under a proprietor of their own persuasion would be frightened away if this colony were given to Sutherland. To complete the purchase begun by the late queen would be a different matter, for the profitability of Barbados and other islands under the Crown was well known, as was the dismal condition of Carolina under a proprietorship.

On William Keith's arrival in America in May 1718 he lost little time in rallying local sentiment against the pretensions of Sutherland. To separate the three Lower Counties from "Mr. Penn's proprietary jurisdiction," he wrote to the Board of Trade, would "inevitably ruine the most flourishing Colony of so small an Extent in America." With his letter, Keith sent the Board a copy of the address he had received when he met the representatives of the Lower Counties in general assembly at New Castle on June 13, 1718, wherein they forcefully expressed their opposition to "the attempt craftly managed at home upon their rights and possessions," that is, Sutherland's petition.

The remainder of the address contained sentiments that are surprising in view of the antiproprietary and anti-Pennsylvania opinions that had recently flourished in this body. "Our present Proprietor Mr. Penn's interest and ours are so interwoven," the assemblymen wrote, and Jasper Yeates, as their speaker, signed, "that they are not to be separated without destroying each other." What a shame that Penn's health did not permit him to appreciate this expression of loyalty! But there was still more to delight the old proprietor, could he have read this address: "As we are situate by nature, we conceive the interest of Pennsylvania and ours to be so much the same that nothing could more contribute to the happiness of us both than an intire Union."

Had it taken the neurotic excesses of Gookin, the inspired greed of Sutherland, and perhaps the artful management of Keith to bring the Lower Counties to this point? No matter. However the result was brought about, Sutherland was stymied and his petitions pushed aside. But for William Penn these expressions of inseparable loyalty, of acknowledgment of his wisdom in encouraging union with the upriver counties came too late. On July 30, 1718, at Ruscombe, in Berkshire, not far from Windsor Castle, the old proprietor died.

Though the administration of William Keith in the Lower Counties began with new expressions of loyalty to Penn and of affectionate attachment to his province, Keith's course was uneven. Before his term was over the last serious effort (prior to the American Revolution) to separate the three Delaware counties from even their few remaining connections with Pennsylvania, as well as from the proprietary family in England, had occurred. Part of the explanation of Keith's conduct lies in his own character, in his ambitions and his needs; another part lies in the tangled nature of the Penn title to the Lower Counties.

Besides the Sutherland petition and the threat of direct Crown control due to the failure of the proprietor to pay that half portion of the income from Kent and Sussex which he had pledged to the Duke of York, other problems about the title to the Lower Counties arose upon the death of William Penn. By a will made in 1712 he had disinherited his improvident oldest son, William Penn, Jr., in favor of the children of his second marriage. To further complicate matters, the will set up two groups of trustees, one for the government of his American domains and the other for the management of lands and other property there. Still another interested group were the mortgagees, the men who had earlier taken a mortgage on Penn's property to save him from debtor's prison.

The key to the situation lay in the capable hands of Penn's widow, the former Hannah Callowhill, who was named sole executrix by his will. She had already gained experience in the management of Penn's affairs in the last six years of his life, when he was incapacitated for business. In the eight years of life remaining to her after his death in 1718, even though she was herself an invalid in the last five of these years, she untangled the main knots in the affairs of the estate.

The sale of Penn's rights to government, under way when the will was written in 1712 but then suspended by his illness even though a down payment of £1,000 had been made, was eventually canceled and the down payment restored to the Crown. With the help of the mortgagees Hannah Penn fought successfully against Sutherland's petition for the Lower Counties, reminding the Board of Trade, which was considering the petition, that the inhabitants held their titles from William Penn; a particular point was made that the Naval Store Company of Bristol had recently made a large investment in a hemp plantation in Kent County from which it had so far no return. The rights of these private claimants could not be lightly ignored, and the board therefore recommended that a decision on the validity of Penn's claims to the Lower Counties should be sought in chancery before any consideration was given to Sutherland's petition.

This recommendation effectively pigeonholed the petition, for no legal decision, in chancery or elsewhere, was ever made between the conflicting claims to the Lower Counties of the Penn family and the Crown. Nothing ever came of occasional efforts to revive the claim of John Gordon, the Earl of Sutherland, before his death in 1733. His petition was never forthrightly denied; it was simply ignored.

A court decision did play a part in solving an intra-family dispute about the proprietorship. The only surviving son of Penn's first marriage, William Penn, Jr., died two years after his father, in 1720. To settle the validity of Penn's will against claims of the children of William Penn, Jr., Hannah Penn went to the Court of Exchequer, which eventually upheld the will in favor of Hannah and her children. By the time of this decision, handed down in 1727, Hannah was dead, but before her death she had acted, according to the provisions of Penn's will, to allocate shares in the proprietorship, one-half share going to her oldest son, John, and one-quarter shares to each of the two surviving younger sons. Although a few minor settlements remained to be arranged, at last, after slightly more than a decade of confusion, of claims and counterclaims to Pennsylvania and the Lower Counties, the proprietary title and power had passed, thanks to their mother's skill and determination, to John, Thomas, and Richard Penn.

Meanwhile, for a decade uncertainty about the authority of the Penns had provided opportunities and offered temptations to the ambitious, impecunious, clever William Keith. Even before William Penn's death his new lieutenant governor was proposing a change in the status of the Delaware colonies, urging that West Jersey, Pennsylvania, and the Lower Counties be brought into one government. By this time he had personally visited all three Delaware counties and begun a process of ingratiating himself with the people, or at least with their leaders, a process which he renewed every year at the meetings of the assembly, where by design he was very obliging and sympathetic, making common cause with the colonists even if it meant flaunting or ignoring the desires of the proprietors.

This became all the easier after Penn's death when William Penn, Jr., tried briefly to insist on his rights to his father's colonies. After learning that these claims were put forward without authority, Keith gradually was emboldened to ignore all the Penns and act like a royal governor which, as far as the Lower Counties were concerned, the Board of Trade insisted he was. He issued commissions and other official documents in the name of the king, without reference to the Penns; he adopted a new seal for the Lower Counties that bore no reference to the proprietors; he dismissed faithful and able James Logan as secretary, and insisted that he, Keith, alone had power to sell lands and dispose of property.

To the dismay of the Penns, this bold deputy encouraged people of the Lower Counties to consider abolishing all arrears on quitrents by statute and to issue paper money, as the assembly did in 1723, when an economic depression caused a decline of trade and a shortage of currency that made the situation of debtors especially difficult. As time went on, Keith increasingly neglected the council, a stronghold of the friends of the proprietors, though he made a point of seeing that two seats on it were filled by residents of the Lower Counties. In approving new courts and a new criminal code, he demonstrated his concern for the people of the Lower Counties, and he spared no pains to tell them so, while at the same time disclaiming responsibility "for other People's Neglect" of them.

It is difficult to know whether ambition or financial need was the compelling motive behind Keith's increasingly independent course. On almost every visit to New Castle he reminded the assembly of his financial dependence on their generosity, and his popularity was recognized by their response. He did indeed need the appropriations he was voted; with their lands mortgaged and their title threatened the proprietors could hardly do other than leave their deputy at the financial mercy of the colonists. There were a few fixed fees that customarily reverted to the executive, the principal one a fee for licenses of public houses (taverns and inns), but these were insufficient to support any governor, and certainly not enough for a young baronet (which Keith became upon his father's death) who liked to live well but was only gradually paying off the debt he incurred in bringing his wife and children to America.

Though his family lived in Pennsylvania, Keith in 1722 purchased an extensive tract in New Castle County near Iron Hill, calling it Keithsborough and building an iron furnace and forge to utilize the ore that was dug from open pits in the vicinity. His apparent success, political and economic, led Keith to think that the regard of the proprietors and their agents was of little importance to him. For two years, from 1722 to 1724, he did not even correspond with the Penns, yet during this time he constantly sought the attention of the Crown, requesting the guidance of "His Majesty's Orders and Instructions."

Evidently Keith expected the Crown to take over the government of

Pennsylvania or at least that of the Lower Counties, and he probably believed that his position was so solid that the proprietary family could not remove him. In 1724, at the height of his popularity, Keith took the most extravagantly independent step of his administration of the Lower Counties when he issued a new charter for the town of New Castle, creating it a city with greatly expanded boundaries (the Christina River on the north and the Appoquinimink on the south), with new courts, distinct from the county courts, new officials, named in the charter, and special representation, independent of its county, in the assembly. To proclaim this remarkable new charter, transforming a town of a thousand people into a city covering forty square miles, the governor and his lady came there with a retinue on the king's birthday, and while cannon were fired to celebrate the occasion they sat down to a banquet with the new city officials. After dinner all the members of the royal family were toasted, but no toast to any of the Penns is recorded. Nor was proprietary authority referred to in the new city charter, which Keith issued in the name of the king.

Sir William had gone too far. In May 1724, the month and year of this ceremony at New Castle, Hannah Penn, though she had not yet heard of this event, sent Keith a letter of reprimand, intimating that she would have dismissed him were she not concerned for his family and giving him specific instructions regarding his future conduct. By the time he received this letter Keith must have thought he could not retreat, particularly in the matter of the New Castle charter. He made the letter public, hoping to encourage popular discontent with proprietary power, and discussed it with his friend Alexander Spotswood, lately governor of Virginia, who visited Keith on his way to England, where his influence might be helpful.

Spotswood did what he could. Finding Hannah Penn determined to get rid of Keith, Spotswood applied to the government, arguing that a replacement was calculated by the Penns to frustrate any inquiry into the debt owed the Crown from the revenue for Kent and Sussex counties. More than that, he questioned the right of the Penns to any political authority in the Lower Counties, where he hoped that Keith would be retained in his present place until conclusion of the controversy among the Penns about the inheritance, still unsettled in 1726, or at least that Keith might stay on as the king's "own appointed Governor for the three lower Counties on Delaware."

Spotswood's petition to the Crown on Keith's behalf was accompanied by another submitted by five of Keith's English creditors, who explained that he had made over his whole salary to them to pay his debts, subsisting only on the fees that were his perquisites of office. But Hannah Penn had sufficient determination and enough friends at court to secure approval of a new governor of her choice, though as to the Lower Counties the old disclaimer was again insisted upon, that approval of this appointment was in no way to be construed as diminishing the right of the Crown to the Lower Counties. Not only Hannah, as executrix of Penn's will, but also Springett Penn, William Junior's son, the heir to whatever claims Hannah's step-children might have, signed this disclaimer in March 1726. The exchequer suit over the inheritance was not yet settled, but the Penns were united in wishing Keith recalled.

The new governor was Major Patrick Gordon, a loyal Scot and a veteran soldier, but probably no close connection of the other Gordon in this history, the Earl of Sutherland. Formally approved by the king in council on April 18, 1726, Gordon arrived in America on June 22, to the joy of the friends and agents of the Penn family, such as James Logan, who was reinstated as secretary on June 24.

There had been fear Keith would refuse to surrender his post and he may have had some action in mind, at least in the Lower Counties, for he issued writs asking the assembly to meet him at Dover (instead of New Castle). Penn's land agent declared he "believed some extraordinary matters" would be attempted, but this assembly seems never to have met; probably Gordon arrived too soon for Keith's plans to mature.

Keith then busied himself attempting to organize an antiproprietary political party with a popular base. He circulated petitions that had as their purpose, according to Logan, "to wrench the Lower Counties from the Prop[rietor]s, and to divide their Trade from the Prov[ince]." He also offered himself as a candidate for the assembly from New Castle County.

Somewhat surprisingly, however, the people of the Lower Counties rallied round the new governor. Perhaps they were frightened back into the arms of the Penns by news Gordon brought. Not only had the Earl of Sutherland renewed his effort to acquire these counties, but Lord Baltimore too had revived his claim to them. Quite obviously any agitation to separate Delaware from the relatively mild administration of the Penns might play into the hands of another claimant to the proprietorship. It was one thing to complain of the Penns' eagerness for an income from the Delaware counties; it was another matter to supplant the Penns with a Scottish lord who wanted to make a profit, or to fall into the hands of Lord Baltimore and the Marylanders, with whom the residents of the Lower Counties shared a long history of border wars and fracases ranging from Lewes to Ogletown.

Though defeated at the elections in New Castle County, Keith succeeded in gaining a seat from Philadelphia in the Pennsylvania assembly and continued his machinations in both governments. Governor Gordon became so annoyed with Keith that, despite his years—he was sixty-two—he challenged Keith to cross the river into New Jersey to settle their disagreements man to man. No duel occurred, but for more than a year Keith was at the center of an intrigue against Gordon and the proprietors. In return, Gordon did what he could to uphold his authority, dismissing several justices of the peace in Sussex County, dropping John French (the Speaker of the assembly) from the council, canceling the city charter Keith had given New Castle, and encouraging a young Scottish lawyer named Andrew Hamilton, who had lands in Kent and in 1727 was elected to the assembly, to take a leading part in that body and in the press in combating Keith's influence.

The struggle with Keith was finally won by forfeit. Without the perquisites and salary of office, Sir William could not keep up his political activities. Dodging his creditors and abandoning his family, he fled down the river from Philadelphia in a rowboat in March 1728. At New Castle he boarded a vessel bound for England and hid until it set sail.

Meeting at New Castle in the fall of this same year, the assembly of the Lower Counties chose Andrew Hamilton as its new speaker. Governor Gordon, in his address to this assembly, announced that the dispute between branches of the Penn family was ended and that progress could now be expected in settling the controversies about titles and boundaries that had been troubling this small colony for decades.

The expected progress was very slow. Early in 1732 the three Penn brothers—John, Thomas, and Richard—now reasonably secure in their role as proprietors, reached an agreement in England with Charles, Lord Baltimore, that they hoped would end the boundary controversy. Baltimore gave up his claim to the Lower Counties and accepted Fenwick Island (the false Cape Henlopen) as the southern boundary in return for compensation on the northern line, which was to be located fifteen miles below the southern edge of Philadelphia. The details of the boundary of the Lower Counties were in general agreement with the decision of the Crown in 1685. A transpeninsular line was to be drawn westward from Fenwick Island to the Chesapeake. From the middle point on this line, another straight line was to be surveyed northward to make a tangent with a twelve-mile circle around New Castle. From the tangent point a line was to lead directly north to an east-west line drawn fifteen miles south of a parallel from the most southern part of Philadelphia.

A further provision of the agreement, settled upon in May 1732, was that each side to it would appoint commissioners, residents in America, who would see that the boundary delineation was begun in October 1732 and completed by Christmas 1733. Lord Baltimore, however, soon came to regret the concessions he had made, and his commissioners found excuses to delay action.

Meanwhile new outbreaks of violence had occurred on the border. One, for example, involved a man named James Newton who had bought land on the western edge of Kent County. Thinking it was in Maryland, he paid taxes on it there at first, but upon learning it had originally been surveyed, "seated," and assessed for taxes as a part of Kent County on the Delaware, he ceased paying Maryland taxes. He refused repeated demands made on him by the tax collector of Dorchester County, Maryland, whereupon, in 1732, the undersheriff of that county, accompanied by "Ten or a dozen lusty, pirt fellows," burst into his house early one morning and carried him off, heading for Cambridge jail. A Kent County constable learned of the seizure and rallied a number of Newton's neighbors. Setting off after the Maryland posse, they rescued Newton "after a Bloody Battle (but no life lost)," as a contemporary told the tale.

While accounts of such incidents were piling up in the correspondence of the Penns, they were troubled to hear that the Crown was about to offer the Lower Counties to Robert Hunter, a popular veteran of Marlborough's campaigns who was now governor of Jamaica but had formerly been governor of New York and New Jersey. From his term in North America Hunter had a considerable claim against the Crown for money he had advanced to assist German settlers on the Hudson. Possibly there was some basis for the rumor he would be recompensed by a gift of the Lower Counties, but Hunter died in 1734 before any such gift had been made. A more persistent threat to the Penn title came, as in times past, from Lord Baltimore, for this worthy, ignoring his agreement to surrender the Lower Counties, renewed his claim to them in August 1734.

In a petition to the king he argued that the words *"hactenus inculta"* (hitherto unpopulated) in his 1632 grant to Maryland had been interpreted incorrectly in 1685 to deny him his rights to the Lower Counties because of the small and impermanent 1631 Dutch settlement at Lewes. In 1638, he noted, his grant had been judged to include Kent Island despite an earlier settlement there by William Claiborne. The grounds of the 1638 decision were that Claiborne's settlement had no prior right in English law and was not meant to be excluded. Why did not the same reasoning apply to Swanendael?

The Board of Trade, in January 1735, agreed that it did and upheld Baltimore. Fortunately for the Penns, the opinions of the Board of Trade had no legal force, being only recommendations to the Privy Council; therefore the Penns asked the council to delay action while they took their case to chancery, as they proceeded to do.

Fifteen years passed before the Court of Chancery gave its decision. When that decision was handed down by the Lord Chancellor, Philip Yorke, first Earl of Hardwicke, in 1750, it upheld the claims of the Penns against Lord Baltimore. Lord Hardwicke carefully avoided consideration of the rights of the Crown to theistm Lower Counties, but his decision put an end to the claims of the Maryland proprietors. The Penns' lengthy possession of the Delaware counties, supported by the agreement Baltimore had signed, destroyed whatever claim Baltimore might have had. Now at last the boundary lines could be surveyed and marked.

Years were still to pass before these boundaries were settled. Commissioners met in the fall of 1750 at New Castle and agreed on the spire of the courthouse there as the center of the twelve-mile circle that is Delaware's northern boundary. Surveyors* proceeded in December 1750 to Fenwick Island (traditionally pronounced Fenicks). Working steadily through the winter and spring they completed a survey of the transpeninsular line that was to form the southern boundary of Delaware.

In the course of the work several controversies arose, the most important concerning the middle point on this line, the point that was to be

---

* William Parsons and John Watson, from Pennsylvania, and John Emory and Thomas Jones, from Maryland.

the southwestern corner of Delaware. Its location depended on whether the survey should stop at Slaughter Creek, which was only two feet deep, or should be extended three miles farther west across Taylor's Island (a peninsula) to the shore of the Chesapeake itself.

Work stopped in June 1751, while an appeal was made to the Lord Chancellor, and the delay was lengthened by the death of Charles, the fifth Lord Baltimore, and by his will, in which he attempted to leave his proprietorship to his daughter and not to his young son, Frederick, who inherited the title. Eventually both title and proprietorship went to Frederick, who let the Penns have their way about the middle point in a compromise that enabled him to escape a judgment making him responsible for all the costs of the long chancery suit.

Work now was begun on the difficult task of running a straight line northward (but not directly north) from the middle point so as to make a tangent with the twelve-mile circle. Local surveyors worked on this line from December 1760 to August 1763, but the difficulty of the work led the proprietors to employ two highly respected English surveyors and scientists, Charles Mason and Jeremiah Dixon, to complete the line.

Soon after their arrival in America in the fall of 1763 Mason and Dixon determined the latitude of the southern edge of Philadelphia, because the Maryland–Pennsylvania boundary was to be drawn exactly fifteen miles south of this latitude. They then moved westward of Philadelphia to the forks of the Brandywine and measured off fifteen miles to the south, which brought them to a spot in the hills of New Castle County, just north of what later came to be known as Milford Cross Roads. Here they erected a post marked "West" to indicate the latitudinal mark from which the northern boundary of Maryland should be drawn.

In June 1764 Mason and Dixon traveled southward to the transpeninsular line, laid out in 1751, and began to survey the west boundary of the Lower Counties, the tangent line. When the tangent point was reached, the surveyors were still several miles below the northern boundary of Maryland, so they continued their survey around the circumference of the circle till they reached a spot exactly north of the tangent point. At this spot (west of Newark) they left the circle and laid out a straight line to the north until they reached the latitude of the post marked West.

After the west line of the Lower Counties was surveyed it still had to be marked with stones that the proprietors sent by water. Every mile on the line was marked by a stone, with a larger stone, called a crown stone,

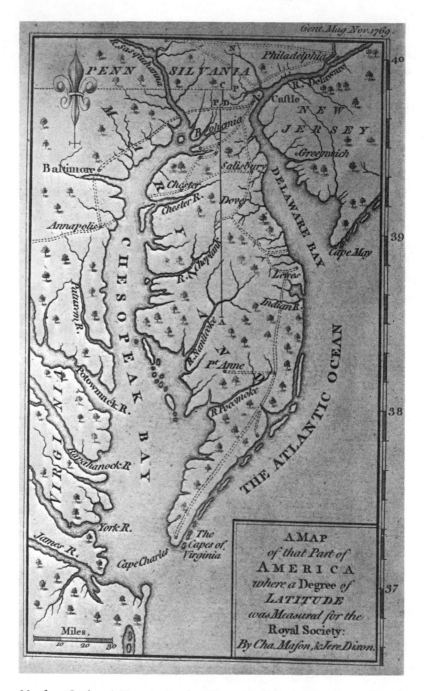

Map from *Gentleman's Magazine*, London, November 1769, showing surveys of Mason and Dixon. Courtesy of the Division of Historical and Cultural Affairs, Dover.

marking five-mile segments. Before the end of 1765 the north-south section of the Mason-Dixon Line (the less famous part of it) was completed, delineating the western boundary of the Lower Counties. By this time Mason and Dixon had already begun the east-west line that was to make their names famous. It was completed in the next two years, but only a small section at its eastern end, between the end of the north-south line and the circumference of the twelve-mile circle, served as any part of the boundary of the Lower Counties. This was the top of the "Wedge," an 800-acre tract of land that was in dispute until the end of the nineteenth century, when it was finally awarded to Delaware. At the request of the commissioners, Mason and Dixon extended their survey all the way across New Castle County to the Delaware River, near Wilmington, but the survey east of the circumference of the circle was not a part of the boundary and so was not permanently marked.

Their work finished, the English surveyors left America in 1768. The Penns and Lord Baltimore united in petitioning the king for his approval of the boundary, which was given on January 11, 1769. Yet it was not until 1775 that the assembly of the Lower Counties finally incorporated the boundary settlement into the lines of the three Delaware counties. The new boundaries ran close to the previously accepted borders in New Castle County, but to the south the new line was considerably beyond the area over which the Penns had heretofore exercised control.

To Sussex County, in particular, completion of the boundary lines meant a significant addition of territory on the west and the south. For instance, much of John Dagworthy's baronial estate, awarded him by Maryland for his services to this colony in the French and Indian War, turned out to be in Sussex. So did two Anglican chapels—Prince George's at Dagsboro and Christ Church on Broad Creek—which were established as chapels of ease in Maryland parishes. So much territory was added to Sussex County, though a great part of it was but sparsely settled, that there was talk of creating a fourth county, New Sussex, and it did become necessary in time to move the courts from Lewes to a more central location.

Not until 1775, on the very eve of the Revolution, did the Delaware colony, the Penns' Lower Counties, assume its proper and final geographical porportions. Politically and culturally, however, the colony had reached maturity decades earlier.

* * *

Entry for June 25, 1764, from the original Mason and Dixon Journal in the Historical Society of Pennsylvania, Philadelphia. Used by permission of the Society.

A warrant of March 12, 1776, signed by John Penn, ordering a resurvey of property that had been ceded to Delaware by ratification of the boundary surveys by Mason and Dixon and their predecessors. Courtesy of the Division of Historical and Cultural Affairs, Dover.

The generally happy relations of Governor Gordon with the assemblies that convened in New Castle following Sir William Keith's departure in 1728 suggest that the people of the Lower Counties appreciated their modest prosperity and their large measure of independence under the mild rule of the Penns. Their situation, without a resident governor and court, without the need of submitting their laws to England, was nearly if not entirely unique.

Perhaps it was the very uncertainty of Penn's title to the Lower Counties and the controversy regarding their boundaries that led these counties to cling to their proprietary connection with a warmth markedly different from the discordant relations of the Penns and their deputy governors with the assembly in Pennsylvania. Just as their exposure to naval attacks led people of the Lower Counties to show more sympathy for imperial defense needs than was exhibited in Pennsylvania, so their vulnerability to border raids from Maryland and to challenges to their land titles because of uncertain boundaries led them to cling more closely to their proprietary connections than they might have done otherwise. It was harder for the Penns to govern the province that was indubitably theirs than the territories where their title was in doubt.

Two of the three Penn brothers came to the Delaware valley in the early 1730s. John, the principal proprietor, hurried back to England in 1735, to defend family interests against Lord Baltimore, but Thomas, the second brother, spent many years in America after his arrival in 1732 and made many visits to Delaware while putting the family's business affairs in order. He might have assumed the governorship upon Patrick Gordon's death in 1736, or even earlier, except that it involved taking an oath, which Penn, as a nominal Quaker, would not do. In later years, he regularly attended the Church of England, like his younger brother Richard, but in the 1730s he was apparently hesitant to take any step that might reduce his influence with the Quakers.

Instead of choosing one of the family to succeed Gordon, the Penns turned to George Thomas, a planter from Antigua in the West Indies, who paid for the privilege of being governor. Because of the controversy in England about the title to the Lower Counties, Thomas's commission was delayed, and in the meantime old James Logan served as acting governor.

Gradually the proprietary connection was becoming increasingly attractive to the people of Delaware. They realized that the Penns were

Christ Episcopal Church in Broad Creek Hundred, near Laurel, erected in 1771. Originally a chapel of ease in a Maryland parish, but left in Delaware after the boundary was adjusted, this plain, unpainted building remains largely unaltered. Courtesy of the Division of Historical and Cultural Affairs, Dover.

their chief defense in England against the historic encroachments of Marylanders. And though in America they looked chiefly to Philadelphia for a market in peacetime and for succor in time of war, it was the proprietorship that furnished a special connection between these Lower Counties and Pennsylvania; it was this that gave them a claim upon a governor who frequently sought their cooperation in common endeavors and who would never be likely to forget their annual, and voluntary, contribution to his support. The Pennsylvania assembly, on the other hand, was a body from which they had seceded, and which they could never rejoin except in a distinctly subordinate role. For the government of their neighbors in Maryland, the assemblymen who met in New Castle had only scorn: we possess, they declared in 1738, "many valuable Liberties and Privileges" which "the Inhabitants of a neighboring Government [they were clearly referring to Maryland] only enjoy in Imagination."

What the residents of the Lower Counties particularly enjoyed was the right to run their own affairs with little if any interference from England. In the mid-eighteenth century few colonies were so independent as these counties; perhaps only Connecticut and Rhode Island, where the people chose their own governors. They owed their good fortune mainly to ignorance of their very existence and to their inconsequence in the grand pattern of an expansive and expanding empire. Even fellow-colonists could overlook their status. For example, when the Albany Plan of Union was drawn up in 1754, the drafting committee declared its intention of including "all the Brittish Dominions on the Continent" but the Delaware counties were not mentioned, being assumed, apparently, to be part of Pennsylvania. (Nova Scotia and Georgia were not mentioned either, but they were then frontier marches, supported by annual parliamentary appropriations.)

In London, however, the Board of Trade was neither wholly ignorant of nor completely indifferent to the status of the Lower Counties. In April 1740, they raised questions about these counties with Ferdinand John Paris, the agent of the Pennsylvania government and of the Penns. Why should the Penns be referred to in Pennsylvania laws, they asked, as "true and absolute Proprietors of the three Lower Countys" as well as of Pennsylvania? Did the Penns not sign an acknowledgment, every time a new governor was appointed, that the proprietary appointment must not be considered to prejudice the Crown claim to the Lower Counties?

"They desired to know," wrote Paris to Thomas Penn, "how [your title] was writ in the Lower County acts. And to see all those Lower County Laws."

While keeping Penn informed, Paris answered these inquiries as best he could, insisting that the phraseology of the Pennsylvania laws was the work of the Pennsylvania assembly, not of the proprietors, but that the title was no innovation (as the board had implied) but had been used in the time of the founder, William Penn, and without objection. Furthermore, the fact that the Penns waived any prejudice to the Crown claim whenever a new governor was qualified did not mean that they gave up their own claim to the government of the Lower Counties. As to the Lower County laws, Paris was helpless. "I told them I was not Agent," he declared, "nor had no authority from those People, that I did not know that I had ever seen two Acts made by that separate Province."

When the Board of Trade persisted by asking why laws of the Lower Counties were not submitted, Paris answered that the grant to the Duke of York by which Penn claimed had not required that laws be laid before the Crown, in that respect being similar to the charters of Connecticut and Rhode Island. Whatever the board thought, no laws were then available for it to examine, and there is no evidence that any were ever submitted in the future.

7

THE FOUNDING OF A CITY AND
THE PEOPLING OF A
COUNTRYSIDE

During the early eighteenth century an agricultural transformation occurred in the counties of Kent and Sussex. The most valuable crop in
these counties at the beginning of the century was tobacco; by 1770
cultivation of this crop had been abandoned in the Delaware counties.*

Perhaps the explanation lies partly in the fact that tobacco is an extrac-
tive crop; planted year after year in the same land it is notably hard on the
soil. It is probable that after a generation of tobacco growing farmers
were discouraged to find their yields decreasing. Yet there remained
plenty of land not yet cleared to which they might have turned. A price
decline that took place in the eighteenth century must have so decreased
the margin of profitability as to cause landowners in Kent and Sussex to
turn to other sources of income.

Some landowners were satisfied to take their main profit from the sale
of timber, and throughout the eighteenth century a brisk trade took
place in boards and shingles and, as cities grew and demand increased, in
firewood. But the new agricultural staples from the Lower Counties, the

---

* Of 29 probate inventories surviving for Kent County in 1774 and published by
Alice Hanson Jones in her *American Colonial Wealth,* I (New York 1977), only one mentions tobacco. This inventory (p. 364), for the estate of James Brown, of Murderkill
Hundred, values his "Tobaco in Sheef" at only 20 shillings, whereas his wheat was worth
over £40 and his corn £37. In neighboring Queen Annes County, Maryland, tobacco was
still a major product in 1774.

crops that farmers grew for market, increasingly came to be corn and, except in Sussex, wheat.

The availability and attractiveness of land in the Delaware counties is demonstrated by the steady movement into them of farmers from neighboring colonies, especially from the Eastern Shore of Maryland. Very likely the declining profitability of tobacco culture was a strong motive in this migration, which led such notable gentry as the Dickinsons, Chews, Mifflins, Rogers, and Mitchells to move to Kent or Sussex from the Eastern Shore of the Chesapeake.

Besides the push toward migration resulting from the decline of tobacco, there was a positive attraction drawing settlers from the Chesapeake to the Delaware counties—the growth of Philadelphia. In the middle years of the eighteenth century, the capital of Pennsylvania, by this time the largest city in English America, offered an unrivaled market. Its own growing population provided an immediate market for foodstuffs, such as meat and wheat and wood, that no city on the Cheasapeake could offer, Baltimore being as yet just a village. Furthermore, Philadelphia merchants sought cargoes for their trade overseas with Europe, with the West Indies, and along the coast of the continent, from the Carolinas to Nova Scotia.

One settler attracted from the Chesapeake to the Delaware in the mid-eighteenth century was Samuel Dickinson, father of John Dickinson. Having married for a second time, he decided in 1740 to turn over his lands in Talbot County, Maryland, to the children of his deceased first wife, and to develop lands he had for several years been buying near the Delaware in Kent County. Dickinson was atypical in the sense that he was wealthier than most of the planters migrating from Maryland to Delaware. His estates in Kent amounted to about three thousand acres, including eight hundred acres purchased as early as 1676 by his grandfather and acquired by Samuel Dickinson from other members of his family. Altogether the Dickinson estate, comprising about six square miles, was a significant portion of the best land in Kent, where the eastern half of the county, accessible to river landings and thus to trade with Philadelphia, had the greatest value.

In this region, on the St. Jones River, Samuel had a new house constructed to which, in January 1741, he brought his second wife, formerly Mary Cadwalader, of Philadelphia, and their two young sons, John and Philemon. This move of Samuel Dickinson's was not only a change from

Portrait of Samuel Dickinson, by Gustavus Hesselius. Courtesy of the Division of Historical and Cultural Affairs, Dover.

Dickinson Mansion, Jones's Neck, Kent County, built 1740 by Samuel Dickinson. Courtesy of the Division of Historical and Cultural Affairs, Dover.

one colony to another but also a change from tobacco culture to grain farming, from the world of the Chesapeake plantations to the neighborhood of Philadelphia, for even though this city was a normal two-day ride away from St. Jones Neck, where the Dickinsons had settled, river-borne traffic was constant and made the connection a close and an easy one.

Many farmers less prosperous than Samuel Dickinson made a similar migration into Delaware. To an extent this was an eastward migration from the Chesapeake Bay that was a small eddy in the great westward movement from the Atlantic Ocean. The Eastern Shore of the Chesapeake had provided many inviting harbors and convenient landings as well as a cash crop that sustained and even enriched early settlers. As they sought new lands for their children or, when the old lands wore out, for themselves, the settlers gradually moved inland from the bay.* From the Eastern Shore this inland migration led settlers gradually into the Lower Counties. In some cases they merely moved up the valleys of such Eastern Shore rivers as the Choptank and the Nanticoke. Other Maryland farmers, and some from Virginia, moved, like Samuel Dickinson, beyond the Chesapeake watershed.

This migration was not merely of white farmers; it also included their black slaves. Slaves had been brought to the Delaware counties since the days of the Dutch, but the greater size of plantations on the Chesapeake made them, as time went on, more of a goal for slave ships. The eastward migration to the Delaware counties, therefore, brought an influx of white and black farmers largely, in both cases, of American birth.

While this movement was going on in Kent and Sussex, which had the largest proportion of new lands available to migrants, a contemporary but different migration was taking place in New Castle County. Here there was little attraction to farmers from Maryland, because the farm-

---

* Very recently Paul G. E. Clemens, in an essay entitled "Economy and Society on Maryland's Eastern Shore, 1689–1733," in Aubrey C. Land *et al.*, eds., *Law, Society, and Politics in Early Maryland* (Baltimore, 1977), 152–170, has argued persuasively that boom times provided an opportunity for poor whites in old Eastern Shore areas to move eastward and establish themselves as independent farmers. Thus, he explains, geographical mobility became the means by which the lower classes sought to achieve social and economic upward mobility. Clemens also makes note of migrations by elements of the wealthy.

lands in most of New Castle had been occupied at least as early as those in the neighboring Maryland county of Cecil or the neighboring Pennsylvania county of Chester. Furthermore the peninsula narrowed and ended here as the Chesapeake Bay came to a head. The natural direction for migrating farmers was westward toward the Appalachians or northward up the Susquehanna valley.

On the other hand, the expansion of the agricultural area into, for instance, the new Pennsylvania county of Lancaster, and the quickening spirit given to economic life by the growth of Philadelphia, increased opportunities for merchants and for the artisans and other non-farming workmen who would cater to the needs of commerce.

For almost a century the small Swedish hamlet of Christina had slumbered beside the river of the same name before a rebirth of commercial vitality occurred in its near vicinity in the 1730s. One notable change in that long period took place in 1698, when a new Lutheran church was begun on a knoll just beyond the graveyard that was northwest of the little riverside settlement. On Trinity Sunday, July 4, 1699, the Reverend Erik Björk, its prime mover, dedicated the new church to the Holy Trinity. An older church across the Christina River at Crane Hook was abandoned, and the center of the religious life of the Swedes in this area was now on the north bank of the river.

West of the hamlet, graveyard, and church stretched only forest, fields, and farmhouses until in the 1730s merchants from Philadelphia began construction of a new village where fast land extended to the high-water mark on the Christina River about a mile upstream from the Swedish settlement. The land that sloped down to the river at this point was bought in 1727 by a Swede named Andrew Justison, whose daughter a year later married an English merchant named Thomas Willing. Justison, like almost all of the Swedes of the Delaware valley in the eighteenth century, was an American by birth and rearing, but the Swedish church and its missionary pastors helped maintain some vestiges of Swedish culture, including the language and religion, which kept the descendants of the New Sweden settlers a distinct ethnic group for more than a century.

Either Justison or Willing or the two men in concert soon divided a portion of Justison's tract into town lots and by 1735 fifteen or twenty houses had been constructed in the development which was then known as Willingtown, including the house of Willing himself, near the foot of

King Street. Apparently Willing attracted new settlers by the promise of a market for the prosperous farms along the Christina, by the easy access this river afforded to the wharves of Philadelphia on one hand and to a large hinterland northward in the Brandywine valley, westward up the Christina River, and also by roads and paths into Cecil County, western Chester County, and Lancaster County.

Philadelphia was the major attraction for the products of the farms of all this area, but Willingtown, being west of Philadelphia, was closer to the farmlands stretching out toward the Susquehanna and merchants at Willingtown hoped to make a profit on goods funneled through their hands to the metropolis. Possibly the developers of Willingtown also had some understanding of the economic possibilities of the spendid millsites nearby along the valley of such tributaries of the Christina as the Red Clay Creek and especially the Brandywine.

Neither Thomas Willing nor his name was to remain identified with the village he and his father-in-law projected. Willing, who was a cousin of the founder of the prominent mercantile firm of Willing and Morris of Philadelphia, soon moved away. He was still a resident of the town he founded in 1736, but leadership there already seems to have passed from his hands into those of an English-born Friend named William Shipley and, in the words of a Quaker historian, "some active business characters" who had come to the new village with Shipley.

Arriving in Willingtown in 1735, William Shipley quickly infused new vigor and new capital into its development. It seems likely that a good part of his interest as well as his capital originated with the remarkable woman, born Elizabeth Levis, who was his second wife. Elizabeth Levis Shipley was a professed visionary and a distinguished minister in the Society of Friends who, in her long life, made many religious journeys of visitation, including trips to New England and the South and one in 1743–1745 to meetings in England and Ireland. In the course of an early journey to visit Quaker meetings on the Eastern Shore, she viewed the site of Willingtown from a hill behind it and felt she recognized it as a place shown her in a vision where she and her husband were to settle and be of great benefit.

William Shipley was sufficiently attentive to his wife's impulses to inspect the site of Willingtown and, pleased by its commercial possibilities, purchase a substantial amount of land there. Perhaps Shipley came to America with money to invest; he had bought a tract of land in Pennsylvania, southwest of Philadelphia, shortly after his arrival in 1725. However, Samuel Levis, Elizabeth's father, died in 1734, and it seems probable that Elizabeth's inheritance allowed William to act upon her vision.

At any rate, after buying his land Shipley went on to construct a market house, a brewery, and a wharf at Willingtown, and in 1736 his name was second, after that of Joseph Pennock, who was his wife's nephew, among the residents and freeholders of Willingtown who signed a petition to Thomas Penn. Willingtown, they said, gave "the pleasing prospect of thriving and increasing [with] divers houses built and others a putting forward . . . near . . . a convenient landing place." They wished to be given the power to regulate their own affairs, particularly their streets and market, and to elect their officials. Besides thirty-five signatures that seem to represent residents of Willingtown, sixty-eight were of freeholders who dwelt in the back country, many or most of them in Chester County. Apparently development of a market town on the Christina met a regional need.

Three years passed before the petition was granted, and in the meantime Willingtown was torn by a quarrel over the market house William Shipley had built in the center of High Street (later Fourth Street), very close to his own home. Some other residents, perhaps earlier purchasers, began to build another market house on Second Street, nearer the Christina River than Shipley's. When Shipley and sixty-three inhabitants of Willingtown "and parts adjacent" sought to stop the new construction by a petition to Penn, they were joined by the pastor and thirty-one members of the congregation of Old Swedes Church. These men declared their satisfaction with Shipley's market house, which stood near the edge of lands belonging to their church. The support the Swedish congregation gave Shipley indicates that the market house quarrel was not simply a squabble between the first settlers (the Willing-Justison group) and the latecomers like Shipley. Willing and Justison were not among the signers of petitions for or against Shipley's market house, but they provided the land for the rival market built at Second and Market streets.

Criticism of Shipley was apparently sufficiently sharp to cause a committee to be formed to collect funds to buy his market house and make it a public enterprise. It is interesting that this committee was composed, designedly, of two men from Willingtown, two from New Castle

County, and two from Chester County, demonstrating again the regional interest in the establishment of this market town. However public Shipley's market became and however much it appealed to farmers in the outlying county and in Pennsylvania, it did not satisfy the inhabitants of the lower parts of Willingtown, for they sought to destroy it by cutting down the large white-oak posts at its corners, until its defenders came to the rescue and forcibly restrained the axemen.

A sketch of the community of Willingtown in 1736 shows it extending from the Christina north to what became Seventh Street. Including Shipley's market house, thirty-four houses or "improvements" are noted, grouped in two main clusters, an upper (northern) one near the market house and a lower cluster between Second Street and the river. A division is evident between a riverside village and a town on a hill above it. (The hill, incidentally, was higher then than later; by 1846, for instance, its height was eight or ten feet less than a century earlier.) Probably Shipley's hilltop town was the easier to reach by cart road from such areas as Kennett Square and Concordville, as well as from the Brandywine valley. The lower town was closer to the upper Christina valley, but settlers up the Christina may have preferred to develop their own river landings and take their goods directly to Philadelphia. Across the Christina from the lower town was a great marsh.

The long passage of time between the petition for a town charter (signed by advocates of the lower market house as well as by Shipley and his associates) and a favorable response was occasioned by the problem of filling the place of Governor Patrick Gordon after his death in 1736. Thomas Penn, the resident proprietor, did not dare personally to issue a charter to Willingtown on behalf of himself and his brothers because he had not taken the oaths required by the Crown of each colonial governor. He had to be particularly careful not to be overly assertive in the affairs of the Lower Counties, where his rights were challenged. Nor could James Logan, who as president of the council was acting governor, qualify as Gordon's successor with full powers because he, like Penn, was a Quaker and could take no oath of office.

In England John and Richard Penn had decided by the spring of 1737 upon George Thomas as successor to Governor Gordon, but Charles, the fifth Lord Baltimore, attempted to prevent this appointment by arguing that the Lower Counties should not be joined with Pennsyl-

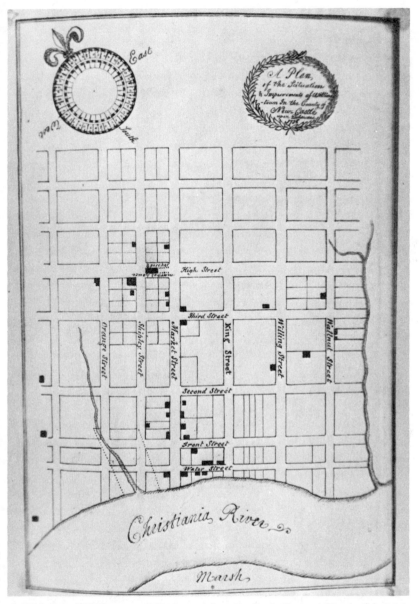

A 1736 plan of Willingtown (Wilmington) from Benjamin Ferris, *A History of the Original Settlements on the Delaware* (Wilmington, 1846).

vania under the same governor or, if they were, that his commission as governor of the Lower Counties should derive from the king directly and not from the Penns. At this time new border violence had erupted that led, on August 18, 1737, to an order from the Privy Council forbidding any new settlement or sales of land in the Lower Counties or on the disputed Maryland—Pennsylvania line. In the spring of 1738, however, Baltimore and the Penns patched up their quarrels temporarily and agreed that the order in council banning further settlement in the Lower Counties should be withdrawn, as it was.

In the same season the Privy Council permitted George Thomas to take his oath as governor in his native Leeward Islands, to which he had returned, and in June 1738, properly qualified as governor of Pennsylvania and the Lower Counties, he arrived on the Delaware. Why the issuance of a charter to the new village on the Christina was still delayed for more than a year is unknown. Probably Governor Thomas was busy with more pressing matters; perhaps the time was needed to allow the negotiation of a compromise between the two quarreling factions in Willingtown.

When Governor Thomas finally issued a charter of incorporation on November 16, 1739, indications are clear that there had been much work done behind the scenes. First, the new corporation was given the name of Wilmington, a name hitherto never used for the community. It seems likely that this name was chosen by Thomas Penn in Philadelphia or by his brothers in England. Spencer Compton, the Earl of Wilmington, had nothing directly to do with the village on the Christina, but as lord president of the Privy Council since December 30, 1730, he was in a position to influence the progress of the Penn-Baltimore quarrel in England, where he was looked upon by the Penn brothers as a friend to their interests.

Another indication of special consideration in the borough charter was a provision that the freeholders and inhabitants should decide in a special meeting "the place or places" where fairs or markets would be held. The charter granted the borough permission to have two markets a week and two fairs a year, and a town meeting held December 10, less than a month after the granting of the charter, divided the markets and fairs evenly between the two market houses. The Saturday market and the spring fair, probably the preferred dates, were voted to Shipley's market house by, it is said, a majority of 146. The lower market house was awarded the

Wednesday market and the fall fair by a majority of only 27, which suggests that the advocates of the former might have carried the day entirely had they not decided on a compromise.

The composition of the officials named in the borough charter also demonstrates the leadership of the Shipley interests. Not one of the men who signed the petition on behalf of the Second Street market was named to an office in the new borough. William Shipley himself was named chief burgess, and Thomas West, a well-to-do and influential Friend, was named second burgess. At least four of the six assistants, who, with the two burgesses, comprised the borough council, were men who had purchased shares in Shipley's market house, and a fifth, Timothy Stidham, was a prominent landholder of Swedish descent. Appointment of a high constable and a town clerk completed the officials of Wilmington, who were to serve only until September 8, 1740, when their successors were to be elected to one-year terms. The powers granted were the usual ones of a municipal corporation: the right to hold property, to sue and be sued, to regulate streets, wharves and markets, to keep the peace, and to manage the other affairs of the borough and its people.

The high constable was to preside at the annual town elections, where the right to vote was reserved to freeholders and to other "housekeepers" renting property worth five pounds or more a year and resident in the town for at least twelve months before the election. Town meetings could be called at will by the burgesses, high constable, and assistants to enact ordinances for the government of the borough by majority vote. The borough authorities had, in general, the powers of justices of the peace, subject to the county quarter sessions court. Permission was granted for construction of a borough courthouse, but the burgesses and their assistants met in private houses until 1774. Then a town hall was constructed on the upper floor of the Second Street market house, which was built of brick and was more substantial than Shipley's slightly older market in High Street. In providing quarters for the town government over the market, Wilmingtonians were following the model of Philadelphia, just as they followed that model in the rectangular plan of their city, built back from the banks of a river.

When the first borough elections took place in September 1740, the ascendancy of Shipley and his Quaker friends was further demonstrated, as he was elected chief burgess, the position he already filled by appointment. His votes, however, were only 61, quite reduced from the so-called "majority" of 146 said to have been cast at the town meeting in December 1739 for Shipley's market. Furthermore the highest vote recorded for any candidate is 96, cast for the reelected town clerk and for Thomas West as an assistant. West had previously been second burgess and possibly was not nominated for that office again because if he had won more votes than Shipley, he would have become chief burgess, and it seems likely that West would not have wished to replace Shipley in this position.

No record is known of votes cast for losing candidates, but since Joseph Way was elected second burgess with only 50 votes it is not likely that the total number of voters was much higher than the 96 who supported Thomas West and the clerk. Apparently, if the figures are correct, there was less interest in this election than in the decision regarding location of the markets and fairs. This supposition seems likely, because feeling on the latter issue had led to violence; once it was settled and the rights of the downtown faction protected by a compromise, town politics became less exciting and the voters turned out less willingly. In future elections, a heated local issue, such as whether the Christina should be bridged at Wilmington (in 1808), would excite voters more than the ordinary choice between candidates, even for high office.

Between the granting of its charter in 1739 and the beginning of the Revolution there was a change in the nature as well as in the number of the inhabitants of Wilmington. As to the number, the population increased from about six hundred in 1739 to between twelve hundred and two thousand people in 1776, a doubling or tripling of size within a generation. This growth made Wilmington, small as it was, the largest community in Delaware, surpassing New Castle which, lacking a protected harbor or a tributary stream that would easily bring produce from the hinterland, exhibited little growth and possibly some shrinkage.

The qualitative change in the population of Wilmington and, for that matter, of its environs, is indicated by the person of the chief burgess on the eve of the Revolution. Whereas the first occupant of this magistracy had been William Shipley, an Englishman by birth and a Friend by conviction, the chief burgess in 1775 was John McKinly, an Irishman and a Presbyterian.

It is important to note the particular sort of Irishman McKinly was. He belonged to the group that in America called themselves Scotch-

Irish, the descendants of Scots (largely from the lowlands) who had been resident in Ireland for several generations. Their movement to America was the largest transatlantic migration to the English colonies in the eighteenth century, just as the English migration had been the largest to these colonies in the seventeenth century.

Though religious considerations played a part, the impelling motive for their emigration was economic. The English rulers of Ireland had established a tax-supported Church of Ireland, protestant but episcopal, a sister denomination to the Church of England, but even the tithes collected from Presbyterian farmers for this church that they did not attend were not as annoying as English landlords who periodically raised rents and English laws that limited or forbade the sale of Irish products, such as beef, in the English market.

While statistics on the migration are sketchy, the smallest figure commonly accepted for the Scotch-Irish immigration is two hundred thousand, which would mean an average of about thirty-five hundred in each of the fifty-eight years between 1717, when the migration began, and 1775, when war interrupted it. Early Scotch-Irish immigrants often went to New England, where Calvinist churches predominated, but they found a cold reception among the English settlers there. In Pennsylvania, a newer colony, on the other hand, they found themselves welcome. Thereafter a decided majority of the Scotch-Irish headed for ports on the Delaware, primarily Philadelphia, but also New Castle, where their vesssels stopped even if but briefly and where thousands of the immigrants from Ulster disembarked. They were often hired or even sold as indentured labor to local planters, with whom they would stay until able to make their way to the cheaper lands in the West.

Here on the Delaware they found an equable climate, orderly government, cheap land, opportunity for advancement, and religious freedom, without the requirement of tithes for any church. The colonies on the Chesapeake or to the south were less attractive because the episcopal Church of England was established in all of them, as it was also in the southern counties of New York. It is likely that competition with slave labor also reduced the attractiveness of the southern colonies.

In 1728, 4,500 persons, chiefly Scotch-Irish, are said to have landed in the Lower Counties (a probable exaggeration) and 1,155 Scotch-Irish in Philadelphia. According to advertisements in the Ulster newspapers between 1750 and 1775, 55 percent of the emigrant ships (including those bound to Nova Scotia and Prince Edward Island) sailed for the Delaware, and the number rose to above 60 percent in years of light migration. The traffic between Ulster and the colonies on the Delaware was facilitated by the demand of the Ulster linen industry for American flaxseed, which was mainly exported from Philadelphia and New York.

Some immigrant ships from Ulster made the new port of Wilmington their goal, but most of the Scotch-Irish landing in the Lower Counties disembarked at New Castle, hoping either to make their way west from there or to find employment at once near their landing place. Within a few decades New Castle County had taken on a distinct Scotch-Irish tint, and the Presbyterian churches scattered across that county from New Castle and Wilmington on navigable waters to Lower Brandywine, Red Clay Creek, White Clay Creek, and the Head of Christiana, farther inland, give evidence, especially through the stones in their graveyards, of the diffusion of these settlers. They also became prominent in the central and youngest county, Kent, and, to a lesser degree, in Sussex, where in 1728 the Anglican missionary at Lewes, the Reverend William Becket, testified that "of late years great numbers of Irish (who usually call themselves Scotch Irish) have transported themselves and their families from the North of Ireland into the Province of Pennsylvania and . . . many families are settled in the County of Sussex."

In the Lower Counties, as well as in Pennsylvania, many immigrants began as indentured servants, having pledged themselves to work off the cost of their transportation to America. If this pledge, or indenture, had been given to a ship captain, it was sold on arrival at New Castle or elsewhere to a farmer needing assistance. Some of these servants, proving intractable or resenting ill treatment, ran off, as newspaper advertisements testify. If they did, their command of the language and their education, often superior to that of native Americans, gave them a good chance of remaining undetected. Those who worked out their service, normally for three to seven years, could use it as a period of orientation to the conditions of this new world.

Whatever the conditions of their introduction, the Scotch-Irish embraced their new life with vigor and much material success. Resenting English institutions and laws, which they blamed for their grievances abroad, they quickly entered politics and became the bulwark of the revolutionary movement as well as of one of the two emerging factions in local politics, the particular faction that developed into the

Original Friends Meeting House, Wilmington. Courtesy of the Historical Society of Delaware, Wilmington.

First Presbyterian Church, Wilmington, at its original location on Market Street. The building has been removed to the Brandywine Park and preserved there with the help of the Colonial Dames. Lithograph by P. S. Duval from a sketch by Benjamin Ferris in the latter's *A History of the Original Settlements on the Delaware* (Wilmington, 1846). These two simple structures represent the two groups (Quaker merchants and Presbyterian immigrants) mainly responsible for the rapid growth of Wilmington in the mid-eighteenth century.

Democratic-Republican party. Because the schools in their homeland were good, at least in comparison with America, and because of their familiarity with the language, they were especially well prepared to enter the learned professions. It is by no means an accident that the first printer, the first chancellor, the first president of the medical society, the founder of the school that developed into the state university, and the first chief executive of an independent Delaware State* were all of this stock. On the other hand, as in the case of most large immigrant groups, their numbers and their ethnic distinctiveness stirred up many resentments among older settlers and eventually a "church party" appeared in Delaware to oppose what its adherents regarded as the pretensions of an "Irish party."

Besides the Scotch-Irish, there was a second large wave of immigrants into the Delaware valley in the eighteenth century. But this wave, the German immigration, flowed almost completely by the Lower Counties. Because they were aliens, the Germans were not permitted to disembark at New Castle but were required to proceed to Philadelphia, where their arrival could be properly registered. A few of the Germans did eventually migrate to the Lower Counties, but their ignorance of English and their desire to stay together in areas where they could be understood, as well as the greater availability of lands in Pennsylvania, kept the number of German migrants to Delaware very small.

A much more important ethnic group in the Lower Counties was the Welsh, including some who settled on a tract of land given them by William Penn on the Maryland border at the beginning of the eighteenth century. This Welsh Tract (not to be confused with another more famous Penn grant bearing the same name in the province of Pennsylvania) began north of Iron Hill and covered thirty thousand acres, running for several miles south of that modest eminence, which is responsible for the Welsh name of Pencader (high seat) given to this area. Among the first Welsh settlers were a congregation of fifteen to twenty Baptist families from Pembrokeshire who had spent two years in Pennsylvania before migrating to New Castle County in 1703. The Baptist meeting house that they built in 1746 still survives, and some stones with Welsh inscriptions are in its graveyard.

---

* James Adams, William Killen, James Tilton, Francis Alison, and John McKinly.

Welsh Tract Baptist Meeting House, at the foot of Iron Hill. Erected in 1746, this building was involved in some of the fighting during the Battle of Cooch's Bridge, September 3, 1777. A number of gravestones are inscribed in Welsh. Courtesy of the Division of Historical and Cultural Affairs, Dover.

The Welsh Baptists were joined on their tract by other Welsh who were Presbyterians and the founders of the Pencader Church at the village now called Glasgow. Many other settlers in the Lower Counties were of Welsh descent but, being members of Quaker meetings or Anglican churches, formed no distinct group in any ethnic sense. The distinguished statesman, John Dickinson, for instance, had three Welsh grandparents.

The Scotch-Irish and the Welsh immigrants to the Lower Counties in the eighteenth century added to the ethnic diversity of this area, though their effect was mainly on New Castle County, where most of them settled. This county was the most attractive to newcomers, not because it had the most land open to settlement (on the contrary, it was the smallest county and had the least available land) but because it had the major Delaware ports, New Castle and Wilmington, because it lay close to the growing colonial metropolis, Philadelphia, and because it was athwart the new routes being developed by land to the interior counties in the west and southwest. At least one Jewish merchant, Abraham Judah, resided in Wilmington in the 1750s, though he had moved to Philadelphia by 1761.

In adding to the population diversity of New Castle County, the new immigrants helped to enlarge the division that developed in the eighteenth century between New Castle and the two southern counties. Kent and Sussex were rural and agricultural; New Castle was, too, but it had an important mercantile element that was growing and it had also the beginnings of an urban society in New Castle town and in Wilmington. New Castle County was also the chief seat of the remaining Dutch and Swedish influence in Delaware. The Dutch, never numerous, merged into other groups, intermarrying first with Swedes and English and then finding themselves in Calvinist communion with the Scotch-Irish. There was no Dutch Reformed church in Delaware in the eighteenth century, but the Presbyterian church in New Castle incorporated a Dutch element within its congregation.

The few hundred Swedes at Wilmington, on the other hand, remained a distinct people, and continued their Lutheran worship until after the Revolution, when the Church of Sweden refused to continue its practice of sending missionary pastors to America. Thereupon the members of the Old Swedes Church completed the long process of their anglicization by calling an Episcopal minister to their pulpit. In doing so they were but continuing a process of change which the Reverend Israel Acrelius commented upon in 1759, when he wrote:

> The times within fifty years are as changed as night is from day. . . . Then many a good and honest man rode upon a piece of bear-skin; now scarcely any saddle is valued unless it has a saddle-cloth with galloon and fringe. Then servants and girls were seen in church barefooted; now young people will be like persons of quality in their dress; servants are seen with *perruques du Crains* [wigs of hair] and the like; girls with hooped skirts, fine stuff-shoes, and other finery. Then respectable families lived in low log-houses, where the chimney was made of sticks covered with clay; now they erect painted houses of stone and brick in the country. Then they used ale and brandy, now wine and punch. Then they lived upon grits and mush, now upon tea, coffee, and chocolate.

Swedish, English, African, Scotch-Irish, or of whatever origin, the whole population of Delaware in 1776 amounted to little more than thirty-seven thousand. Small as this was, it was larger than the population of Philadelphia (a superiority that was soon lost) and larger than that of Georgia. In relation to the whole of the new nation that was arising, Delaware, in terms of numbers, was then of more significance than it was ever again to be.

8

THE REVIVAL OF FAITH AND LEARNING

Like neighboring Pennsylvania, Delaware was one of the few colonies without an established church. By Penn's charter, freedom of worship was granted to every person acknowledging one God, though in practice there was a distinct Protestant bias to the government. The charter permitted only Christians to hold office, and statute law effectively disqualified Roman Catholics by the requirement of an oath denying papal authority.

The Protestant bias in the government of the Lower Countes was a passive matter and the Church of England, the ancestral church of most of the English settlers, had a difficult struggle to maintain its existence. In few places was there a sufficient concentration of worshippers to support a clergyman. Every Anglican minister in the colony was invited to serve more than one congregation, but the distances and the roads made it difficult to be in more than one church on a Sunday. If the minister at Christ Church, Dover, for example, responded favorably to requests that he also officiate in the northern part of Kent County, at Duck Creek, as well as in the wooded south of the county, he could occupy his pulpit in Dover only two Sundays each month.

There were never enough clergymen to satisfy the need. Every one of the Anglican clergy in the Lower Counties was a missionary, sent under the auspices and at the expense of the Society for the Propagation of the Gospel in Foreign Parts, the Anglican missionary society. It was difficult, indeed practically impossible, to raise a local clergy in the colony, because a college education was required and for many decades the only Anglican college in America was at Williamsburg, which had little connection with the Delaware valley. Furthermore, an Anglican clergy-man had to be ordained by a bishop, and there were no Anglican bish-ops in America. The absence of a bishop also made it difficult for Amer-icans to be confirmed, and without confirmation there could be few communicants—only those church members who had been confirmed abroad.

Five Anglican clergymen were the largest number in the Lower Coun-ties at any one time, and the consequence was that most of those residents who through family tradition were of Church of England affiliation in practice were unchurched. The few Anglican clergymen made some ef-fort, as they were ordered, to baptize blacks as well as whites, and since most of the substantial farmers who held slaves in the Lower Counties were nominally Anglican, a great part of the African element was brought into the Christian community by the ceremony of baptism and, probably less commonly, by some religious instruction. Yet among both English and African groups in rural Delaware there remained a fertile field for a vigorous missionary effort.

A vigorous missionary effort was initiated in the year 1739, when the Reverend George Whitefield landed at Lewes on October 30. Whitefield, then only twenty-four years old, had been affiliated at Ox-ford University with the Holy Club founded by Charles Wesley; in scorn, its members were called Methodists because they were methodical in their devotions. After a brief missionary trip to Georgia, Whitefield had returned to England for ordination and had preached there to large, enthusiastic audiences before he set out again for America.

He arrived at Lewes by pilot boat and found his repuration was known. He was invited to preach on the next afternoon (a Wednesday) in St. Peter's, the Anglican church, where, according to his journal, "per-sons of different denominations were present, and the congregation was larger than might be expected in so small a place, and at so short notice." Whitefield's success in reaching "persons of different denominations" and in attracting an audience "larger than might be expected" at Lewes on October 31, 1739, was repeated on many occasions through the next two decades, when he made five more trips to America. On Saturday, December 1, 1739, he reported that two thousand people heard him preach from a balcony in New Castle (where the total population was fewer than two thousand) and later on the same day another crowd of equal size heard him at Christiana, a small village. At noon on the next day he spoke to "upwards of ten thousand people" in rainy weather near White Clay Creek Presbyterian Church, at a place where the minister, Charles Tennent, had erected a tent to shelter him.

Perhaps Whitefield exaggerated the numbers of his auditors since there were, after all, scarcely ten thousand people in all of New Castle County in 1739, but evidence abounds that he did draw extraordinarily large crowds and that he preached with much conviction and to great effect. Apparently he knew how to reach ordinary people; though he had gone to Oxford he was of modest background—the son of an innkeeper—and his message was warm and emotional, catholic in its appeal, with little attention to sectarian dogma or denominational distinctions.

He would, moreover, preach almost anywhere that a crowd could be collected—in a field, a public hall, a city square—and on any day in the week. His methods and his message however, won him only a cold response from his fellow Anglican clergymen, such as the Reverend William Becket, of Lewes, who condemned Whitefield for leaving the church building, on a second visit to Lewes, "to go and preach in an open Balcony," as though afraid he had thrown about "hell and damnation, fire and brimstone enough to have burnt a wooden frame." "I conclude," Becket added, "that enthusiasm is a sort of wild fire that leads men into ponds and ditches and for all that the muddy fellows think they are in a good road."

Partly because of the frigid reception the local Anglican clergy gave him, Whitefield had little lasting effect on the Anglican population of the Lower Counties or of neighboring colonies. He did inspire a religious society at Lewes, composed of Anglicans, Presbyterians, and Quakers, which was meeting twice a week in 1740 (it has been called the first Methodist society in America), but his influence in the area was not lasting. Except for the town of Lewes, Whitefield made little effort to reach people in the two southern Delaware counties, where the Anglican population was greatest.

On the other hand Whitefield had considerable influence among the Presbyterians of New Castle County, as well as in neighboring colonies. The beginnings of Presbyterianism in the Lower Counties can be traced to services held by Dutch Reformed ministers at New Castle as early as 1654. A Scotch-Irish immigrant, Francis Makemie, who had settled on the Eastern Shore of Virginia, began the organization of the Calvinists of

Dutch, English, and Scottish descent into a presbytery, and when, after his death, the Synod of Philadelphia was established in 1717, one of its four divisions was the presbytery of New Castle, which included all the churches of New Castle County, as well as many to the west and south. Briefly, from 1735 to 1742, and again a few years later, there was also a presbytery of Lewes.

The great Scotch-Irish immigration of the eighteenth century enormously strengthened Presbyterianism, especially in New Castle County, where it became the largest denomination. Many ministers came with the new immigrants, but since the Presbyterians did not require episcopal ordination and indeed opposed the institution of episcopacy itself, it was easier for them than for the Anglicans to create ministers in America. One handicap to their growth, however, was their demand that ministers be educated.

Schools were in short supply in the middle colonies; therefore the Presbyterians were quick to found academies of their own. Thomas Evans, a Welsh immigrant who was pastor of the Pencader Presbyterian Church at Glasgow from 1723 to 1742, conducted an academy there. The Reverend William Tennent, father of the minister who was Whitefield's host at White Clay Creek, had a school called the Log College in Bucks County, Pennsylvania, which was more notable for the zeal of its students than for their learning. Tennent and his followers argued that a personal conversion was more important than knowledge, and to them, therefore, the fervent nondenominational sermons of Whitefield had great appeal.

Many Presbyterian ministers were shocked by the idea of exalting enthusiasm above reason and theological knowledge. In 1741 these conservative churchmen expelled Tennent and the enthusiasts from the synod, thus beginning a schism between what were called Old Side and New Side Presbyterians. One of the Old Side ministers, the Reverend Francis Alison, concerned to assure a continued supply of educated young men for the ministry, opened a school at New London, Pennsylvania, in 1743, and soon secured financial assistance from the synod.

Alison, whose educational credentials were widely praised, attracted an excellent group of students, but in 1752 he left New London to become rector of a nondenominational academy in Philadelphia. His own school was taken over by the Reverend Alexander McDowell, who moved it first to his manse near the Rock Church, in northeastern Cecil

Reverend George Ross, Scottish-born Anglican rector at New Castle. Engraving by Samuel Sartain from a painting by Gustavus Hesselius. Photocopy made at the Eleutherian Mills Historical Library and used by permission of Immanuel Church, New Castle.

County (Maryland), and then, in the early 1760s, to the crossroads village of Newark in New Castle County, a village that had been recognized in 1758 by a charter from the governor permitting a weekly market and a semiannual fair.

From the very beginning the course of studies in this school was the equivalent of that of most of the colonial colleges. Alison, McDowell, and their graduates sought to have the quality of the work recognized by a charter that would empower the school to grant a baccalaureate degree. The proprietors, however, turned down this request, arguing that the nondenominational College of Philadelphia, chartered in 1755, would take care of all collegiate needs in their domains. Alison and his Old Side friends settled finally for the best charter they could get, which was for an Academy of Newark, granted by Governor John Penn in 1769. By its terms Alison became chairman of a self-perpetuating (and long-lasting) board of trustees.*

The great schism among the Presbyterians was settled in 1758, by which time the emotional evangelists of the New Side far outnumbered the conservatives of the Old Side. The latter, however, were tenacious in their desire to preserve a school of their own in case the old battle erupted once again, and they carefully fostered the Newark Academy as a resource against revivalist enthusiasts, who had replaced the Log College with the College of New Jersey, later Princeton, as their chief academy. For this purpose fund-raising teams were sent south to the Carolinas and the West Indies. Two graduates of Alison's school, Dr. Hugh Williamson and the Reverend John Ewing, were sent to England, where they solicited funds with some success from such notables as Dr. Samuel Johnson and the king himself.

The Academy of Newark was the one school in the Lower Counties which regularly attracted students from a broad area, for through its Presbyterian sponsorship its reputation and its influence were widespread. Another institution which came to rival the Newark Academy but always attracted a more local clientele was the Wilmington Academy, which was also chartered by the Penns, four years later than Newark, in 1773. In

---

* The board remained in existence for over two hundred years until 1976, when it turned over the property it administered to the University of Delaware. The academy, however, had ceased functioning as a private school in the late nineteenth century.

this same year a stone school building was constructed on what was then the north side of Wilmington, above Eighth Street, between King and Market. The Lutheran pastor, Lawrence Girelius, was the first president of the board of trustees, which also included the Reverend William White, of Philadelphia, later a Protestant Episcopal bishop, and a number of prominent merchants and professional men, largely from Wilmington.

The fact that ministers, Alison and Girelius, presided over the charter boards of trustees of the two incorporated academies in the Lower Counties indicates the importance of the church in educational affairs. Anglican priests had small parish libraries, distributed religious tracts sent them by the Society for the Propagation of the Gospel, and frequently added to their scanty incomes by teaching. Presbyterian ministers, who could expect no help from overseas, usually sought an outside source for funds and often this meant establishing a school of some sort as, for example, the Reverend Matthew Wilson, a graduate of Alison's school and a onetime teacher there, is said to have done at Lewes after filling the pulpit of its Presbyterian church. Wilson also helped support himself by the practice of medicine.

Though the Quakers had no clergy to serve as school teachers, they were assiduous in establishing schools so that their children of both sexes could learn to read plainly, and to write and cipher. They had little interest in any advanced instruction; none of the colonial colleges was founded by Quakers. Their need was to allow their young people opportunity to read the Scriptures and to have the skills essential for a mercantile career. The oldest existing school in Delaware is the Wilmington Friends School, probably founded as early as 1740, but there were once schools at many other sites where the Friends had meetings.

A great part of the people were illiterate, as the number of marks in place of signatures on legal papers attests. The first and second generations of natives in the Lower Counties probably had a higher rate of illiteracy than the immigrants from Europe, where schools were more abundant. But gradually, as the ordinary people improved their economic condition, they saw to it that their children received some elementary education. The heavy Irish immigration promoted the cause of education, for young Irishmen could be hired and boarded around by farmers who collaborated in erecting a schoolhouse in some convenient location. In some cases the schoolteachers were purchased: that is, they were indentured servants whose contract could be bought, probably at New Castle, from a shipmaster who had transported them to America. "Let us go and buy a school master" was said to be a remark heard among Delaware farmers when they saw an immigant ship coming up the river.

In such circumstances it is not strange that the office of schoolteacher was held in low repute, as a position to be taken only until a better was available. Some teachers proved to be ill fitted for the place; where the chief consideration was the availability of a cheap but literate man there was little concern about his character or his experience.

As population grew, an increasing number of teachers opened schools of their own. Among the most famous was John Filson, who kept an elementary school in Wilmington before the Revolution but had to give it up after returning from the army because a wounded arm prevented him from disciplining children. It did not, however, keep him from achieving fame on the Kentucky frontier, where he is remembered as author of the first book on Kentucky, as well as the ghost writer of Daniel Boone's memoirs.

Most of the small communities had a school of some sort. In 1772 the assembly set aside part of the market square in New Castle for a schoolhouse and appointed five trustees to supervise its construction. A schoolhouse was erected at Christiana Bridge in 1769 at a cost of over £100. Many of the schools took in girls as well as boys, and there is a belief that Lewes had the oldest school for girls in the colonies. Lewes may have applied some income from the Great Marsh, its commons, to education. It had a building constructed as a Latin school, but when an Anglican missionary, the Reverend John Andrews, wrote from there in August 1768, all attempts to operate it had failed. "There is not a Grammar School within the County," wrote Andrews, "and it is a thing extremely rare to meet with a man who can write a tolerable hand or spell with propriety the most common words in the English Language."

Vocational education was provided within the family or by the apprenticeship system. Even lawyers and physicians normally read law or studied medicine by apprenticeship to a practicing attorney or physician. Sometimes young men went for this training to Philadelphia, where the local college offered the first medical course in America in the 1760s. A few fortunate young men (such as John Dickinson) went abroad to study law in London at the Inns of Court or (like Henry Latimer and George Monro) to study medicine in Edinburgh.

James Adams, a Scotch-Irishman, came from Philadelphia to Wilmington in 1761 to set up the first printing press in the Lower Counties. He announced his intention to publish a newspaper, the *Wilmington Courant,* in 1762, but no copies are known to exist and the paper may never have appeared. No other newspaper was even projected in the Lower Counties before the Revolution; the first newspaper that can be authenticated was the *Delaware Gazette,* published in Wilmington in 1785 by Jacob Killen, who had learned the trade with Adams and was a son of the Scotch-Irish chancellor of Delaware, William Killen.

About one-third of all the titles of works printed in Delaware in the eighteenth century came from the press of James Adams, who had no local competition in the colonial period and remained active for a third of a century. A good number of the remaining titles were printed by his former apprentices, including three of his sons. In printing, as in many fields related to literature, the proximity of Philadelphia stifled local initiative in the Lower Counties. Philadelphia newspapers, as their advertisements indicate, were the chief reliance of those residing in New Castle, Kent, and Sussex who felt any need for such a medium of information. The General Assembly of the Lower Counties recognized the local circulation of Philadelphia newspapers by ordering notices to be placed in them.

The most famous literary work by a colonial Delawarean was John Dickinson's *Letters from a Farmer in Pennsylvania to the Inhabitants of the British Colonies,* which were sent anonymously to a Philadelphia newspaper, the *Pennsylvania Chronicle,* in 1767 and 1768 and were reprinted in many other journals from New England to Georgia. Soon the letters reappeared in pamphlet form, including editions published in London, Dublin, and Amsterdam. At the time of writing, Dickinson was a resident of Pennsylvania, but he had retained interests in Delaware and shuttled back and forth between the Lower Counties and Philadelphia. Dickinson won great fame (and an honorary degree from the College of New Jersey) as a result of this work, which was the most popular polemical publication in the colonies until Thomas Paine's *Common Sense* was printed in January 1776. On the other hand, Henry Brooke of Lewes, David French of New Castle, and John Parke of Dover, produced essays and poetry that are remembered only by historians and students of literary curiosities.

Painting had a more notable development than literature in the three

Lower Counties, owing to the work of a father and son, Gustavus and John Hesselius, and their connection with Old Swedes (Holy Trinity) Church. Gustavus Hesselius came to America in 1711, when he was twenty-nine, accompanying a brother who had been appointed pastor of Old Swedes. Subsequently the painter made his home primarily in Philadelphia, where he could find patrons, but he painted throughout the area, going as far south as Virginia. His son, John, born in America and baptized at Old Swedes, lived in New Castle for a time and is remembered both for his own work and as the first teacher of Charles Willson Peale. Still a third member of the same family was Adolph Wertmüller, a court painter in Sweden, who came to Delaware near the end of the eighteenth century, married a granddaughter of Gustavus Hesselius, and settled on a farm beside Naaman's Creek.

A settled rural society could patronize distant writers, but it needed painters, cabinetmakers, and silversmiths close at hand. Painters were usually itinerant visitors, but cabinetmakers and silversmiths set up shops in the locality. The earliest known silversmith was Wessell Alrichs, of New Castle, who worked at the beginning of the eighteenth century and also served in minor public offices, as sheriff and justice of the peace. A few decades later Johannes Nys (or de Nys) was active in Kent County, and by the end of the colonial period a number of silversmiths were at work in the Lower Counties, among whom the most notable were Bancroft Woodcock and Joseph Warner, of Wilmington. Even in rural Sussex County there was at least one such artisan, William Parker.

Duncan Beard, who had a shop near Odessa, was both silversmith and clockmaker. Charles Bush, an Irish-born cabinetmaker, was one of the first residents of Wilmington. His contemporary, John Williams, of New Castle, would for a fee make almost any article of wood. John Bell plied the cabinetmaker's trade in Dover until his business failed in 1760.

The neglected farmers of the rural Lower Counties, those not close to churches or meeting houses, were finally rescued from their cultural isolation by a tardy portion of the Great Awakening, the Methodist revival of the 1770s. Whereas Whitefield, after his initial reception at Lewes, had concentrated on the crowds who assembled to hear him in cities and towns and the more densely populated farming regions nearby and found his readiest welcome among the Presbyterians, the Methodist preachers sent to America by John Wesley in 1769 and thereafter went everywhere and spoke to anyone who would listen.

Though Whitefield and the Wesley brothers were ordained ministers of the Church of England, the first of the Wesleyan preachers to come to America were laymen, part of a group directed by John Wesley to carry the gospel to areas without ministers, whether in the growing mill towns and cities of England or in the backwoods of America. These preachers came not as proselytizers for a new denomination but as spokesmen for the old faith, striving by their enthusiasm and zeal to reawaken religious life where it had been allowed to lie dormant if not to die. Very seldom were these missionaries college-bred, for if they were their zeal might have led them to become ordained and then settled as pastors of an established parish. Seldom were they married, for if they were they could not easily accept Wesley's challenge to carry the message to America. Normally the preachers were bachelors of limited education, but zealous and devoted to their mission and willing to travel where needed.

The first Methodist preacher to come to Delaware (after Whitefield, if he could be considered a Methodist in his American years) was an exotic of his kind. Although most of the preachers were young and peaceful, this man, Captain Thomas Webb, was an old soldier who unbuckled his sword and placed it beside him before beginning to preach. Most of the preachers learned to concentrate on the countryside where plain farmers of English descent, who were out of reach of any settled minister, welcomed their visits, but Captain Webb spent most of his time in Delaware in Wilmington, New Castle, and their environs.

Here the English population was proportionately small and often already attached to a church or a meeting. Later Methodist ministers found success in rural lower Delaware and throughout the Delmarva Peninsula where the English proportion of the population was high and where the African slaves also represented a neglected element in society that welcomed the attention of enthusiastic preachers.

As early as 1770 the printing press of James Adams gave evidence of the effect of the Methodist revival, for in that year Adams reprinted a sermon by Charles Wesley and two others by one of Wesley's friends. The greatest inspiration for Methodism in Delaware came from Francis Asbury, who arrived in America in 1771 and remained on this continent until his death in 1816. Asbury was at first only one of many Methodist preachers sent from England, but the onset of the Revolution caused almost all of the others to return. Asbury remained; however, he objected to state laws requiring all men to take oaths of allegiance, including a pledge to take up arms if called upon, so he spent almost two years in Delaware, where the laws were less severe, though even here he felt it necessary to go into hiding for about five weeks.

Except for this period, Asbury was constantly in motion. A bachelor and homeless, he rode circuit over eastern North America, from Canada to Georgia, covering in his lifetime about 300,000 miles. He found a particularly favorable reception on the Delmarva Peninsula, and especially in Kent County, Delaware, where he had spent twenty months in refuge. Perhaps because he was himself an English tenant farmer's son and had left school when only thirteen, he could approach the ordinary farming folk of Kent and its neighboring counties with sympathy and understanding, and with such success that he is said to have won 1,800 converts during his stay in the Delaware counties.

Here too Asbury and other Methodist preachers met a generally favorable response from Anglicans—even from the clergy, who welcomed them as missionaries performing a needed service in preaching to the people. Samuel Magaw, Anglican rector at Dover, went out into the country to appear at Methodist meetings, while Asbury, never offering communion himself until after the Revolution, came to Magaw's church to take communion when in Dover.

Since to qualify a man as a preacher the Methodists required neither episcopal ordination nor advanced education, but only a good character, a fervent zeal, and a willingness to work for nothing more than subsistence, the first English missionaries, by communicating their enthusiasm, produced a new group of American preachers almost overnight. When most of the English missionaries returned to their homeland at the beginning of the war, a new group of ministers, all Americans, was ready to replace them.

To reach people in the back country of the Lower Counties and throughout the peninsula, the Methodists employed two devices new to this area—the circuit rider and the camp meeting. Clergymen of other faiths had served congregations or families at such distances that they spent much time in travel, but the Methodists, following the example set by John Wesley in England, utilized the itinerant ministry on a larger and more regular scale than anyone had done previously in Delaware. Normally they assigned two preachers—a veteran and a neophyte, both bachelors—to an area as large as a county and sent them off on continual perambulation through a year or so, the length of their appointed stay. At first they preached in the homes of sympathizers; in public buildings, such as courthouses where available; in taverns; or outside, in fields or village greens—wherever they could gather an audience. In a short time well-to-do converts began to build chapels to shelter Methodist meetings from inclement weather. The Kent circuit, begun in 1774 or earlier, was the oldest on the peninsula, and Barratt's Chapel, near Frederica, and White's Chapel, near Whiteleysburg, were two of the numerous meeting houses that began to be a part of the Kent landscape.

The early Methodist preachers were generally pacifists and almost all abolitionists, who took particular pains to preach to African slaves as well as to their white masters. As a result of their efforts and of the crippling effect of the Revolutionary War on the Church of England, the greater part of the rural population of the Lower Counties was made Methodist within one generation. By 1800 it is estimated that not only was Methodism the prevailing denomination in Delaware but Methodists formed a larger proportion of the population of Delaware and of the entire Delmarva Peninsula than of any other portion of the United States.

A meeting between Thomas Coke, an emissary newly arrived from John Wesley, and Francis Asbury at Barratt's Chapel in 1784 was a notable event in the history of Methodism. Coke brought Asbury Wesley's recommendation that the American Methodists form their own organization and cut their overseas ties, for Wesley, as a minister of the Church of England, supported the organization of the Christian church on national lines. A conference was quickly called in Baltimore, where the Methodist Episcopal Church was formed. What had begun as a revival movement within the Anglican church emerged as a separate denomination.

Besides the Methodists, another group actively proselytizing in Delaware in the 1770s was the Baptists. In 1779, Francis Asbury, in one of his rare witticisms, noted in his journal: "I found the Baptists were fishing in troubled water (they always are preaching water to people) and are striving to get in all the houses where we preach."

The Welsh Tract Church was the mother church to a number of Baptist congregations in Delaware—at Wilmington, Duck Creek, and Mispil-

lion, for instance. In Sussex County, however, during the years of the
Revolution two Baptist preachers from Virginia, Elijah Baker and Philip
Hughes, won many converts among the unchurched residents of English
descent. One of the most famous of the eighteenth-century American
Baptist ministers, the Reverend Morgan Edwards, historian of his
church and a founder of Brown University, spent his last years on a Welsh
Tract farm. However, before he moved to the Lower Counties he had
given up his active life in favor of his writing, and he played no important religious role thereafter. Nor were the Baptists, indeed, ever a major
sect in Delaware, perhaps because they never attained an organization as
efficient as that of the Methodists.

The Quakers, too, remained small in number, though their mercantile
prominence, their entrepreneurial adventurousness, and their developing philanthropic interests allowed them to play a leading part in the
economic and, to a lesser degree, the cultural life of the Wilmington
area. There were active Quaker meetings in Kent County as well as in
New Castle, but only a few Quakers resided in Sussex.

In 1766, John Woolman of New Jersey traveled to meetings on the
peninsula and sought, with some success, to rouse Quakers to sensitivity
concerning the dangers of ease and luxury and particularly to declare the
sinfulness of slaveholding. The preaching of Woolman and other Quaker
reformers gradually had effect as the Philadelphia Yearly Meeting, the
organization to which the Quakers of Delaware belonged, concluded,
first, that trading in slaves was wrong and must be forbidden to Quakers,
and then, in 1776, took the further step of forbidding slavery altogether.
In the Lower Counties the chief Quaker proponent of abolitionism, as
well as of pacifism, was Warner Mifflin of Camden (formerly Mifflin's
Cross Roads), in Kent County, who became internationally renowned for
his activities during and after the Revolution.

When John Woolman passed through this area he found along the
border between Maryland and Delaware a group of people called Nicholites. These were the followers of Joseph Nichols, who was born near
Dover in about 1730 and began preaching in the early 1760s. His followers called themselves Friends and were sometimes called New Quakers,
but they were an independent denomination, not originally connected
with the Society of Friends. The Nicholites emphasized the Inner Light
and opposed an ordained ministry, higher education, luxuries of dress,
and slaveholding. In their attitude toward slaveholding they were in

advance of even their Quaker neighbors; the members of at least one family of former slaves were admitted to full membership among the Nicholites. The latter were not formally organized until December 1774, which was after Joseph Nichols's death. Thereafter their growth was primarily on the Eastern Shore of Maryland and in the Carolinas, and in both areas they joined with the Quakers at the end of the century.

Like the Nicholites and, for that matter, the Methodists, the strength of the Catholics in the Lower Counties seemed at first to be centered firmly on the Delmarva Peninsula rather than to flow outward from the Delaware River settlements of New Castle and Philadelphia, where the Anglicans, Presbyterians, and Quakers had their oldest places of worship. Some of the first Catholics in the Lower Counties may have come directly to the Delaware River valley as part of the English migration of the late seventeenth century, but it is likely that many if not most of them moved into the Delaware counties from Maryland, where the first Catholic settlement had been made in 1634.

Under the Penn regime in the Lower Counties there was no hindrance in the way of free practice of the Catholic religion such as existed in most of the other colonies. By the middle of the eighteenth century Catholic services were being held with some regularity in the neighborhood of Dover and Odessa by priests from the Jesuit mission of St. Xavier's on the Bohemia River in Cecil County and, after 1764, from a mission established at Cordova, in Queen Annes County, by Father Joseph Mosley, also a Jesuit.

In Pennsylvania and Delaware, as in Maryland, Jesuit missionaries often purchased land in the name of one priest and on it erected a small chapel or church. In 1745 a farm near Hazlettville, in Murderkill Hundred, Kent County, was registered in the name of Father Thomas Poulton, a Jesuit from the Bohemia station. A chapel and probably a school were erected on the property, which was most likely the first Catholic establishment in Delaware. The Jesuits gave up this property in 1785, concentrating their efforts in the mid-peninsula area on the Cordova mission.

Another early Catholic chapel may have been erected in lower New Castle County, but the permanent base for Catholicism in Delaware was at Coffee Run, near Mount Cuba, in Mill Creek Hundred, northern New Castle County, where services may have been held as early as 1747. In 1772 Cornelius Hollahan, a Catholic farmer, sold a two-hundred-acre farm at this location to Father Matthew Sittensperger, a German Jesuit stationed at St. Xavier's, Bohemia, who was known in America as Father Manners. The purchase was actually made in the name of Father John Lewis, the head of the Jesuits in English America, to avoid any problem from having the land in the name of an alien. A church called St. Mary's was built here, and in time it became the center of an itinerant mission.

The French alliance and the presence of French troops during the Revolutionary War helped give Catholicism increased prestige in this area. The resumption of Irish immigration after the war and the arrival of Catholic refugees from France and especially from the French West Indies in the 1790s significantly increased the number of Catholics in Delaware and occasioned the establishment of Catholic churches in New Castle and Wilmington. The really large growth in the Catholic population, however, did not come until the great migrations of the middle and late nineteenth century.

9

THE ECONOMY—OLD PATTERNS AND
NEW BEGINNINGS

Slavery reached its apogee and began to decline in the Lower Counties at some time prior to the American Revolution. When the first federal census was taken in 1790 there were 8,887 slaves and 3,899 free blacks in Delaware. Inasmuch as the overwhelming majority of the Africans had been slaves when they entered Delaware it is obvious that a strong manumission movement was under way. The rate at which it was taking place may be estimated from the figures for the first three censuses:

	Free Blacks	Slaves
1790	3,899	8,887
1800	8,268	6,153
1810	13,136	4,177

The 1790s were a period of intense abolitionist enterprise and possibly speeded up a movement that had begun earlier. In the decade between 1810 and 1820 the movement toward liberation came to a temporary halt, but it was resumed in the next decade. By 1840 there were only 2,605 slaves in Delaware, whereas there were then 16,919 free black residents, and by 1860 the number of slaves had declined to 1,798, while the free black population had increased to 19,829.

The accuracy of the statistics in early censuses is suspect, but the general tendency is clear, and one wishes for colonial statistics that would help ascertain when the movement began. Probably the same forces, whether of soil exhaustion or of diminishing demand, that caused the decline of tobacco culture in the Lower Counties also decreased the value of blacks as slave labor. The statistics just cited suggest that free black labor had economic value, for the total number of blacks was steadily increasing, even while the number of slaves declined. This may, however, have been a post-Revolutionary development. In the absence of useful statistics, it is impossible to say authoritatively whether the total black population was increasing in the decades prior to the Revolution; yet in view of what is known of the immigration from the Eastern Shore it is likely that it was, for many slaves moved with their Maryland masters into the Delaware counties.

Yet some slaves were still being imported by sea into the Delaware valley in the eighteenth century. A student of the Pennsylvania slave trade (Darold D. Wax) found that the number of slaves brought to market in the Delaware valley rose to a peak in the decade from 1755 to 1765, even though Quakers were dropping out of the business. Previously local merchants had imported slaves in small numbers from the West Indies, as in the case of the nineteen blacks brought from Barbados to Philadelphia in June 1701, along with a cargo of rum, molasses, sugar, and lime juice, in the *Constant Alice,* of which Hercules and James Coutts, of New Castle, were part owners. At the height of the trade, however, Philadelphia merchants sought larger numbers of slaves and sent ships directly to Africa. How many or what proportion of these slaves reached Delaware is unknown, but certainly some did. In 1762, for example, the Philadelphia firm of Willing, Morris and Company advertised for sale at Wilmington 175 "Gold Coast Negroes" just imported from Africa.

In 1790, the first census showed that almost 22 percent of the total population was composed of blacks, and later censuses showed the black proportion of the population rising until the heavy Irish and German migrations of the nineteenth century reversed the trend. Whether this trend that is clearly visible in the years 1790–1810 was also characteristic of the mid-eighteenth century is by no means certain. After 1790 whites could leave Delaware for new opportunities in western Pennsylvania, Kentucky, or Ohio, far more easily than blacks, whether free or slave, so it seems likely that the growing proportion of blacks in the Delaware population was due to white emigration rather than to black immigration.

There seems to have been no special legislation regarding blacks in the counties on the Delaware until 1700, when an act was passed making special, and discriminatory, regulation for their trial and punishment and forbidding them from carrying weapons or assembling in large numbers. Other similar laws were passed in subsequent years as fears of slave insurrections grew. In 1741 Governor George Thomas used the possibility of "Domestic Insurrections of the Negroes," along with fear of raids by French or Spanish pirates, as excuse for urging the colonists to provide for their defense. The assembly, in response, agreed that the danger of such insurrection was real, the slaves having "of late . . . given . . . too much Reason to fear that they will become troublesome to us in like manner as Negroes have been in some of our neighbouring Governments."

By this date, it is evident that a number of blacks in the Delaware counties had attained freedom, because the laws begin to make specific reference to them. In 1731, for instance, a law required masters manumitting their slaves to assume any cost the county was put to for care of the freed men.

This law suggests that masters were suspected of freeing the aged and the infirm, who were of no value, in order to be absolved of expense for their care. To provide for such cases a law in 1740 required the former master to post a bond of thirty pounds for every slave freed who was infirm or over thirty-five. In 1767 the amount of the bond was doubled, and the requirement was extended to all manumissions, whatever the age and physical condition of the slave being freed. It seems likely, however, that little attention was paid to this requirement of a bond, for in 1787 the requirement was abandoned, the legality of all previous manumissions was recognized, even though a bond may not have been posted, and masters freeing slaves who were in good health and between twenty-one and thirty-five years old were released from any requirement to give security. In practice, distinctions of age and decrepitude were ignored thereafter, and even blacks illegally manumitted were considered free.

Meanwhile many residents of the Lower Counties had become concerned about the morality of slaveholding, and particularly about the buying and selling of slaves, which, together with the obvious horrors of the transatlantic slave trade, aroused sensibilities of the free population sooner than slaveholding itself. In 1767, the Kent County delegates to the General Assembly, with Caesar Rodney taking a leading part, proposed legislation forbidding any further importation of slaves. Their proposal failed, but as the years passed an increasing number of thoughtful people came to support the position taken by Rodney and the Kent delegates of 1767. Some men were moved mainly by religious arguments against slavetrading, as well as slaveholding, which were expressed vigorously through these years by leaders of many denominations. Others were moved primarily by the increasing emphasis upon man's natural rights to life and liberty, as well as by other appeals to reason made as part of the increasing struggle against unpopular English laws. Perhaps religious and rational arguments against slavery were increasingly successful in the Lower Counties because the economic need for slave labor was declining. At any rate, in 1775 the General Assembly passed the bill forbidding further slave importation that it had rejected in 1767. But still it did not become law; Governor John Penn, influenced by English policy, refused to approve it.

By 1775, however, the influence of English policy and English governors was limited. In the next year the Lower Counties proclaimed their freedom from England, and in the constitution they quickly drafted they inserted a provision, which they declared unamendable, that no slaves should hereafter be brought into Delaware.

Unfortunately, no penalty was provided for anyone disregarding this constitutional provision, and it remained ineffective, though wartime conditions made slave imports unlikely. Soon after the war was over, however, the legislature moved to strengthen the constitutional provision against slave importation and considered additional action against slavetrading and even against slaveholding.

Slavery existed in all the colonies before the American Revolution, though warm weather and an extended growing season made slaveholding more economical in the southern colonies than in the North. In scarcely more than two decades after the Revolution, however, all the states north of Delaware had provided either for the immediate or the gradual abolition of slavery, whereas no such provisions were made in any of the states south of Delaware. Since considerations based on religion or on rational thought about the rights of mankind were as likely, in themselves, to move southerners as northerners, economic differences, based on geography and climate, are the logical explanation of the different behavior of the two sections in the new nation. In this case, Delaware was in a pivotal position as the central state, a border land between North and South.

Among the forces working most actively to improve the lot of the black population of Delaware was the Society of Friends. In 1758, the Philadelphia Yearly Meeting, with which the Delaware meetings were affiliated, declared its opposition to all phases of the slave trade, the importation, the sale, and the purchase of slaves. From this position in opposition to trade in slaves it moved quickly to opposition to slaveholding itself, first recommending that all Friends free any slaves they possessed and finally, in 1776, making this recommendation compulsory.

One Delaware Friend who was deeply affected by Quaker sentiments on this issue was Warner Mifflin. Born in 1745 on the Eastern Shore of Virginia, he had moved while young to Kent County, where his father owned almost two thousand acres of land in the vicinity of Camden. When he was a boy of fourteen, working in the field with his father's slaves, one of them asked him whether it was right that they should toil to support him and send him to school and that by and by their children must do the same for his children.

The question disturbed Mifflin. Moved by what Quakers would call an inner light, Mifflin, when the power to take action became his, freed all the slaves within his command and tried to persuade his neighbors to do likewise. In time he became convinced that mere manumission was not enough since he had already unjustly profited from slave labor; thereupon he paid his former slaves for work they had done while in bondage.

His concern on this subject led him to travel widely to Quaker meetings from Rhode Island to North Carolina, conveying his conviction regarding the sinfulness of slaveholding. He was the author, moreover, of many petitions on this subject addressed to state legislatures and to Congress.*

The Quakers were not the only ones whose religious sensibilities were aroused by the practice of slaveholding in colonial America, though they maintained their antislavery opinions more consistently and over a longer period than other denominations. The early Methodist preachers sent by John Wesley from England also opposed slavery vigorously; the American preachers, however, who succeeded the original missionaries did not all share in this aspect of their zeal.

Richard Bassett, who had inherited a large part of Augustine Herrman's estate called Bohemia Manor and also practiced law in Dover, was an early Methodist convert who freed all of his numerous slaves. After the legislature postponed action on a bill for the gradual abolition

---

* For his vigorous advocacy of abolition and also of pacifism, Warner Mifflin gained an international reputation before his death in 1798 of the yellow fever (probably contracted while nursing the sick in Philadelphia).

of slavery, written by John Dickinson and recommended in a petition signed by more than two hundred Quakers in 1786, Bassett the next year introduced a bill that did succeed in blocking any legal trade in slaves across the narrow borders of Delaware.

This bill, as enacted in 1787, put teeth in the constitutional prohibition on the importation of slaves by providing that any slave brought into Delaware automatically became free, whereas the person bringing him across the state line would be fined £20, half of the fine to be awarded to the informer calling the incident to attention. Even more important, the law prohibited the exportation of slaves for sale. A farmer moving out of the state permanently might take his slaves with him, but no longer could a Delawarean sell his slaves to dealers for use in Maryland or elsewhere out of state. The legislature, informed that free blacks as well as slaves had been exported and sold, set the penalty at £100, half to go to the informer.* This same law promised free blacks the right to hold property and to have legal redress for injuries but specifically denied them the right to vote, hold office, or enjoy the other privileges of a free man.

Abolition continued to be put off, but in 1789 antislavery forces won further concessions from the legislature when they warned that a ship was fitting out at Wilmington to enter the slave trade. It was illegal to prepare ships for this nefarious trade in Pennsylvania, and the legislature quickly nipped in the bud any idea of making Wilmington the home port of a slaver. The same law also made provision for jury trial for blacks accused of capital offenses.

The act of 1787 that prohibited any trade in slaves across the boundaries of Delaware assured the decline of slaveholding in Delaware, even though Delawareans refused to take the final step of passing an abolition law. As the economic value of Delaware slaves decreased, either from a decline in the productivity of the soil under conditions of intensive farming or for other reasons, a Delaware slaveowner could not sell his slave for the highest price available in America unless willing to take his chances on smuggling a slave out of state illegally.

---

* The provisions of this law were later strengthened, for example, by a 1793 law providing for the whipping and mutilation (cutting off part of the ears) of anyone kidnapping free blacks. Probably this provision was so savage that it was not properly enforced.

Charcoal sketch by an unknown artist of Richard Bassett, most prominent Methodist layman in Delaware, based on Alfred Rosenthal's copy of a portrait by Charles de Saint-Mémin. Photocopy from the Historical Society of Delaware, Wilmington. Used by permission of the Division of Historical and Cultural Affairs, Dover.

To prevent and expose any such temptation, as well as for abolitionist purposes generally, Warner Mifflin, Richard Bassett, and others of like mind organized a society in 1788, with headquarters in Dover, the Delaware Society for Promoting the Abolition of Slavery, for Superintending the Cultivation of Young Free Negroes, and for the Relief of Those Who May Be Unlawfully Held in Bondage. Another similar society was organized in Wilmington in 1789, with James A. Bayard, later a distinguished senator, among its members.

One surprising feature in the progress of emancipation in this state is the forwardness of Kent County, where many of the blacks gained freedom early. Of 29 Kent County probate inventories and estate accounts for 1774 listed by Alice Hanson Jones (in *American Colonial Wealth,* I, 353–401) only eight list slaves. Andrew Caldwell, Esquire, was the largest slaveowner, possessing, at the time of his death, five adults and four children. The other seven slaveowners, a blacksmith, a tanner, a carriagemaker, a shipowner, a widow, and two farmers, had a total of twelve adult slaves and eleven children, and one of the latter was owed his freedom in ten years. It is notable that sixteen yeomen or farmers had no slaves. (Statistics for neighboring Queen Annes County, Maryland, are very different in this respect.) The decline of slavery in Kent County was demonstrated by the first federal census in 1790:

	New Castle	Kent	Sussex
Slaves	2,562	2,300	4,025
Free Blacks	639	2,570	690

The persistence of slavery in Sussex County can be accounted for by the fact that Sussex was decidedly the largest county in area and also, in terms of tax returns, the poorest. Since slave labor in this area was primarily agricultural, it had a greater usefulness in Sussex, where distance from the Philadelphia market gave less incentive to farmers to turn to a money economy than in the more prosperous counties of New Castle and Kent. Furthermore, the Quaker influence was decidedly smaller in Sussex than in the other counties. Then too, since Sussex is the southernmost of the Delaware counties, there were factors of climate and geography favoring the continuance of slavery.

But from these same factors one would expect slaveholding to persist in Kent County longer than in New Castle. Kent was larger and more nearly devoted to agriculture; it lay to the south of New Castle, farther from Philadelphia, and it had fewer Quakers. However, the Quakers residing in Kent had remarkable leadership, including not only Warner Mifflin, but also John Dickinson, the county's largest landholder. For most of his life Dickinson was not a practicing Quaker, and he never joined that society formally, but the Quaker influence upon him was strong. His mother was a Quaker, as were his wife and his children, and his father had been a Quaker until he separated from the society after a quarrel.

Kent was also a center of early Methodist influence, the site of the first Methodist circuit on the Delmarva Peninsula, the place where Francis Asbury sought refuge during the Revolution. The peculiar mixture of Quaker and Methodist influences in Kent, along with the individual efforts of Mifflin, Dickinson, and Bassett, apparently created an antislavery sentiment that prevailed over geographic and economic conditions. Even on the eve of the Civil War, Kent retained its leadership; the 1860 census showed 203 slaves in Kent County, 254 in New Castle, and 1,341 in Sussex. By that date the number of free blacks exceeded the number of slaves in every Delaware county.

The progress that was possible for a Delaware slave, as well as the handicaps he would face, are illustrated by the career of Richard Allen, who has preserved the account in his autobiography, entitled *The Life, Experience, and Gospel Labors of Richard Allen.**

Allen, one of the two or three most distinguished men ever to rise from the bonds of slavery in the Lower Counties, was born to slavery in 1760 in the prominent Chew family of Philadelphia and Kent County. As a boy he was sold, with his mother, to another Delaware planter named Stockley, and this man, for reasons unknown, gave Allen the opportunity to buy his freedom. This was the way in which many slaves won their freedom, but exactly how Allen raised the money is not clear. Some slaves were "rented out": that is, allowed to work for a money wage and to keep part of their earnings. Allen may have raised money in a manner he described, though not necessarily speaking of his own experiences: "The slaves would toil in their little patches many a night until

---

* This work, not published until 1887, is more readily available in a second edition appearing in 1960.

midnight to raise their little truck and sell to get something to support them more than what their masters gave them." It is doubtful, however, that Allen could raise all of the £60 he needed from working a small truck patch late at night. More likely he worked as a slave at tasks he turned to after he became free, when he cut cord wood, labored in a brick yard, carted salt from salt works at Rehoboth, and did days' work of any sort.

As a slave, Allen had been converted by Methodist preachers, and as a free man after moving to Philadelphia he became a leader in the Methodist church. Ordained a deacon by Francis Asbury in 1799, he later led a schism that grew out of racial prejudice and obstruction in the church. The result of the schism was the establishment of the African Methodist Episcopal Church, in which Allen became a bishop.

A similar schism in Wilmington led a black preacher named Peter Spencer to found another African Methodist church. Spencer's denomination, centered in Delaware, never became as large as Allen's and less is known of Spencer's own background since he left no autobiography. The important point is, however, that the blacks of the Delaware counties were at least as greatly moved by the Methodist revival of the late eighteenth century as were the whites. The Methodist church seems to have provided a means for them to exhibit a degree of both economic and intellectual independence, since they did not remain content to follow white preachers or to worship in edifices built and controlled by whites.

Of course, not all Delaware blacks were Methodists. A notable exception was Absalom Jones, founder of a Protestant Episcopal church for blacks in Philadelphia. Jones was born in Sussex County in 1746. After he moved to Philadelphia he became associated with many fraternal and philanthropic movements there, including a Free African Society, established in 1787, in which he and Allen were leading figures.

The slave was not the only unfree laborer in the Lower Counties, where a substantial part of the working force was made up of indentured servants. Analysis of advertisements for runaways appearing in colonial newspapers between 1728 and 1767 indicates there were more than three times as many white servants as blacks fleeing their masters in Delaware. This does not prove there were three times as many whites as blacks in servitude; it was probably more tempting for whites to run away because they could conceal their identity fairly easily, and for this same reason masters

Portrait by an unknown artist of Reverend Richard Allen, founder of the African Methodist Episcopal Church. Courtesy of the Moorland-Spingarn Research Center, Howard University, Washington.

Portrait by Raphaelle Peale of Reverend Absalom Jones. Courtesy of the Delaware Art Museum, Wilmington.

may have felt it necessary to advertise for runaway whites. Over the same years newspaper announcements of captured fugitives being held in jail until claimed also show a majority of whites over blacks—not as large a majority of whites as in the advertisements for runaways, but a significant plurality since it is likely that black runaways were more frequently apprehended than runaway white servants. These statistics suggest that unfree white servants were at least nearly as numerous as black slaves in Delaware in the mid-eighteenth century.*

Some white servants entered this rank involuntarily, having been transported to the colonies as convicts and then sold to work off sentences imposed on them for crimes committed in England. (American convicts were also sold into service.) Few convicts, however, were sent to the Delaware valley; in 1739 the importation of anyone convicted of a "heinous crime," such as murder, burglary, forgery, perjury, or any other felony, was forbidden by the assembly at New Castle under penalty of a £5 fine on the person responsible, who was also required to provide security in the amount of £50 for the imported convict's good behavior for a year. Shipmasters thereupon began avoiding enforcement of the law by unloading any convicts among their passengers at Reedy Island, below New Castle; but the law was stiffened in 1749, one of the provisions of the new law setting a fine of £10 pounds upon anyone who purchased a convict—that is, purchased his services—however he entered the Lower Counties.

Most of the indentured servants in Delaware were European immigrants who could not afford the voyage to America and therefore signed a contract, called an indenture, with a ship captain who agreed to bring them over the ocean for whatever compensation he could get when he sold the contract in the New World. The terms of labor were usually between three and seven years, for which time the immigrant agreed to work for food, shelter, and clothing, but without any other pay.

Many of the indentured servants in the Lower Counties were Scotch-Irish, but some were of Catholic Irish, English, or German stock. The farmer in need of a hand would travel to New Castle, where most immigrant ships stopped, to buy a servant. On May 21, 1752, for instance, Randle Mitchell, a New Castle merchant, advertised in the *Pennsylvania Gazette* that a vessel was in port carrying a load of English servant men,

---

* For this information on runaways the author is indebted to the late H. Clay Reed, who collected the data, and to Lambert Jackson, who analyzed it.

including "tradesmen of different kinds, to be sold cheap for ready money."

Women, as well as men, were sold as indentured servants, but the term commonly refers to whites only and not to blacks. It was a major grievance of local planters, as expressed through their delegates in the colonial assembly, that servants were frequently enlisted in the military companies formed for service in the colonial wars of the mid-eighteenth century. Governor George Thomas, for instance, angered planters in 1739 by promising freedom to all indentured servants who would enlist, and when the assembly of the Lower Counties the next year voted £1,000 for feeding and transporting troops, including those raised for an expedition against the Spanish fortress of Cartagena in South America, the assemblymen asked that all servants enlisted in the counties they represented be first released.

The indentured servant, during his period of service, was likely to be worked as hard as a slave. He had the great advantage, however, of knowing that his term was of limited duration. Nor was the fact that a man had served out an indenture an impenetrable bar to his later advancement. Many young men of education and ambition found entering indentured service their best means of getting to America. James Annesley, heir to the earldom of Anglesey, served for a time, by a series of misadventures, as an indentured servant in the Lower Counties, and a novel, *The Wandering Heir,* by Charles Reade, was later based on Annesley's experiences.

Besides the unfree labor of slaves and indentured servants, much of the work on farms in the Lower Counties was done by hired hands, black and white, paid before the Revolution about three shillings, ninepence, for a day's work in Kent, though the wage depended on the task. Many farmers rented their lands, some of them on shares. The average farmer probably lived humbly, like William Shurmer, of near Little Creek, in Kent County, who dwelt in 1762 "in a Loansom Cottage, a small Log House that serves for Kitchen, Parlour, Hall & Bed Chamber."

Newspaper advertisements indicate that the average farm in New Castle County, at least from 1728 to 1746, was slightly more than two hundred acres in size. Larger landholdings were common in Kent and Sussex, though only a small part of the total acreage was likely to be cleared—or drained, if near the bay—for farming.

In Sussex County, in 1728, according to the Reverend William

Becket, the people lived half a mile to a mile apart, except for the fifty-eight families in Lewes. Their "business" was said to resemble that of English farmers; they commonly raised wheat and rye, plus Indian corn and tobacco, and they kept horses, cows, sheep, and hogs.

Such general farming remained characteristic of the Delaware counties through the time of the Revolution, though tobacco, as has been said, had by then been abandoned. Rye, oats, flax, hay, and garden vegetables, such as potatoes, cabbage, peas, and beans were also grown, as well as orchard crops, though corn and wheat were the staples, the crops most often grown for sale. The wheat of the upper peninsula was of an especially fine quality, often commanding a higher price than other wheat. Sheep and cattle, on the other hand, were small, being allowed to run almost at large in the marshes and forests of Kent and Sussex. The cattle were often driven to New Castle and fattened there—on grass, not grain—for the markets of Wilmington and Philadelphia. For the sheep, salt grass was stacked on poles about four feet above the ground, and in winter the sheep were driven under the shelter and ate the hay from between the poles. Practically every farmer had a few hogs, and some also had geese, turkeys, and bees.

Because land accessible to water was most valuable, there was an economic encouragement to the draining of tidal marshes. The Dutch settlers may have given a very early impetus to embanked fields, particularly in the area south of New Castle. In the eighteenth century the development of markets in Wilmington and Philadelphia gave new incentive to the farming of land below sea level in southern New Castle County, where large crops of wheat, rye, and oats could be produced.

In Sussex County there seemed to be unlimited resources of cedar and pine. Large quantities of shingles and boards were shipped to Philadelphia from the Indian River area, where the inhabitants also developed an export trade in cider to Philadelphia. In Kent and New Castle oak, hickory, poplar, walnut, maple, and ash were the predominant woods. Orchard crops were produced in small quantities throughout the Delaware counties.

The bays of Sussex County were the center of a profitable shell fishery. Especially valued were oysters from Rehoboth Bay, where it was said that one man in a day could take thirty bushels. A traveler in 1775 noted the existence of a great herring fishery on the Christina, and all the small streams of the Lower Counties were filled with fish once a year when "those Sea rovers [came] up the fresh watered Creeks and revelets to Propegate their Spaties," in the words of a contemporary petition for their protection.

Caesar Rodney's younger brother Thomas described the life of the white inhabitants in the mid-eighteenth century, before the French and Indian War, as "very simple, plain, and social." "Almost every family," he continued, "manufactured their own clothes." They ate their own beef, pork, and poultry, along with wild game, fruits, and butter and cheese of their own making, and they grew wheat and corn enough at least for their own needs. Milk, cider, beer, and peach or apple brandy were their beverages, tea, coffee, and chocolate being hard to find. Honey, instead of sugar, was the customary sweetening of even "the best families." In that period "the largest farmers . . . did not sow over twenty acres of wheat, nor tend more than thirty acres of Indian corn, and there was very few of this sort, so that all the families in the county had a great deal of idle time." The "land being fertile supplied them plentifully by a little labor." They had time for many social gatherings, "at which . . . the young people would dance, and the older ones wrestle, run, hop, jump, or throw the disc or play at some rustic and manly exercises. On Christmas Eve there was an universal firing of guns, and traveling round from house to house during the holiday, and indeed all winter there was a continual frolic at one house or another, shooting match, twelfth [night] cakes, etc." With the beginning of war in 1754 prices began to rise, produce became more valuable, and "in a few years the country became engaged in more pursuits and put on quite a new appearance. . . . The old habits and customs gradually wore off. . . . What little remained till then was expelled by the Revolution which . . . naturally wrought a far greater change than the former war."

In those times dinner was eaten in the middle of the day and was, even for slaves, a full meal of meat, bread, and vegetables. Meat was also eaten at breakfast, but not at supper, which was the lightest meal. Salt pork and bacon, often boiled, were the commonly used meats in winter, but fresh meat was available in summer and fall and was more often roasted than boiled. Vegetables of all kinds were used, often made into sauces to be served with the meat.

Wealthy people made their bread of wheat, but the poor ate corn bread. Whereas in mid-century coffee and tea were seldom used, by 1788 customs had changed so much that a distinguished but censorious physician, James Tilton, could write: "There is . . . an excessive use of tea and coffee in this state. Every housekeeper that can afford it breakfasts upon one or the other; and the genteel people generally indulge in the parade of tea in the afternoon."

The genteel people would mean the large landholders, the wealthiest merchants, and some of their friends in the professional classes, especially the Anglican clergy. In Delaware, however, there was only a slight distinction between these folk and the more numerous yeomen farmers who tilled their own soil. Both groups lived relatively simple lives, and the richest family, the Dickinsons, dwelt in a house that does not seem grand when compared to the homes of Virginia's tidewater aristocrats. "There is nothing of the Virginia character among our people," wrote a politician, in playing down any elements of aristocracy, and though his statement was didactic in purpose, it was basically true.

Waterways were the key to the commerce of colonial Delaware. Such roads as existed were generally in poor condition and led only to landings where produce could be put on board vessels for easier and cheaper transport to market by water rather than by land. A post road from Philadelphia to Wilmington continued on southward through New Castle to Dover via Odessa or Middletown, and then on to Lewes, with another road diverging at Milford toward Dagsboro and Snow Hill, the latter in Maryland. Travelers going to the western shore of Maryland left Wilmington for Newport, Christiana, and Elkton. Various roads crisscrossed these routes, especially at Christiana, where there was a bridge across the Christina River at the head of navigation.

At the river landings farm produce was picked up, mostly by shallops —shallow-draft sloops operated by just a man and a boy—and carried to New Castle, Wilmington or, most often, Philadelphia. These shallops navigated streams that today seem too small for commerce, but in the eighteenth century water was not diverted from its natural course and the streams were relatively deep. The Christina, for instance, was navigable for sloops of fifty tons for ten miles above Wilmington.

Since waterways through most of the Lower Counties flowed eastward into the Delaware, the commerce of this area fell naturally into the orbit of Philadelphia throughout the eighteenth century, as it did for long afterward. The notable exception was southwestern Sussex County, where the Nanticoke River and other streams led to the Chesapeake, but this area was on the periphery or even outside the jurisdiction of Sussex authorities until several years after completion of the Mason and Dixon survey.

In addition to the river commerce, Wilmington principally, and New Castle and Lewes in diminishing degree, were the home ports of some ocean-going vessels. Many of these were employed primarily in the coastal trade to New York or farther north, even to Newfoundland, and to the south, especially to Carolina, but by 1789 Wilmington was also the home of eleven vessels in the West India trade and six in the Irish trade.

The chief export to Ireland was flaxseed, because the Irish found it most profitable to harvest their flax or fiber for manufacture into linen, while importing their seed. Flour, timber, and potash were also sent to Ireland, and in return linen, glassware, and, of course, immigrants came to America.

As early as 1742 the brig *Wilmington,* owned by William Shipley and several partners, entered the West India trade, carrying outward mainly flour, but also lumber and wood products, corn meal, beef, pork, and similar goods and bringing back sugar, rum, molasses, cotton, and coffee. Despite the existence of some direct overseas commerce, however, the larger part of the overseas trade from the Lower Counties was conducted indirectly, via Philadelphia.

The importance of water-borne traffic to the Lower Counties encouraged the early development of a shipbuilding industry. Some shipbuilding was carried on along almost every navigable stream, on the Broadkill and the Mispillion as well as on the Christina. Though the foundation of an enterprise which eventually would gain for the Delaware valley a reputation as the American Clyde, it was on a very small scale in the eighteenth century, as indeed was almost all of the manufacturing carried on in the Delaware counties.

The production of iron had been undertaken in Governor Keith's day, based on ore deposits at Iron Hill. Keith's furnace was abandoned before the Revolution, but Sussex County, utilizing bog iron deposits, developed a small iron industry after Jonathan Vaughn and some partners from Pennsylvania constructed the Deep Creek Furnace and the Nanticoke Forge (at Middleford) about 1763.

The most important manufacturing in the Lower Counties, as in the other colonies, was undoubtedly domestic manufacturing, the processing of food (preserving, smoking, etc.) and the production of clothes, gear, and implements carried on within every rural family. But the branch of manufacturing with most significance for the future was the milling industry, centered in the grist mills along the Brandywine.

Mills for the grinding of grain were built even in the Swedish period and proliferated with the expansion of population, as the names of Milton, Milford, Millville, Milltown, and Mill Creek attest. The first mills were small affairs, operated by one miller, aided by his family, grinding a farmer's corn or wheat or barley for a fee. Though such custom mills continued in use into the twentieth century, the significant development was the appearance of merchant mills—larger enterprises operated by a merchant miller who bought the farmer's grain and sold the flour, sometimes owning the vessels that brought the grain to his mill and took the flour to a market.

The most important merchant mills were constructed on the Brandywine, at the head of navigation on that stream. Here by 1788, according to Dr. James Tilton, it was "the prevailing opinion . . . that we have the largest and most perfect manufacture of flour within a like space of ground known in the world." Tilton meant his comment to apply to the state of Delaware as a whole as well as to the Brandywine mills in particular, but the Brandywine mills were considered preeminent.

The beginnings of milling on the Brandywine were quite modest: the first mill was probably a barley mill erected in the seventeenth century by the sons of Dr. Tymen Stidham, a Swedish settler who owned most of the south bank. In the 1740s, soon after the founding of Wilmington, some of Stidham's property came into the hands of Oliver Canby, who built a grist mill there and was the first of the several Quaker millers who made that area famous for its flour manufacture. Thomas Shipley, son of the Wilmington developer, began, with some associates, construction of a mill race along the southern side of the Brandywine in 1760. Completion of the race allowed construction of mills with overshot wheels, using water power more efficiently than undershot mill wheels. Soon Joseph Tatnall, a distant connection of Thomas Shipley, had constructed a mill race on the rocky and more difficult north bank. By 1770 eight mills were clustered together within a quarter mile below the new Brandywine bridge. Vessels carrying two thousand bushels of wheat could unload immediately beside the mills and then load again with a cargo of flour.

The mills prospered from their location beside a steady and regular flow of water and also from their proximity to some of the best wheat-growing country in the America of that day. Joseph Tatnall and his son-in-law Thomas Lea owned two sloops which they used to bring wheat and sometimes corn to their mills and to carry their product to Philadelphia. They ground one hundred thousand bushels of wheat yearly but employed only six men, largely English and Irish immigrants, as mill hands, together with another twenty-four men who worked on the sloops or as coopers making barrels.

These statistics apply to the post-Revolutionary period when the efficiency of the Brandywine mills had been improved by the inventions of Oliver Evans. Born near Newport in 1755, Evans was apprenticed to a wheelwright but soon began working in a mill operated by his brothers. In the 1780s he developed improvements in milling machines—elevator, conveyor, hopper-boy, drill, and kiln-drier—that helped carry flour through the milling process with little need for human labor. Many of his inventions were patented by act of the Delaware legislature in 1787, as well as by other states and the federal government later, and Evans's connection with the most up-to-date practices in milling was further solidified by the publication in 1791 of his book, *The Young Mill-Wright and Miller's Guide.* As he sought contracts to install his improvements in mills throughout the area, it was of great advantage to him to be able to assert that his inventions had been adopted by the Brandywine millers.

The Brandywine mills were superior only in degree to those in other areas of Delaware, notably the mills on the Red Clay Creek. Besides grist mills, saw mills existed throughout Delaware, and fulling mills, in which woolen cloth, woven in the home, was softened (and, as time passed, often dyed), were erected in many places in the eighteenth century, near Rockland in 1733 and near Milton by 1758. Tanyards in Odessa, Wilmington, and elsewhere were necessary to produce the leather needed in an agricultural society for uses as varied as men's breeches and shoes and horses' harnesses.

A roster of manufacturers and artisans in the Wilmington vicinity in 1791 lists 59 coopers, 55 wool and cotton card makers (the cards were necessary to untangle and straighten out yarn before it was spun in the home or a shop), 51 carpenters and joiners, 58 tailors and weavers, 42 shoemakers, 28 hat makers, 28 blacksmiths, 30 printers and book binders, 22 carriage makers, plus brick layers, brick makers, cabinetmakers,

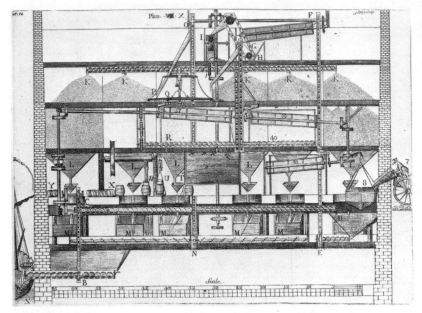

Sketch from Oliver Evans, *The Young Mill-Wright & Miller's Guide* (Philadelphia, 1795) demonstrating the automatic milling machinery Evans invented to move flour from a farmer's cart through the mill and into the hold of a vessel. Such machinery was employed at the Brandywine mills. Courtesy of the Eleutherian Mills Historical Library, Greenville.

silversmiths, shipwrights, etc.—a large number of skilled artisans in view of the small population.

Still, as this was the chief center of manufacturing in Delaware, the total number employed in such trades was small compared to the number of farmers. Yet the future lay with the miller, with such a man as Joseph Tatnall, who was to become president of his state's first bank and its first canal. In the Wilmington area by 1791 there were 12 grist mills, 6 saw mills, 1 barley mill, and also 1 snuff mill, 1 slitting mill, and 1 paper mill. On the Brandywine, which fell a total of 120 feet in a stretch of less than five miles, the steady water flow would attract other manufacturers in the early years of the new nation. Textile mills and powder mills would be reared on the banks of a river that flour millers first made famous. In time, Bancrofts and Du Ponts would supplant Canbys and Leas, and eventually the colonial relationship would be reversed and Delaware agriculture would become ancillary to Delaware manufacturing.

10

THE ANGLO-FRENCH WARS

The outbreak of war between Great Britain and Spain in 1739 had only a modest effect on the quiet tenor of life in the Delaware counties. The clearing of fields, construction of roads, embankment of streams, draining of marshes, location of mill sites went on quietly, in war as in peace. Thinking men, however—and members of the assembly were necessarily thoughtful about these matters—realized that the long low coastline of Delaware left it open to maritime aggression at any moment. The defense of their plantations against a foreign fleet or even a privateering vessel was more than they themselves could supply. Their reliance had to be upon outside assistance.

By the circumstances of the case this small colony was driven to respect its proprietary connections at the very time its neighboring province of Pennsylvania was stirred by an effort to break this somewhat medieval bond to a profiteering family. Pennsylvanians, made self-confident by the increasing wealth and power of their prosperous commonwealth, might think of cutting their connection with the Penn family and establishing their ties directly with the Crown and with Parliament, with whom they came to believe their own appointed agent could represent them better, and less selfishly, than the Penns.

But their own good sense led men in the Lower Counties to be less confident about upsetting the proprietary apple cart. In 1726, at a time when Hannah Penn was struggling to retain her family's inheritance in Delaware, James Logan complained to her of mistakes that had been made: "In taking a Title at first to those Counties that was not legal and then not perfecting it while practicable. In not fixing the line with the L. Baltimore when it might easily be done and in heaping things called

Privileges on a People who neither know how to use them, nor how to be grateful for them." But soon after Logan surrendered to George Thomas the governorship he had filled temporarily from 1736 to 1738, the Delaware counties became notable for the support they gave the new governor.

Not immediately, for at the beginning of Thomas's administration a number of more or less minor difficulties marred relations between the governor and the assembly. For instance, in April 1739, he complained that the Delaware assemblymen were passing bills faster than he could examine them. Many old laws were lost, they explained, and others were lying around the county offices in disorder; the assemblymen thought they should revise the laws they could find and replace those that were lost.* Then finally they could have their laws printed, as the governor urged them to do.

Besides his difficulty in learning what the laws were, George Thomas had several small controversies with the representatives of the Lower Counties over such issues as the right to license ferries and to collect fines. The one serious difficulty that hampered the relations of Governor Thomas and the people of the Lower Counties was the enlistment of servants after war with Spain erupted in 1739.

This war, which began only one year after Thomas's arrival on the Delaware, lasted throughout the remainder of his administration and paradoxically helped to calm relations between the governor and his assembly. The clue to the good relations Thomas came to enjoy with the Delaware assembly lay in the difficulties he encountered with the Quaker-dominated assembly in Pennsylvania when he sought men or money for military needs.

In the Lower Counties, Governor Thomas gave way to the assembly by promising to have all servants released from the army. His power was limited in this respect, but fortunately he succeeded in persuading the military to release indentured servants enlisted in the company raised there, even though these men had been promised freedom.

When Thomas at once praised the zeal of the Lower Counties for raising, victualing, and transporting troops and warned them that in their defenseless state they were "exposed even to the Insults of a few Privateers, or to the Domestick Insurrections of the Negroes," the assembly promptly passed a militia act. Every freeholder and taxable

---

* Many of the early eighteenth-century Delaware laws have never been found.

The Cape Henlopen Lighthouse, from a lithograph based on a sketch by J. Queen. Built at the expense of Philadelphia merchants in 1767, the interior was burned by the British during the Revolution but restored immediately afterwards, in 1784. Undermined as the coastline gradually receded, the lighthouse was finally toppled by encroaching waves in 1926. Courtesy of the Division of Historical and Cultural Affairs, Dover.

from seventeen to fifty was required to enlist and to provide himself with arms, with a few classes excepted—Quakers (upon payment of a two-shilling, sixpence, fine to the Poor Fund), magistrates, physicians, lawyers, millers, ministers, and the infirm. Ferdinand Paris, in London, was impressed: "I wish you had sent me a printed copy," he wrote a correspondent; "that would be of use here, to show that the Quakers in the lower Countys, are not so unreasonable as those in the upper."

Paris probably did not realize that in the Lower Counties the Quakers were a small minority with limited political influence. It was certainly not their doing that made the assemblymen in New Castle so responsive to Governor Thomas's requests as they were when they established a watch, backed by an armed citizenry, at the port of Lewes or when they forbade pilots to board incoming ships unless licensed by the governor. Even the governor's repeated requests, stimulated by orders he received from England, for the collection and publication of the laws were finally answered in the early months of 1742, when Benjamin Franklin "by Order of the Assembly" published the *Laws of the Government of New-Castle, Kent and Sussex upon Delaware.* * In small matters, too, the assemblymen were cooperative, responding, for example, to the governor's suggestion that they make a regular provision for the support of the judges of the Supreme Court.

Despite the expense and trouble of coming to New Castle, Governor Thomas found relief there from his constant quarrels with the Pennsylvania Assembly. In view of "the Harmony which has subsisted between me and the Representatives of the People here," he wrote at New Castle in October 1742, "it will not be doubted but that I have at all times a very real Satisfaction in meeting them." Efforts had been made, he declared on another occasion, to carry the war against him into the Lower Counties, but to no avail. He was happy to caution the Pennsylvania assemblymen, when they made some remarks regarding his compensation: "you have no more to do with what related to that Government [the Lower Counties] than you have with the Income of my own private Estate."

Nor did the Privy Council, though no one would have said this, have much to do with what went on in Delaware. Governor Thomas had, indeed, been instructed to collect all the laws in force in the Lower

---

* This first volume of laws passed by the Lower Counties Assembly bears the date 1741 because at that time the new year did not begin until March 25.

Counties and transmit them to England. It seems likely that he did transmit the edition that Franklin printed in 1741/42, but there is no known notice of any official action taken regarding it, or even of its receipt. Certainly no attempt was made to disallow any of the laws of the Lower Counties, or to approve them either.

Thomas also passed on to the assembly instructions he received to account for all the paper money issued and to suggest how it might be discharged. Speaker David French gave Thomas an account of the bills of credit the Delaware counties had circulated, and the assemblymen were pleased, when Thomas sent this account to England, to have him argue that the best way of discharging these bills was to follow the method the assemblymen had already prescribed.

The Delaware counties had first issued paper money in April 1723 at the instance of Sir William Keith, who had approved Pennsylvania's first issue a month earlier and was quick to recognize the utility of providing a medium of trade in these colonies. The problem here was that they were constantly short of money, which was drained from them by England because of their continuing need of English imports, such as textiles and other manufactured goods. The first paper money emission amounted to £5,000, which was quickly raised to £11,000 before the year was out.

The bills proved to be very popular, as Keith correctly figured they would be, and also safe, as Keith hoped, though his record as a debtor makes the fiscal soundness of his measures more surprising than their popularity. Printed by order of the assembly, the bills were turned over to trustees of loan offices established in each of the three county seats. These trustees put the bills in circulation by lending them in sums of £12 to £60 to borrowers who would mortgage their real estate in return. The mortgage contracts called for repayment in eight years in equal annual installments, plus interest at 5 percent. More than the convenience of a medium of exchange was provided; the interest money, as Keith undoubtedly realized, became, with an excise tax on liquor sales, the main basis of colonial finances, including the source of the annual appropriation made to the governor.

It is no wonder that paper money bills had a certain popularity with colonial governors, despite the fear in England that this increase in the money supply would cheapen payments by American debtors to English creditors. In fact, these paper money emissions operated as a "land bank," for borrowers put up their land as security, appraised very conservatively at about 50 percent or less of market value, and received

Two examples of Delaware paper money, one from the colonial government and one issued after independence. Courtesy of the Division of Historical and Cultural Affairs, Dover.

the new bills as a loan. In the absence of any private commercial banks, the government was providing a genuine and a popular service, and it was making a profit. By 1729, when the imminent retirement of the first bills led to a new emission, there had been only two foreclosures, both of small plantations.

At this time Patrick Gordon was governor and, under pressure from the proprietors, he was reluctant to permit new emissions. Paper money, however, had become so popular that he could not withstand the demand for it. An emission of £12,000 was voted, with the period of repayment extended from eight to sixteen years. In just five years, however, in 1734, there was successful pressure for a further emission of £12,000, and then in another five years, in 1739, Governor Thomas was persuaded to agree to a £6,000 emission, which was orginally intended only to replace bills that were ragged and torn. The allocation of the bills authorized in 1739 (£2,400 to New Castle County, £2,000 to Kent, and £1,600 to Sussex) indicates the relative activity of the economy and is similar to the allocation in 1729, the only other such detail surviving.

The original intent of using the new bills only to replace defaced old ones was departed from in a way the governor could hardly complain about in 1740, when £1,000 in these new bills was allocated for the use of the king in supplying the troops raised for the Spanish campaign. Thereafter frequent emissions were voted—in 1743, 1746, and 1753, for instance—but especially in war years. The small £3,000 issue authorized in 1753 was the only one in peacetime, whereas once the French and Indian War began there were numerous emissions—£2,000 in 1756, £12,000 in 1758, £27,000 in 1759, £4,000 in 1760—and then none until the beginning of the American Revolution.

Until the Revolution, when the Continental Congress destroyed the value of paper money by its large and unsecured emissions, the people of the Lower Counties were very happy with their paper money. Supported by statutes which required its acceptance as legal tender within the Delaware counties and supported also by the willingness of Philadelphia merchants to accept it, the Delaware currency maintained a good reputation and an approximate equality with the paper money of Pennsylvania and New Jersey.* The new emissions were not, of course,

---

* The local money had, however, depreciated in comparison with English money. In 1774 the exchange rate was 174 pounds of Delaware, Pennsylvania, or New Jersey money for 100 pounds sterling.

The Ridgely House on the Green, Dover. The first section was built in 1728 by Thomas Parke, father of the poet John Parke. Acquired in 1764 by Dr. Charles G. Ridgely, it is occupied by his descendants today. Courtesy of the Division of Historical and Cultural Affairs, Dover.

completely in addition to earlier emissions; in part, they merely replaced bills paid in and destroyed as borrowers settled their accounts. The amount in circulation grew fairly steadily, particularly in wartime, but the population was also increasing and commercial life was growing at an even faster rate than the population.

Though the utility of the bills as a circulating medium was their chief justification, their value to the government was by no means inconsiderable as a source of support both for the ordinary expenses of peacetime and for extraordinary expenditures in time of war. English fears of a runaway inflation that would cheapen the payments of American debts led to instructions to governors which helped slow down emissions and discouraged the assemblies from overenthusiastic reliance on paper. In wartime, however, the governors relented. Once the governor approved a bill passed by the assembly of the Lower Counties, it became the law; no power in America or England would attempt to gainsay it.

In 1744 the war that had begun with Spain in 1739 was widened and made more frightening for colonists on the Delaware when France, too, became an open enemy. Spain had been chiefly concerned with protecting its extensive empire; the entrance of France into the war increased the likelihood of a maritime attack on the almost unprotected coast of the middle and northern English colonies.

There was particular reason for the Delaware counties to be fearful, considering that in effect they consisted of little more than one hundred miles of shoreline beside navigable water. For several years, however, until 1747, there was no serious threat of attack. A French privateer from Louisbourg did appear off Cape Henlopen in the fall of 1744 and seized several merchant vessels before being captured in November. The watch at Lewes continued to function, the militia to drill, and the pilots were warned to be wary. In June 1746, Governor Thomas called for the enlistment of four hundred men in Pennsylvania and the Lower Counties to march to Albany for service on the northern frontier.

A company of one hundred men, commanded by Captain John Shannon, was recruited in the Delaware counties, the home of his lieutenant, Jacob Kollock, Jr., and of his ensign, Robert Bull. A roster of the one hundred enlisted men reveals that most of them were immigrants—fifty from Ireland, twenty from England, Scotland, or Wales, and one a German. Since Governor Thomas ordered Captain Shannon to enlist only

Protestants, it seems likely that most of the Irish natives were Scotch-Irish. One other detail concerning this company is furnished by a 1749 payroll bearing the names of thirty-seven men, of whom twenty-five (68 percent) were illiterate and signed with a mark. It may have been that only the humblest and poorest free men would volunteer for service in an army that was expected to invade Canada.

However, the invasion of Canada for which these troops were called up never took place. Shannon's company reached Albany by September 1746 and served in that vicinity for a year. In September 1747 their camp was swept by an epidemic that destroyed their effectiveness, and the company was disbanded in November.

By this date the war (commonly called King George's War in America) had been brought home to the Delaware counties at last. On Sunday, July 12, 1747, a band of approximately twenty Frenchmen or Spaniards landed at the head of Delaware Bay near Bombay Hook and looted Edmond Liston's house, carrying away four slaves. From Liston's they went on to the neighboring plantation of James Hart. Hart tried to resist them, but their shots wounded his wife and he had to surrender. After they took what they wanted, they ordered him to guide them to other plantations, but he wore them out trudging through swamps and woods and they returned to their vessels. A few days later the same band seized a ship off Cape Henlopen.

In September two French vessels, one of them a thirty-gun privateer from Haiti, entered Delaware Bay, taking two prizes and throwing fear into a wide area before they sailed away. The coming of winter brought temporary relief from such maritime attacks and gave opportunity for the organization of local defenses. Efforts were made to strengthen the battery at New Castle, where there were four cannon but only a meager supply of gunpowder and cannonballs. At Wilmington a bomb-proof magazine and battery were erected at the Rocks, where the old Swedish fort had stood. Plans were made to move the public records from New Castle to Christiana Bridge.

At Lewes the watch was maintained and a militia force was supposedly kept in readiness by laws requiring every freeman in the area to keep "a well-fixed firelock or musket," with twelve charges of powder and ball, three flints, and a priming rod. The Lewes pilots, restricted in their work, complained of the practices of pilots based at Cape May and Philadelphia. In New Castle and Kent counties volunteers called "associators" formed themselves into regiments and companies whose officers received commissions from the governor.

Their fears seemed justified in May 1748, when a French privateer captured a brigantine in Delaware Bay. Even worse, a Spanish privateer of fourteen guns sailed up the river later in the same month, deceitfully flying a British flag, and unsuccessfully attacked a Jamaica ship lying near New Castle. To prevent surprises, Abraham Wiltbank, a Lewes pilot, was ordered in June 1748 to cruise in the river and bay on watch for the enemy. Fortunately, the Peace of Aix-la-Chapelle was concluded this year and brought the conflict to an end.

In May 1747, a year before the war ended, Governor Thomas announced his resignation and imminent departure for England. At the same time he also announced the death, in October 1746, of the principal proprietor, John Penn, the bachelor eldest son of Hannah and William Penn. John Penn had willed his half share of the proprietorship to his next brother, Thomas, who already had a quarter share and therefore now became the principal proprietor, sharing the title with his younger brother Richard, who held the remaining quarter share.

Thomas Penn was well acquainted with the colonies on the Delaware, where he had lived from 1732 to 1741, and being a man of good business habits he was able to utilize the peaceful interlude that began in 1748 to continue the process, begun in the time of his mother, of converting the proprietary claims into a very profitable investment. Despite his best efforts, quitrents were never very successfully collected, least of all in the Lower Counties, but the Land Office in Philadelphia, which served both Pennsylvania and the Lower Counties, did a thriving business.

From the secretary of the Land Office, normally also the provincial secretary, a warrant had first to be secured by anyone desiring to establish title to a tract of new land. The warrant was an order for a survey, which could be made by the surveyor general or, more likely, by a deputy. In general the applicant could pick out any parcel of unsurveyed land he pleased, of any shape, as long as Indian title had been cleared and no prior survey and title had been taken to it. He was expected to choose a moderate quantity, which in most cases meant two hundred or three hundred acres, and when he paid for the land a patent was issued which was his deed or title.

The price of the land varied. By the end of King George's War the price had risen from £5 per hundred acres in 1713 to £15, 10 shillings. This high price seems to have driven some settlers from the Penn colonies to Virginia and the Carolinas, so the price was gradually lowered, first to £10 per hundred acres and then to £5. Sale was also made with the understanding that a quitrent was due, varying from a half penny per acre in 1755 to a penny per acre in 1765, but in the Lower Counties this proved very difficult to collect.

When George Thomas resigned the governorship, his place was temporarily filled by the president of the council, Anthony Palmer, who was, like Thomas, originally from the West Indies. King George's War had ended before November 1748 when the new governor, James Hamilton, arrived. Son of that Andrew Hamilton who won fame as the defense attorney in the Zenger trial (in New York) and was long a spokesman for the proprietary interests in the assemblies of both Pennsylvania and Delaware before his death in 1741, James Hamilton was the first governor to have been reared in this area. A lawyer, too, he was rapidly making a reputation of his own, though still in his thirties.

In the Delaware counties, his administration was relatively calm. A new seal was adopted, bearing the words "Counties on Delaware." The new calendar went into effect in 1752, when the new year began on January 1, instead of on March 25, as heretofore. The transpeninsular boundary line was run, a new collection of laws was printed, and the increase of trade was indicated by the passage of an act providing for the care of roads by overseers appointed in each hundred* by the justices of the peace.

But while enjoying an uneventful administration in the Lower Counties, Hamilton's effort to do the proprietors' bidding in Pennsylvania involved him in a series of quarrels with the assembly over such issues as taxation, frontier defenses, and paper money. His patience at an end, he gave notice in 1753 that he would resign the governorship in 1754.

Once again the Penns turned to an American as governor. Their choice

---

* The hundred is an ancient English term of uncertain origin for a subdivision of a county and was applied in Penn's time to constabularies or tax districts. Though once found in several other colonies, including Maryland, the hundred survives only in Delaware, where it resembles the township in Pennsylvania and New Jersey and the town in New England, but has lost practically all political significance. The council on April 9, 1690, instructed magistrates and grand juries of the counties to divide them into hundreds, but the term was already in use in the colony.

this time was Robert Hunter Morris, a member of a wealthy and distinguished family of New York which also held a large amount of property in New Jersey, where his father was governor. Robert Hunter Morris* was well past fifty years old in 1754, about ten years older than Hamilton, and he already held one distinguished place, that of Chief Justice of New Jersey, to which his father had appointed him.

Morris had gone to England in 1749 to collect arrears on his deceased father's salary and stayed there until he found a new appointment for himself. Returning to America to assume his new position in the fall of 1754, Morris hoped that as a rich, handsome, sociable bachelor he would be able to enjoy the prestige involved in being governor of two colonies. But his timing was unfortunate. The quarrels that had erupted between Hamilton and the Pennsylvania assembly were not to be brushed aside lightly. Instead, the outbreak of a new war intensified old disputes and raised new issues.

The new conflict was the French and Indian War, which erupted in the forests of western Pennsylvania in the year 1754, two years before it developed into a worldwide struggle called the Seven Years War that lasted until 1763. For the Delaware counties this meant another time when fear of naval attack encouraged a desire for a close relationship with the empire and a willingness to make some sacrifices, in men and money, for imperial war needs. The contrast was striking between the assembly at New Castle, dominated by members of the Church of England, willing to support the war effort and generally friendly to proprietors who were seeking to settle their boundaries, and the assembly at Philadelphia, dominated by Quakers, on principal opposed to all military endeavors and further annoyed by the efforts of the proprietors to control the governor and through him to prevent taxation of proprietary estates.

This latter issue seems never to have arisen in the Delaware counties, apparently because they had no proprietary estates of any significance. Unsurveyed land belonged to the proprietors, but apparently it was not rated for purposes of taxation. The area of the Delaware counties was so small comparatively that there were no rich wildernesses into which settlers were eager to push. The lands that were unsurveyed were generally lands thought to be of little value, relatively infertile or inaccessible.

---

* He should not be confused with Robert Morris, the "Financier of the American Revolution," who was much younger and was not related to this man.

There were also properties of uncertain status lying on the western fringe of the Delaware counties or at their southern verge, lands that might belong to Calverts or to Penns, as no one could be sure until the boundary was finally drawn and adopted, which was not until 1775.

In these circumstances, Robert Hunter Morris, who found himself in an unhappy situation in Pennsylvania, was able to get along in a relatively smooth manner with the assembly in the Lower Counties. In 1754 the Delaware assembly appropriated £1,000 to the king's use; in 1755 it made a second appropriation, this time of £2,000 to the Crown, and sent provisions to the army that was marching across the Appalachians under General Edward Braddock. The militia law, which had lapsed in peacetime, was revived in March 1756, and a lottery was begun to raise money to provide additional cannon for the battery at New Castle.

On one issue—the export of provisions and other supplies—Morris met with some resistance, even in the Delaware counties. He proclaimed an embargo in 1755 on shipments from Philadelphia and New Castle because the assemblies had not taken action and he feared vessels leaving these ports might, by seizure or by the temptation of great profit, wind up supplying French strongholds in America. The "bread colonies" of the middle Atlantic coast could find a good market in French and Spanish islands in wartime when the connection of the latter with their homelands was made perilous by the British fleet. The temptation of illicit profits was so great that the governors had to urge colonial assemblies to pass embargo laws that would prohibit the exportation of arms.

In seeking these embargoes the governors ran into the problem of intercolonial jealousies. Philadelphia merchants did not want New York merchants to hold an advantage over them. Merchants in Wilmington and New Castle did not want their trade interdicted unless Philadelphia trade was restricted too. The best measure Morris could win from the Lower Counties assemblymen in the spring of 1756 was an embargo act lasting until July 20 and no longer, unless Pennsylvania would extend its embargo. In that case the Lower Counties were willing to extend their embargo to October 22, when a new assembly would be in session.

The catastrophic defeat of Braddock's army in 1755 increased the pressure on Morris until it was more than he chose to bear, and he resigned. The Penns negotiated with a young man named Thomas Pownall, who had achieved a modest reputation as an authority on American affairs,

The New Castle waterfront. From a watercolor by Yves le Blanc, painted July 4, 1797. Formerly in the possession of the Hon. Richard S. Rodney. Used by permission.

besides having a brother who occupied the strategic post of secretary to the Board of Trade. Pownall turned them down, wisely concluding that the need to balance the proprietors' instructions against the assembly's demands made the governor's burden intolerable. They then turned to William Denny, a clergyman's son and an Oriel College, Oxford, graduate who had been making a career of the army, a useful background for the situation in Pennsylvania in 1756.

After his arrival in America, Denny was more successful in his relations with the military authorities, as might have been expected, than he was in smoothing the relations between the Penn family and the people of their colonies. And, in general, he worked more compatibly with the assemblymen of the Lower Counties than with those of Pennsylvania.

The Pennsylvania assemblymen bridled when Denny challenged them with the greater spirit of cooperation that he met with in the Lower Counties, where four thousand men were organized in militia units and vigilant justices were sending constables to collect fines from those not enlisting (even though they claimed conscientious objections as Quakers), jailing at least one man and seizing the property of others. The Pennsylvanians argued that their colony, with its frontier defenses, had to protect the Lower Counties and New Jersey from the French and Indians, but the Lower Counties responded that they were a frontier in their entirety against attack by the sea.

The exchange of messages between Governor Denny and the two assemblies contains several items of interest. "I am sorry," Denny told the Pennsylvania assembly in June 1757, "that you do not think the Militia Act of the Lower Counties worthy of your Imitation. It is certainly thought a good one by the Lords of Trade, who have rejected a warm Application made against it." His suggestion that the Board of Trade even considered a law of the Lower Counties is interesting; perhaps the proprietors made sure that this law was seen so that one of their colonies, at least, would seem to be doing its part.

Governor Denny indignantly rejected an accusation of the Pennsylvania assembly that he had conspired with the assemblymen of the Lower Counties "to keep their transactions from the public View and thereby load us [the Pennsylvania assembly] with their Defects, as that Government may be accounted a Part of this Province, though entirely independent"; nobody, Denny answered, would mistake the conduct of any other assembly with theirs.

The Pennsylvanians continued to charge that the Lower Counties were not properly sharing the defense burden. "Their Lands are rich," the Pennsylvania assembly told the governor, "many of their farmers [are] wealthy, and [they] have all the Advantages of our Market, to which they bring their Commodities at little Expence." In short, the complaint ran on, the Delaware counties ought to pay at least one-tenth of all the defense expenditures of Pennsylvania.

This charge by the Pennsylvania assemblymen met with the sort of reception at New Castle that might have been predicted: "We are," declared the assembly of the Lower Counties, "independent of them (which we esteem no small part of our Happiness) and will ever assert & support that Independency."

In due time the *London Chronicle* published this declaration by the Lower Counties assembly, which included a summary of their measures in support of the war. Benjamin Franklin, who was in England, observing that no proceedings of this assembly had ever been printed in London before, was sure he knew who was responsible for this innovation. "It is plainly done by the Proprietary Tools," he wrote, "to continue the Prejudices against the Province."

The same assembly that boasted of its independence renewed the militia act in the fall of 1757, this time for the duration of the war, and voted £4,000 for His Majesty's use from a new paper money issue of £20,000. Since the Delaware counties were not attacked by an alien army, the organized militia was never called into combat, but in 1758 three companies, of approximately a hundred men each, were raised and sent to Carlisle, Pennsylvania, to join the army which was advancing on Fort Duquesne under General John Forbes. These soldiers helped construct a road over which the army advanced, occupying its objective in the fall of the year without a battle, as the outnumbered French withdrew.

Statistics that survive for two of the companies from the Lower Counties show that the average soldier was between twenty-four and twenty-five years old, with the ages ranging from fifteen to thirty-five. Most of the men were foreign born, and of this group the overwhelming majority was Irish. The greater part of the Irish, as far as can be determined, came from Ulster and were undoubtedly Scotch-Irish, as their names, as well as their county origins, indicate. A breakdown of the origin of these troops follows:

American born		92
Lower Counties	34	
Pennsylvania	9	
New Jersey	3	
New York	2	
New England	2	
Maryland	36	
Virginia	3	
America, but no		
indication of		
colony or area	3	
European born		105
Ireland	68	
England	23	
Scotland	5	
Wales	6	
Germany	2	
Portugal (Madeira)	1	

At least some of the soldiers listed as from Maryland might have been considered natives of the Lower Counties had the boundary survey been completed. A higher proportion of Irishmen was in a company commanded by John McClughan, their fellow countryman, than in Benjamin Noxon's company, the second for which statistics survive. Probably they were reacting to the strong anti-Irish feeling developing in the Lower Counties.

This feeling may explain the treatment of Captain McClughan. Benjamin Chew, the Dover (and Philadelphia) attorney who was a Quaker turned Anglican, like the younger Penns, whom he served, complained to the provincial secretary of "McCluckan," calling him "a low lived Creature, & an obscure Person previous to his late Promotion." When three more companies were enlisted a year later, McClughan was the only veteran captain applying for a commission, and though it was at first given to him it was later withdrawn to give preference to three less experienced men. Yet McClughan had been supported by his commander in the late campaign, by all six assemblymen from his county (New Castle), and by a distinguished Scotch-Irish immigrant, the physician and minister John Haslet, who declared that McClughan was not only an honest man but a better officer than any other two men from the Lower Counties.

Most of the soldiers listed their occupation as laborer, by which they meant farm laborer, it seems clear. A few men in every company listed themselves as craftsmen of some sort, especially weavers, carpenters, cordwainers, coopers, millers, and tailors. Of course, much depended on where the company was enlisted. Some details survive for two companies enrolled in 1759. One, Captain John Wright's, was apparently raised in Sussex County. It included many more native Americans (fifty) than immigrants (six), and included more natives of Sussex County than of any other place, as this list demonstrates.

Place of birth

Sussex County	22
Kent County	3
New Castle County	0
Total, Lower Counties	25
Maryland	16
Virginia	5
Other American colonies	4
Ireland	4
England	1
Holland	1

The average age in this company was lower than the average in a company intended to serve with a Pennsylvania regiment and raised at about the same time by Captain James Armstrong in New Castle County (22.7 as against 25.9). The difference is particularly striking in the number of those thirty or older; there were four in Wright's company and eighteen in Armstrong's. It seems likely that immigrants joined the army at a higher age than native Americans, probably because they were more footloose and perhaps because they were insecure and needed the support, economic or social, that the army might give them. Of the eighteen over-age soldiers (over twenty-nine, that is) in Armstrong's company all but two were born abroad; the oldest was forty-three-year-old Arthur Simpson, born in County Tyrone, Ireland, who listed himself as a schoolmaster. Half of the four over-age soldiers in Wright's company were born abroad.

Besides raising troops for frontier service in 1758 and 1759, the Lower Counties made further appropriations for defense and suffered continued interference with their trade from a renewed embargo and from the havoc created by the appearance of a French frigate off Cape Henlopen. Defenses along the river, especially at New Castle, were strengthened, and Pennsylvania sent an armed vessel into the bay to patrol the shipping lanes.

Governor Denny, caught between obeying his instructions from the proprietors and securing needed legislation from the assemblies to provide troops and supplies for the war effort, took the course that might have been expected of a soldier. He decided that the needs of imperial defense should come first and approved bills to this end even though they meant compromising his instructions. The worst problems he had were in Pennsylvania, but even in the Delaware counties he was persuaded reluctantly to approve in 1759 the reissue of £20,000 in bills of credit in order to procure a new emission of £7,000 for the king's service. This was in addition to an £8,000 appropriation in 1758, which included a bounty of £5 for every volunteer. The 1759 assembly at New Castle disappointed Denny by providing for only 180 soldiers instead of the 300 he requested, but, on the advice of the commanding generals in the area, he assented.

The advice of the generals did not satisfy Thomas Penn; he felt Denny allowed himself to become a tool of the colonial assemblymen, who held the purse strings on Denny's salary as well as on army appropriations. Consequently in October 1759 the proprietors dismissed Denny, replacing him with James Hamilton, who had already served as governor from 1748 to 1754. Hamilton is said to have accepted the governorship only after receiving a promise he would not be given instructions that made his task impossible. His burden, however, was immeasurably easier than Denny's, for in 1759–60 the British conquest of Canada effectively ended the war in North America, though it continued in Europe and elsewhere until 1763.

11

THE EVE OF THE REVOLUTION

No peculiar causes, no special or unusual complaints moved the people of Delaware to rebellion against their king. Their situation was anomalous and their colony did not even have a proper name, neither "The Territories of Pennsylvania" nor the "Three Lower Counties on the Delaware" being authoritatively established (to paraphrase Judge Richard S. Rodney,* the leading student of these matters). Their great fear was of losing their identity, of forfeiting the large measure of independence they had attained under the proprietors and the Crown.

In general the people of Delaware shared—or at least some of their leaders did—in the complaints common in neighboring colonies. The passage of time, the succession of one generation after another on American soil, far removed from England, had created a separate people in more than a geographic sense. The ideas and beliefs that moved colonists elsewhere became familiar to leading Delawareans, filtered for them through Philadelphia, with which city they had almost constant intercourse. Suspicions of ministerial corruption and parliamentary tyranny, grievances raised by English commercial and economic policies were quickly transferred to Delaware by way of the wharves and ships, the offices, the counting houses, and the printing presses of Philadelphia.

The importance of Philadelphia to the Lower Counties can hardly be overemphasized. The people of New Castle, Kent, and Sussex sent their goods to market in Philadelphia and their sons to school or to apprentice-

---

* See his "Early Relations of Pennsylvania and Delaware," recently reprinted in *Collected Essays of Judge Richard S. Rodney on Early Delaware* (Wilmington, 1975), p. 53.

ships there; they read Philadelphia newspapers; on at least one occasion the assembly of the Lower Counties in ordering notices to be posted at certain specified strategic locations included "the Coffee-House in Philadelphia" among them.

Philadelphia was also the seat of the governor (strictly speaking, the deputy governor) and his council. The latter body had little to do with the Lower Counties by the mid-eighteenth century. A few of the councilmen, such as Benjamin Chew and William Till, had property or positions in the Lower Counties, but except for such men the council seldom came to Delaware. The council did share with the governor in the commissioning of justices and if the governor died or resigned the president of the council became the acting executive in the Lower Counties in company with the speaker of their assembly and the ranking justice of the peace in each county. Neither the president nor this board had any power to approve legislation; in the absence of a qualified deputy governor bills simply could not be enacted into law.

The governor normally visited the Lower Counties only when the assembly met, which was once or twice a year. He then came to New Castle, took quarters at an inn, received the assembly, approved the speaker of their choice, gave them any suggestions he had, and waited to receive the bills they passed. He had the power of absolute veto over legislation, but he was more likely to suggest the amendment of a bill he did not like than to veto it. It was important to the governor to work harmoniously with the assembly, if only because at the end of the session he looked forward each year to the passage of what amounted to a salary bill for himself, though it was phrased as an appropriation for the governor's support, as indeed it was.

Despite the fact that seeds of revolution were germinating then, the 1760s appear to have been an especially harmonious period in the history of the Lower Counties. Early in the decade they were delighted to be compensated to the extent of almost £7,000 for their contributions to the imperial defense, and in greeting Governor John Penn in March 1764 the assembly at New Castle used the occasion to praise their late governor, James Hamilton, "whose mild and just administration had greatly endeared him to the good People" they represented.

John Penn, son of the junior proprietor, Richard Penn (and, of course, nephew to the senior proprietor, Thomas Penn), was a member of the third generation of the proprietary family, and his arrival in America in

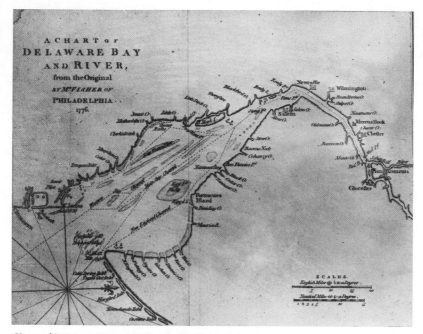

Chart of Delaware Bay and River by Joshua Fisher (1776 edition). Note the position of Cape Henlopen, as agreed to in the boundary settlement of 1732. Courtesy of the Delaware Division of Historical and Cultural Affairs, Dover.

1763 began a dozen years of direct family administration ("rule" would be too harsh a word to use for the light reins of the Penns on the Lower Counties). In 1771 Richard Penn, the proprietor, died, and Governor John Penn, heir to his father's one-fourth share in the proprietorship, returned for a brief time to England. As governor he was succeeded for two years by his brother, a second Richard. John Penn returned to the Delaware valley and reassumed the governorship in 1773, remaining in America not only until the overthrow of the colonial regime in 1776 but to the end of his life in 1795, when he was buried at Christ Church, Philadelphia, a fitting place of interment for this man who had written, "I consider myself more American than English."

The brothers John and Richard Penn were members of the Church of England, a fact that made them eligible for the governorship.* The Anglicanism of the brothers could not have harmed their influence in Delaware, however it may have strained their relations with the Quakers of Pennsylvania. Governor John Penn, a reserved and distant man, made important allies by marrying the daughter of William Allen, the chief justice of Pennsylvania. Allen had married James Hamilton's sister, so by marriage John Penn was related to his predecessor as governor. Hamilton, as president of the council, was also John Penn's temporary successor in 1771 during the months between Penn's departure and the arrival of Richard Penn, who also married an American.

It is clear that as far as the chief executive was concerned, the colonial government was stabilized for the last fifteen years, with only three governors, all interrelated and with strong American connections. For the Lower Counties, the stability was very important, encouraging a quiet, steady increase in prosperity, connected with the growth of Philadelphia and the expansion of the market at home and abroad that Philadelphia provided. The governors, for their part, were careful to reward their friends in Delaware with appointments in their power, especially as judges of the supreme court and justices of the peace. Through these appointments the governors, indirectly, wielded great authority, but

---

*The principal proprietor, Thomas Penn, attended services of the Church of England regularly in the latter part of his life, and his young son, John, who succeeded Thomas as the principal proprietor upon the latter's death in 1775, was reared in the established church. Since Thomas Penn's son John was only fifteen when his father died he never exerted any political authority in his colonies.

this authority was limited by the fact that the appointments were made to the important men in the Lower Counties and were usually extended for the life of the appointee.

The power of the justices of the peace was supreme in matters of local government, and for most purposes they held judicial power as well. Individually they performed many duties, including taking depositions and issuing warrants. Collectively they not only set the county tax rate (with the help of the grand jurors and assessors) but carried out various other administrative tasks, such as setting the price of bread and beer, and four times a year they met to judge cases of many sorts, civil and criminal. They comprised the court of general sessions and gaol delivery, the court of common pleas, the orphans' court, and the court of equity, often functioning on successive days in different capacities. Appeal from these courts lay to a supreme court of four judges (three before 1760), who could not serve in lower courts. Two of the judges of the supreme court constituted a quorum, and they met twice a year in each county. Appeal was possible from the supreme court to the Privy Council in England, and though this was rarely done, probably because of the expense, such an appeal is known to have been taken by David Finney and members of his family in 1774. Whether it was tried in England is not known, but the fact that Finney was a lawyer himself undoubtedly encouraged him to initiate the appeal.

The most important political force in the Lower Counties was not the Crown, not the proprietors, not the governor, but the unicameral assembly which met in New Castle annually on October 20 and very often again in the spring. Each fall eighteen assemblymen, six from each county, selected a speaker from their own ranks. Though the speaker's powers were few, he was, in the absence of any higher ranking official, the first citizen in the colony. Andrew Hamilton, John and David French, Thomas Noxon, Ryves Holt, Benjamin Chew, Jacob Kollock, John Vining, Thomas McKean, and Caesar Rodney were among those who gained distinction from occupying this position.

The members were elected annually on October 1, when the qualified voters of each county assembled at the county courthouse to cast a ballot, written but not secret, for six representatives at large in each county as well as for two candidates each for sheriff and for coroner. Theoretically the governor selected a sheriff and a coroner from the two leading candidates in the poll (this was supposedly a double nomination rather than an election) but the governor seems to have customarily chosen the leading candidate for each post.

The election of assemblymen, however, was final and not reported to the governor. Only the assembly itself received an official report on the election of its members. At that election the sheriff presided in each county (or, in his absence, the coroner), assisted by an election inspector representing each hundred.

A qualified elector had to be at least twenty-one and to have resided in the Lower Counties at least two years; he was also required to own fifty acres of land of which twelve acres were cleared or to have other property worth £40. Everyone qualified was required to vote, unless sick, on penalty of a twenty-shilling fine, and the polls were kept open until everyone had a chance to cast his vote.

No tickets were printed and no organized parties existed but there was, nevertheless, a great deal of politicking. The terms "court party" and "country party" referred to factions that contested the elections, the chief difference between them being that one group was in office and the other group out of office. Apparently these factions often made up tickets which they urged upon voters as the latter arrived at the county seat on election day. Identification with the different factions frequently changed, and both factions would unite on some candidates. The object of the faction was to gain office and influence; family relationships, personal friendships, ethnic or religious connections, and local objectives were dominant. Apparently the sheriff's office was sought most enthusiastically, probably because a profit could be made from it and because the sheriff had great influence, running the county elections and choosing the grand jurors, who were influential in a number of ways, such as in setting the county tax rate. Because the sheriff's office was very popular, only three successive terms were permitted; thereafter the ex-sheriff must be out of office for three years before he was eligible again. No such limitation existed on reelection to the assembly.

At the same time that the assembly had limited the sheriff's term, in 1739, it had also prohibited candidates for sheriff from offering bribes of any sort, including liquor and entertainment, with a heavy fine of £10, plus costs, prescribed for each offense. The law was apparently ineffective, for a Dover clergyman, the Reverend Charles Inglis, later the bishop of Nova Scotia, reported in 1760 that candidates commonly invited the populace to public meetings at least once a week for nearly two months before the annual elections. Free liquor, Inglis charged, was the chief attraction, and the meetings were "nothing but Scenes of Drunkenness and Debauchery." On the day of election the residents of the county seat were especially influential. They were on hand to welcome and influence, if they could, the arriving rural voters, and could volunteer to write out ballots for the illiterate.

Few details are recorded about the conduct of preliminary local elections in the hundreds, traditionally known in the Delaware counties as the "little elections." A 1766 statute provided for the annual election on September 15 of an assessor and an election inspector in each hundred, with the tax collector for the hundred, an appointed official, conducting the election, assisted by two freeholders of his choosing. It was the duty of the election inspector to prepare a list of qualified voters for the county election on October 1. Before 1766 the voters of each hundred chose an inspector after they arrived at the county seat on election day. Probably the number of voters was becoming so large that choice of an inspector beforehand was advisable so he could prepare himself to be an arbiter if questions arose about the qualification of voters from his hundred.

The assessor was a member of the county levy court, the body that each year decided how much money had to be raised by the county property tax and exactly what tax rate (how many pennies on a pound of assessed property) was needed to raise this much money. The levy court consisted of the justices of the peace, at least eight members of the grand jury, and the assessors. Since none of these officials except the assessors (and they only after 1766) was elected, there were complaints that men should have a more direct voice in choosing those who taxed them. Governor Richard Penn in 1773 attempted to rebut this complaint by arguing that the grand jurors were indirectly chosen by the people, since the sheriff, who named them, was an elected official. In answer, the assembly, led by Speaker Thomas McKean, cited the fact that levy court commissioners, as well as assessors, had long been elected annually in Pennsylvania. It was not right, they argued, that the grand jurors, being named by the sheriff, should then sit in judgment on his accounts. And as to the justices of the peace, it was "unconstitutional and unsafe" that these magistrates appointed by the governor should have any power of setting taxes. Furthermore, "their power in these Counties being much greater than that of the Justices of the Peace in England, or any other of His Majesty's

Dominions," they overawed the grand jurors and the assessors, who, for fear of giving offense, agreed too easily to any proposal made in the levy courts by the justices.

Despite the argument of the assembly, Governor Penn persisted in rejecting this bill, which had been requested for several years. Not until well after the Revolution did the levy courts of the Delaware counties become wholly elective.

Before the peaceful course of life in the Lower Counties was suddenly interrupted in 1765 by news of the Stamp Act, an effort by Parliament to raise a revenue in America, the antiproprietary party in Pennsylvania, led by Benjamin Franklin and Joseph Galloway, had been bitterly disappointed not to find support in the Lower Counties for their petition asking the Crown to take over the government from the proprietors. Franklin sought to weaken the Penns' claim to Delaware by arguing that the proprietors had collected an immense sum in quitrents there which should have been paid to the Crown.

He had in mind the old royal grant to the Duke of York, which specified that half of the income from Kent and Sussex should be paid to the king. Accidentally or purposely Franklin overlooked the fact that this clause had never applied to the area around New Castle. He declared that this sum had amounted to £18,000 by 1722 and also referred to an initial payment the government made Penn before his death, exaggerating the amount and ignoring the fact that it had been repaid. In rebuttal, a defender of the proprietors declared that the Penns had never in eighty years received as much as £5,000 from all three of the Lower Counties.*

As speaker of the Pennsylvania assembly, Franklin in the spring of 1764 signed a complaint to the governor, charging him with favoritism in not calling upon the Lower Counties to furnish any share of the soldiers recently requested by the commander of British troops in America. Franklin's political allies, Joseph Galloway and Samuel Wharton, raised similar charges of favoritism. The proprietors, they said, had exerted their influence to have a recent Pennsylvania paper money act voided by the Crown, while permitting a similar act passed in the Lower Counties

---

* As late as 1773 this claim to half of the quitrents was revived by John Hurst, a London merchant, who unsuccessfully appealed to the Crown for a grant of the money due from the Delaware counties, declaring he had discovered this legal claim in 1770 after it had been forgotten for eighty years.

to go into effect unnoticed. "The Ministry must certainly be surprized," wrote Galloway, "to find a Government carried on and Laws made for upwards of 60 Years, without Transmitting any of them for their Approbation."

It particularly galled the antiproprietary party that the assembly at New Castle in 1764 had unanimously agreed to an address to the king written by Benjamin Chew, an ally of the Penns, expressing satisfaction with proprietary rule. Though the assemblymen had insisted on its being worded so as to avoid the appearance of meddling in the affairs of Pennsylvania, Chew explained privately to Thomas Penn that it was nevertheless intended "by a side Wind" to counteract the antiproprietary petition of the Pennsylvania assembly.

Galloway raised old arguments to the effect that the Duke of York had granted William Penn only his right to the soil of the Lower Counties but no right to govern them, and the Board of Trade intermittently raised similar questions. As late as 1770, for instance, this board again protested reference in Pennsylvania laws to the Penns as "true and absolute proprietaries of the province of Pennsylvania and of the Counties of New Castle, Kent and Sussex on Delaware." This was "highly improper and unwarrantable," the board declared, insofar as it related to the Delaware counties. The board, of course, could not protest a similar phrase that was used in the laws of the Lower Counties because it did not see these laws.

But even the assemblymen sometimes forgot that this was so. "Your Majesty has a Negative upon our Laws," declared the assembly in 1768 when petitioning the king against taxes recently imposed by Parliament. They were wrong. His Majesty had no such negative, except perhaps in theory. He could indeed dismiss the governor, but he never did. After all, the king's advisers on the Board of Trade and the Privy Council rarely saw any documents pertaining to the affairs of the Lower Counties, and out of sight, out of mind, is a true description of the situation.

In 1765, however, according to George Read, "The scene in America . . . greatly changed. . . . Political disputes were [formerly] confined to parties formed in the respective colonies. They are now all resolved into one, and that with the mother country. The stamp-act . . . hath raised such a ferment among us . . . that I know not when it will subside."

The reaction in the Delaware counties to the Stamp Act was so carefully concerted, so obviously the work of a few men, that it can be viewed only as part of a continental movement to thwart this extension of the parliamentary taxing power. Though the call that moved Delawareans to action came from Massachusetts—a summons to send delegates to a Congress in New York—the action that it provoked in the Lower Counties was probably affected more directly by Philadelphians, for example, by John Dickinson, who had moved to Pennsylvania and steadily gained influence there. Dickinson did not get along with Benjamin Chew and so was not immediately identified with the proprietary party, but in 1764 he had won attention by publishing *A Speech on a Petition for a Change of Government of the Colony of Pennsylvania,* in which he argued that the proprietary government, whatever its failings, was a useful buffer between the colony and the leadership of the English Parliament.

It was that leadership which was responsible for the Stamp Act. Therefore the proprietary party was quite sympathetic to the movement for an intercolonial meeting of protest. When news of the forthcoming Congress arrived in the Lower Counties, the assembly had already adjourned, and Governor Penn, however he and his advisers felt about the Stamp Act, could hardly be expected to call a special session.

Consequently in September 1765, the assemblymen of each county signed a letter nominating three of their members to attend the Congress. Two of the three letters, those of the Kent and Sussex assemblymen, bore different dates but were almost identical in their wording. The letter of the New Castle assemblymen took a stronger tone, expressing assurance of "the Hearty Approbation of any future House of Assembly" and complaining of parliamentary taxation as an infringement of their liberty.

Each of the three letters nominated the same three delegates, one from each county, an instance of the careful coordination of this movement. The delegates were likely choices: Jacob Kollock, of Sussex, had been speaker of the recent assembly; Caesar Rodney, of Kent, was a young (thirty-six) landed gentleman of a politically distinguished family who had time, means, and spirit for public service; Thomas McKean, even younger (thirty-one) than Rodney, was a Scotch-Irish lawyer, tutored by Francis Alison in his native Chester County, Pennsylvania, who had come to New Castle to study with his distinguished cousin, the attorney David Finney. All the assemblymen signed the nominating letters except the three nominees.

Apparently Kollock never went to New York. He was much older than

John Dickinson. Engraving by B. Prévost after a drawing by Pierre Eugène du Simitière. Courtesy of the Division of Historical and Cultural Affairs, Dover.

Thomas McKean. Engraving by T. B. Welch after a painting by Gilbert Stuart. Courtesy of the Historical Society of Delaware, Wilmington.

the other two delegates and the assembly, which reelected him speaker, was due to meet in New Castle shortly after the date set for the convening of the Stamp Act Congress. But Rodney and McKean did proceed to New York early in October and entered enthusiastically into the work of the Congress, which petitioned the king and Parliament for the redress of grievances, among which they mentioned prominently taxation without representation and trial without jury.

In the Delaware counties men wrote of the need for economic independence or even, as a dreadful possibility, of rebellion. The grand jury at New Castle refused to function in February 1766, unless the court agreed to proceed without using stamped paper. At Lewes in March a riotous crowd forced the county officials and the collector of customs to pledge themselves similarly to disregard the Stamp Act. These local actions were probably unnecessary since popular pressure in Philadelphia had forced John Hughes, who had been appointed stamp agent for Pennsylvania and the Lower Counties, to promise not to distribute stamped paper.

At news of repeal of the Stamp Act, New Castle "was illuminated . . . and really made a pretty Appearance from the Water." The assembly approved a report on the Congress presented by McKean and Rodney and then adopted resolutions expressing their loyalty to the king but, at the same time, their insistence on the traditional rights and liberties enjoyed by his subjects in England, including trial by jury and taxation by consent of representatives of their own choosing.

For about two years the relations between the Lower Counties and the mother country were undisturbed, until new problems raised by the Townshend Acts were discussed in the assembly that met in New Castle in October 1768. The Townshend Acts, passed by Parliament in June 1767, provided for a tariff on lead, painters' colors, tea, glass, and paper entering the colonies. In the Delaware valley some time passed before the danger inherent in these duties, which provided revenue to support British officials in America, was fully evident.

The antiproprietary party in Pennsylvania, seeking to replace the authority of the Penn family with royal government, was reluctant to find fault with Parliament because such fault-finding would diminish the zeal of Americans for the direct rule of the king. Though the Lower Counties were never enthusiastic supporters of the antiproprietary party, they were not wholly immune to this party's political intrigues. For example, by the influence of Benjamin Franklin, an antiproprietary leader, Jacob Kollock, Jr., was appointed collector of customs at Lewes instead of the proprietary candidate, David Hall. Even George Read had sought Franklin's help for appointment as collector at New Castle in 1766, and it was no advantage to the royal cause (or to the antiproprietary party) in the Lower Counties that the appointment went to George Walker. Walker was not a candidate of the proprietary party either, but, according to Franklin's son, was "a drunken Fellow and a stranger."

Read might seem indelibly tied to the proprietary party by his appointment as attorney general for the Lower Counties, a post he held to 1774, but his predecessor in this office, his brother-in-law, John Ross, who was at the same time attorney general of Pennsylvania, had been an ally of Franklin. A stronger influence on Read, however, was John Dickinson, who had been his close friend since they studied law together in John Moland's office in Philadelphia. Dickinson had been speaker of the Lower Counties assembly in 1760, but since his election in 1762 to the assembly in Pennsylvania, his political activities were chiefly in that province. In the late fall of 1767 he began publishing in a Philadelphia newspaper his *Letters from a Farmer in Pennsylvania to the Inhabitants of the British Colonies,* a vigorous attack on the Townshend duties. Though these letters first appeared anonymously, their authorship was soon an open secret. Attorney General Read's participation in the struggle to have the Townshend Acts repealed becomes clear in the light of this friendship. However, even Franklin and many of his antiproprietary allies abandoned their quiet acceptance of the Townshend duties after August 1768, when the British secretary of state for the colonies told Franklin there was no prospect of royal government for Pennsylvania (or the Lower Counties).

However little influence this party had in the Lower Counties, the influence of Philadelphia opinion was very great, and the growing opposition to the Townshend duties led the assembly that met in New Castle in October 1768 to reestablish a committee of correspondence. It consisted of McKean, Rodney, and Read, who had formed a similar committee in 1766 to thank the king for repeal of the Stamp Act. Now they were instructed to prepare a petition to the king, proposed by McKean, protesting parliamentary legislation depriving them of their right of taxing themselves through their own assembly—meaning, of course, the Townshend Acts—and also lamenting the outcome of a controversy be-

George Read. Engraving by Samuel Sartain after an 1860 painting by Thomas Sully based on an earlier portrait by Robert Edge Pine. Courtesy of the Historical Society of Delaware, Wilmington.

tween the New York assembly and the Crown that had led to a suspension of the former body. Besides passing a resolution expressing its feelings, the New Castle assembly empowered its speaker to respond favorably to the speaker of the Virginia House of Burgesses, which had proposed a cooperative effort to secure repeal of the Townshend Acts.

Instead of a congress, the unhappy colonists in this case resorted to a boycott of British goods, but the people of the Delaware counties were slow to join this movement, which was adopted in the main American ports at an unsteady pace. After an agreement to exclude most British goods was finally adopted by the merchants of Philadelphia, those of northern New Castle County towns and villages, including Wilmington, New Castle, Christiana, Newark, Newport, and Hamburg Landing agreed to abide by it. Apparently merchants of the upper Chesapeake Bay adopted a less inclusive boycott, for George Read appealed to the people of lower New Castle County to hold to the Philadelphia agreement instead of departing from their usual avenues of trade to turn to the Chesapeake. This they could easily do by utilizing the old route linking the Appoquinimink to the Bohemia.

The close proximity of Chesapeake Bay to the Delaware River was, indeed, at this very time the subject of an investigation that was eventually to have memorable consequences. With the particular encouragement of a Philadelphia merchant named Thomas Gilpin, who owned property on the Brandywine, on the Susquehanna, and on the Chester River, in Maryland, a group of Philadelphians of varied intellectual interests who had organized themselves as the American Philosophical Society for Promoting Useful Knowledge, undertook surveys of possible routes for a canal across New Castle County to the Chesapeake. Besides the Appoquinimink-Bohemia route, they considered other routes, including one linking Duck Creek (on the boundary of New Castle and Kent) with the Chester River, and another connecting the Christina River with the Elk. Decades passed, of course, before construction began, but these surveys of 1769 and 1770 are a reminder of the easy connection with the Chesapeake Bay that caused George Read concern.

Read's proposals, to abide by the Philadelphia non-importation agreement, were adopted in August 1769 but apparently were not altogether respected, for in the spring of 1770 a system of inspection was inaugurated to enforce the agreement. In each of several New Castle County towns a committee of inspection was established to keep watch on all goods traded and to report to a larger committee whenever it had information that boycotted articles were being sold.

In 1769 the assembly, stimulated to action by reception of a set of resolutions adopted by the Virginia burgesses, declared once again that the sole right of taxation was vested in them, with the consent of a governor approved by the king and holding office at the king's pleasure. They also denounced the idea of moving anyone overseas for trial (as the customs officials threatened to do in smuggling cases) because thereby the defendant lost his privilege of trial by a jury drawn from his neighborhood—from which, of course, it was difficult to get a conviction —as well as the likelihood of any success in summoning defense witnesses. And once again they petitioned the king for a redress of their grievances.

Some of the grievances were quickly redressed, as Parliament in 1770 repealed the duties imposed by the Townshend Acts, except for the tax on tea. It seemed such a minor point that the boycott movement quickly broke down and normal trade with Britain was restored until a sequence of events following upon the Boston Tea Party in December 1773.

In these years of resumed trade and prosperity there was, however, a new degree of disharmony which disturbed relations between the governor and the assembly. Between 1765 and 1770 the governor very rarely rejected a bill presented to him by the assembly of the Lower Counties. Often he proposed amendments, to which the House agreed in most cases; when the House stood its ground and explained its rejection of an amendment, the governor gave it up. The one case in which the governor issued a flat rejection was a private bill regarding an estate inherited by a minor; it was not an important matter, and the assembly let it drop.

In the years from 1770 to 1775, however, several important bills were rejected by the governor. The minutes of the assembly for this period, unlike those for the previous half decade, are incomplete, but five bills are known to have been rejected. One of these may have been rejected by accident: in November 1770, when the assembly was almost ready to adjourn until spring, Governor John Penn asked for additional time for consideration of a bill concerning election regulations, the details of which are unknown. Before the assembly convened again, Governor Penn had left for England and in the absence of a qualified successor no legislation could be passed.

By the time Richard Penn arrived in October a new assembly had been elected. In June 1772, it did pass a bill regarding the conduct of elections —prescribing the oath to be taken and the duties to be perfomed by the election inspectors—but whether it was the bill John Penn needed time to consider is not known. In this same assembly, however, Richard Penn rejected two other bills. One was a bill extending and altering the excise tax on spirituous liquor, a chief source of colonial revenue. The other was a bill obliging justices of the peace to hear and determine actions of debt under the value of forty shillings. In neither case are any details known, but the significance is that legislation was not proceeding as smoothly in the Lower Counties as it had in earlier years.

In April 1773, a bill of undoubted significance was turned down by Governor Richard Penn—a proposal to make the levy courts elective, as they had long been in Pennsylvania. Surviving petitions from electors to their assemblymen testify to the popularity of this measure, which they expected to free them from taxes they regarded as enormous. No public debts have been created recently, no buildings constructed, no extensive repairs made, yet taxes are rising, read a petition from Kent County. A petition from Sussex argued that the levying of county taxes by a board dominated by appointed officials, the justices of the peace, "is the corrupt fountain from whence this Current of oppression flows."

Possibly Richard Penn, if his term had continued, would have run into increasing trouble with the assembly of the Lower Counties. When John Penn returned to the governorship in the fall of 1773 the assemblymen declared they felt "a particular satisfaction in being governed Personally by one of our Proprietors, whose true interests and that of our Constituents are so intimately Connected." They were referring to the fact that John Penn had inherited his father's one-fourth interest in the proprietorship, and they apparently looked to him as a buffer against a ministry and Parliament whose acts they resented.

Through these years a notable development in the assembly was the emergence of a Presbyterian party. Thomas McKean, John Haslet, and such allies as William Killen and John McKinly were frequently found voting together and in a minority. They represented an emerging force, the voice of the new immigrant element in the Delaware counties, especially in New Castle and Kent, but their importance lay in the future when they gained allies among older elements in pressing a vigorous anti-English policy.

In the less than three years of proprietary rule that remained after John Penn's return in 1773 there was no major quarrel between the governor and the assembly. The governor did reject one measure—the bill, passed by the assembly in 1775, to forbid further importation of slaves—but a major achievement of his term was a measure on which Penn and the assemblymen were in complete agreement. This was the extension of the boundaries of the colony and the individual counties to the new lines established by the surveys between 1750 (the beginning of the trans-peninsular survey) and 1768 (the end of the Mason-Dixon survey).

On April 8, 1775, Governor Penn issued his final proclamation (there had been a preliminary proclamation in 1774, afterward withdrawn) of the extension of the authority of the government of the Lower Counties, as well as that of Pennsylvania, to the new boundary lines. On September 2 he approved an act of the assembly of the Lower Counties incorporating all the residents within the new boundaries into this government with full rights and privileges.

It was hardly realized at the moment, but these final acts completing the long boundary controversy also marked the end of the reliance of the people of the Delaware counties upon the Penns. With their boundaries now secure, the Delaware counties no longer needed to fear their neighbors. Their new concern was to march in step with other colonies, to insist upon their equal standing, their representation in intercolonial congresses, their close association with their neighbors. Too small to stand alone, the Delaware counties could see that they were no longer dependent on proprietor or king or Parliament for preservation from aggressors. Their new dependence was on the neighbors they had once feared. Their policy must now be to ally themselves closely but with equality in a confederation of their peers.

12

INDEPENDENCE AND UNION

The Delaware counties were eager to be represented at the Congress called to meet in Philadelphia in the fall of 1774 to protest the coercive measures adopted by Parliament after the Boston Tea Party. Carefully coordinated mass meetings were held in each county. At these meetings speakers condemned British acts, called for a collection to aid the people in Boston who were impoverished by the closing of their port, recommended the establishment of county committees of correspondence, and urged the speaker of the assembly, Caesar Rodney, to convene the members quickly so they could choose delegates to Congress.

Why it was not enough to have the assemblymen in each county agree on delegates, as they had done in 1765, is not clear. Perhaps the unanimity that existed in 1765 was lacking. Or perhaps there were objections to the sort of delegation such a method of selection was likely to produce. In 1765 one member had been chosen from each county, and if the county representatives met separately to agree to a ticket, it would be unwise to propose a ticket on which any one of the counties was not represented.

It is not possible to know with certainty who was directing these events, but it seems likely that the leadership came mainly from northern Delaware. New Castle County was more prosperous than Kent, which in turn was more prosperous than Sussex, and New Castle therefore had a greater number of lawyers and men of affairs to take a position of leadership. By its geography and by its commercial activities New Castle was closer than Kent and Sussex to neighboring colonies; it contained the main ports of the Delaware colony, the largest towns, the most prosperous mills, and it was on the main route by land from Virginia and Maryland to Philadelphia and the North. News came here more rapidly than to Kent or Sussex. The electric spark of dissidence that ran through the colonies in 1774 touched New Castle very quickly.

The men most responsible for coordinating affairs in Delaware in 1774 were probably members of a committee of correspondence established by the assembly in October 1773, in emulation of a similar committee set up in Virginia. The assembly appointed five men to this committee: Thomas Robinson, of Sussex County; Caesar Rodney, of Kent; and three men from New Castle County, Thomas McKean, George Read, and a Wilmington physician, John McKinly, who had been a major in the militia in 1756. It seems likely that McKean, Read, and Rodney were the active members of this committee. Robinson turned out to be a loyalist, and it may have been fear that Sussex County would nominate him for Congress that led more rebellious men to insist on a nomination made by the assembly as a whole. On the other hand, Robinson himself claimed, in an interrogation in England after the war was over, that he was named to the Continental Congress but refused to accept the appointment and argued in assembly against any appointment being made. Perhaps this is so; the records are sparse and give no hint of his nomination.

The first step toward participation in the Continental Congress was a mass meeting held in New Castle on June 29, 1774, with Thomas McKean presiding. (McKean had moved to Philadelphia in May 1774 but retained his New Castle residence and his membership in the assembly there.) Kent County held its meeting on July 20, but Caesar Rodney reported there was some dissatisfaction that the special convention of the assemblymen he was asked to call was to be held in New Castle. It was, of course, the place for ordinary sessions of the assembly, but this was not an ordinary session, not even an official assembly. It was a special convention of assemblymen, and downstaters bridled at the thought that New Castle wanted to monopolize affairs. Dover, after all, was more central. More trouble might be expected in Sussex, where it was rumored, according to Rodney, people were so offended at New Castle for fixing the time and the place that they were likely to choose their own delegate to Congress, somewhat in the fashion of 1765, when the aged Jacob Kollock, since deceased, had been named the Sussex representative in the congressional delegation.

With the help of Thomas McKean, who made a long impassioned address at a mass meeting in Lewes, Sussex County fell into line, adopting resolutions supporting a special convention of the assemblymen, which Speaker Rodney thereupon called, as directed, for New Castle on August 1. Speaker Rodney himself, Thomas McKean, and George Read were chosen delegates to Congress. They were the same useful trio who had often served the assembly on committees of correspondence. Two of the three had formed the active delegation representing the Lower Counties at the Stamp Act Congress. Read was attorney general, Rodney was the speaker, and McKean was a former speaker, now practicing law in two colonies and serving simultaneously as a stimulant to intercolonial cooperation.

Read and Rodney were almost as much at home in Philadelphia as McKean. Rodney had gone to school there and Read had clerked in a Philadelphia law office. They were both on friendly terms with Governor John Penn, his brother the former governor, and members of their circle. Rodney thought Richard Penn "a great friend to the Cause of Liberty," playing host each day to some of the delegates to Congress; Governor John Penn, as Rodney wrote, "wishes his Station would admit of his acting the same part."

One of the ways in which the Penns had kept the friendship of Delaware assemblymen was by accepting their recommendations when important appointments were to be made. In the fall of 1774, during the sessions of the First Continental Congress, this practice was continued, for when Read announced his resignation of the post of attorney general, Governor Penn accepted Speaker Rodney's nomination of Jacob Moore, of Sussex County, to the place. Even at this late hour the relations between the Delaware counties and the proprietors were harmonious.

In March 1775, the three Delaware delegates reported to the assembly at New Castle, of which all three were members, on the actions taken by the Continental Congress in the previous fall. These were, primarily, the adoption of (1) petitions to England protesting the legislation passed by Parliament in retaliation for the Boston Tea Party, and (2) an agreement (called the Association) to boycott English goods. The assembly approved the report and reelected the three men to a Second Continental Congress that was scheduled to meet in May. At the same time the delegates were instructed to seek reestablishment of relations with Great Britain on a constitutional basis, to avoid anything disrespectful to the king, and to insist on an equal voice for their colony in all decisions. The last point was of very great importance to the Delaware counties, which were forced to move as rapidly as their neighbors in order to maintain their identity and independence.

Before the Second Continental Congress met, fighting had begun in April 1775 at Lexington and Concord, and the war was under way. In the Delaware counties militia regiments began to be organized, and the Delaware congressmen joined their colleagues in voting to adopt the troops surrounding Boston as a continental army. When a new assembly convened, it reelected the three delegates, approving their support of military measures, but urging them to continue to seek reconciliation with the mother country.

It was this continued insistence on an effort at reconciliation that led Thomas Jefferson to conclude in the spring of 1776 that Delaware and several other colonies, including Pennsylvania and Maryland, "were not yet matured for falling from the parent stem" though "fast advancing to that state." Many residents of the Lower Counties were convinced resistance to Britain had already gone too far. In February 1775, Robert Holliday, a Kent County Quaker, deeleclared in a letter published in a Philadelphia newspaper that nine out of ten would gather around the king's standard if it were raised in Kent County. In the same county not long afterward one Daniel Varnum told a friend that "he had as lief be under a tyrannical King as a tyrannical Commonwealth, especially if the d———d Presbyterians had the control of it."

Committees of inspection and observation were established in each county to deal with such utterances and all other instances of apparent disloyalty to the official attitude of the assembly and the Congress. Partly they superseded county committees of correspondence chosen at the mass meetings in the summer of 1774. In the fall of that year when Congress decided to boycott British goods, it became of the first importance to have committees on the local level that would use whatever pressure they could to enforce the boycott. Apparently these committees were elected in special hundred or county meetings attended by those voters who were enthusiastic supporters of Congress and the boycott; therefore the committees represented the most zealous and militant elements in the population.

The committees encouraged the formation of military units, which chose their own officers and were generally supervised by a Council of Safety, established at a meeting of officials from all three counties in Dover in September 1775. In December Congress asked this committee to raise a battalion of troops for the Continental Army. This battalion, generally referred to as the first Delaware regiment, was quickly organized under the command of Colonel John Haslet.

Meanwhile a few Delawareans had already gone off to war. Allen McLane, a leather breeches maker at Smyrna (then Duck Creek Cross Roads) went south to fight with the Virginia militia against Lord Dunmore at Norfolk. Several Delawareans were in the Continental Army that invaded Canada in the fall of 1775, including John MacPherson, Jr., a young New Castle lawyer, who lost his life in the attack on Quebec.

After a year of war, many colonists were ready in the spring of 1776 to make the break with Britain complete. In May Congress had asked the colonies to suppress all English authority in their governments and, if they needed to do so, to establish new governments independent enough to deal with the critical affairs at hand. This was practically a demand for colonial independence, and on June 7 Richard Henry Lee called on Congress to be more explicit by declaring that "these United Colonies are, and of right ought to be free and independent states." Lee's demand was a bit premature, since several delegations to Congress, like the delegation from Delaware, were instructed to seek reconciliation; therefore debate on this resolution was postponed to July 1, to allow time for instructions to be changed.

These actions in Congress caused considerable reaction in Delaware. The argument was made that the Lower Counties were practically independent, that no change in their government was necessary. On the other hand the governor did represent the king as well as the proprietor, and however little time he spent in Delaware and however much he listened to the wishes of the assembly, he did have important powers of appointment and he did have an absolute veto on legislation, a veto the Penns had used as recently as 1775, in the case of the bill banning the importation of slaves.

On June 15, 1776, the assembly at New Castle, with Caesar Rodney presiding, took decisive action. A day earlier it had heard Thomas McKean explain the actions of Congress; now it voted to sever all relations between the Delaware government and the Crown. All officials would continue their duties in the name of the three counties until a new frame of government could be prepared. New instructions were given the delegates to Congress who were not told how to vote on Lee's resolution for independence but were freed of any requirement to seek reconciliation.

In essence, the Delaware counties had taken their stand with Congress and against the king. There was, indeed, very little independence that they had to gain by this action, perhaps not enough to be persuasive of itself. But their small size made it necessary that they move along at the pace of their neighbors, particularly if they wished—and on this they continued to insist—that their delegates have equal standing with those of other colonies.

The Lower Counties did not dare to lag behind. The same factors that made them support the British Crown when it called on them to contribute men or money to the wars with the French, the same factors that made them loyal to a proprietary government that defended their boundary against the claims of Maryland now determined the choice the Delaware counties had to make. They were too small, too dependent on their neighbors to make any other.

Still, when Congress, in committee of the whole, voted on Lee's resolution for independence on July 1, the Delaware response was indecisive. Two Delaware delegates were present—Thomas McKean, who supported the resolution with enthusiasm, and George Read, who voted in the negative. The vote followed a debate of the issues in which the principal antagonists were John Adams, lengthily and vigorously arguing for independence, and John Dickinson. Dickinson was no loyalist and no pacifist; he held at that time a commission in a Pennsylvania regiment with which he saw service. Later, when Delaware was invaded, he turned out voluntarily with the Delaware militia. But now, as a Pennsylvania delegate, he counseled delay in any decision that would make a long war inevitable. His arguments affected George Read, or perhaps it was their long friendship, begun when they were law students together.

Lee's resolution was sure to carry by a majority vote of the states, the members being polled individually but only the vote by delegation counting—a procedure that Delaware and the other small states had insisted on throughout the history of the Continental Congress. But a mere majority vote was not enough; it would have the appearance of weakness. Therefore, after only nine of the thirteen states had supported the resolution in committee, a final decision was postponed overnight, till July 2, while an effort was made to get a unanimous vote of the states.

McKean meanwhile had sent an express for Caesar Rodney, the third member of the Delaware delegation. Rodney, as speaker, had been tied up at the assembly meeting in New Castle, and when it was over he had

Statue of Caesar Rodney by James Kelly, in Rodney Square, Wilmington. Not intended to be an exact representation, the statue symbolizes Rodney's hurried trip to Philadelphia to break a tie in the vote for independence within the Delaware delegation to the Continental Congress. Courtesy of the Historical Society of Delaware, Wilmington.

led the Kent County militia into Sussex, where a large band of loyalists had gathered, possibly as many as fifteen hundred. The loyalists had been persuaded to disperse and Rodney had returned to his home in Jones's Neck when he received McKean's summons.

There was no question as to how Rodney felt about independence. "The Continuing to Swear Allegiance to the power that is Cutting our throats . . . is Certainly absurd," he had told John Haslet in May. On hearing from McKean that his voice was needed to cast Delaware's vote for independence, he rushed to Philadelphia, riding through thunder and rain, in time to allow Delaware to vote aye in the roll call on July 2.

The tradition that he rode on horseback (rather than in a carriage, as might have been expected of a forty-seven-year old man who suffered from asthma and a cancer of the nose, particularly on a stormy July night) depends on the memory of Thomas McKean, who wrote, many years later, that he met Rodney, booted and spurred, on the steps of the Pennsylvania state house (Independence Hall) before the vote. Thomas Rodney declared that his brother left his farm home in a carriage, and another observer (Allen McLane) wrote long afterward that Rodney arrived in a carriage. Perhaps he rode horseback part of the way.

Thanks to Rodney's arrival, to the change of mind of a South Carolina delegate, and to the actions of Dickinson and another Pennsylvania delegate opposed to Lee's resolution who purposely absented themselves from the vote on July 2, the resolution was passed by a vote of twelve states to none. The New York delegation, still instructed to seek reconciliation, withheld its vote to give the decision the appearance of unanimity. There was no recorded vote two days later, on July 4, 1776, when a document drafted by Thomas Jefferson was adopted, explaining the decision for independence in terms so memorable that the date of this declaration obscured the action taken on July 2. When a fine copy of the Declaration of Independence was prepared for signatures, George Read signed the document, risking his reputation and perhaps his life in the struggle for independence on which the states were now decisively embarked.

John Dickinson did not sign the declaration. He regarded the decision of July 2 as premature, but he never faltered in his support of what he regarded as a just war. His position, however, was used against him by his political enemies in Pennsylvania, and after the British, on occupying Philadelphia, burned his home, he returned to Kent County, where his reputation was not seriously harmed by his arguments for moderation and deliberation, sentiments that were popular in the Lower Counties. Here he was drafted, more or less against his will, back into political office, first as a member of the legislature and then, in 1782, as chief executive. From that new beginning, he returned to an active role in Pennsylvania politics, but eventually retired to Delaware, building a mansion in Wilmington. Here until his death in 1808 he lived a quiet life, respected by his neighbors, though his sympathy for the French Revolution and for the Jeffersonian party (in which he ran, unsuccessfully, for Congress in 1807) meant that he remained somewhat out of step with the Federalism of Delaware.

Dickinson's friend George Read more closely represented the sentiment of his colony. Though slow to cut the ancient bond to England, Read's decision to sign the declaration exhibits the attitude of the Delawarean, reluctant to break with old connections, which had left the Lower Counties an enviable degree of independence with security, yet unwilling to lag behind the neighboring colonies when a new connection was being made.

Soon after the decision for independence, the assemblymen, at Rodney's call, ordered the election of a constitutional convention, to meet in New Castle in August. The presiding officer and dominant figure in the convention was not Caesar Rodney, who was defeated in the special Kent election, but the moderate George Read, though the irrepressible Thomas McKean was also active in its deliberations. The document the convention drafted, the first state constitution in the union that was written by a body elected specifically for this purpose, was, as might have been expected, no great departure from the frame of government the Lower Counties had enjoyed for seventy years.

The notable change was that the power of the legislature was enhanced and that of the governor diminished. The legislature was made bicameral, a somewhat conservative step that put Delaware in tune with the other states. The office of governor, the one foreign and autocratic element in the colonial politics of the Lower Counties, was abolished. In its place a new office was created, that of a president and commander in chief who was a creature of the legislature, elected by it to a three-year term, without any veto power (thus disposing of that check on the legislature), and dependent, in those few important decisions that were left to him, on the approval of a four-man Privy Council that was also chosen by the legislature. In calling up the militia, for example, in convening the legislature in special session, or in laying an embargo on exports, the approval of a majority of the Privy Council was required. Nor was this weak executive allowed any but a circumscribed voice in important appointments. He had no vote at all in the choice of military officers; and in naming the important judges he had but one vote, like a legislator, except in case of a tie. In the choice of justices of the peace he was given the power with approval of his Privy Council to choose from a double number nominated by the lower house of the assembly.

The election laws were not altered by the constitution, and it is obvious that in general the Delaware counties, now newly named "The Delaware State," wished to continue their political life with as little change as possible.

After the fall elections set the new government into motion, the prevailing conservatism was made evident in the new assembly's choice of a delegation to Congress. McKean and Rodney, advocates of a decisive, vigorous policy, were dropped, whereas George Read was reelected, and as one of his two new colleagues the assemblymen chose John Dickinson. Dickinson refused to accept the election, but not until a year had passed did the assembly again turn to McKean and Rodney. The events of 1776 make it clear that though the Delaware counties cooperated with their neighbors in revolution against Great Britain, the demand for a change in the conduct of Delaware affairs was less than overwhelming.

Colonel John Haslet, serving with the Continental Army in New Jersey, was so disgusted at hearing that Rodney had been dropped from the congressional delegation "when they had to go a begging in order to replace you" that he refused to return to Kent County when his regiment disbanded, having served out its short enlistment time. Within two months he was dead, killed on the battlefield at Princeton.

In the year 1777 the war was brought home to Delaware in such a way that many people were shocked out of their apathy and forced to take sides. In September of this year the British army under Sir William Howe marched through the northwestern corner of Delaware en route to Philadelphia. Not only for the few weeks when British troops were in Delaware, but for the eight months that they occupied Philadelphia and controlled the Delaware River, the Delaware counties were on the front line of the war.

Knowing that a British army was moving by sea from New York to the Chesapeake, Washington marched his troops to Wilmington and then advanced to the Red Clay Creek, expecting to face the British there as they came from their landing place on the Elk River. On September 3, 1777, Howe's army was advancing from Glasgow (then Aikentown) toward Christiana when it ran into a picked force of just under one thousand American light infantry in the woods along the road at the foot of Iron Hill.

In this Battle of Cooch's Bridge, as it is called from the scene of the hottest fighting, the role of the outnumbered Americans, commanded by William Maxwell, was merely to harass the main body of the British and make their advance difficult. At the end of the engagement, however, the British camped in the area for three days, bringing up supplies from their landing place, and then struck off north to Kennett Square, in Pennsylvania, instead of northeastward to Wilmington.

When Washington moved his army to contest the British advance, the Battle of the Brandywine resulted, fought around Chadds Ford and Birmingham Meeting, on September 11. The British victory was complete. On the night after the battle they seized Wilmington, capturing the first president of the Delaware State, John McKinly, as well as the state treasury, seals, and records of many sorts that had been stored on a vessel in the Christina for safekeeping.

For five weeks, until October 16, 1777, some British troops occupied Wilmington while the main part of Howe's army seized Philadelphia and began operations against fortifications the Americans had erected on the river north of Chester. Meanwhile the British kept a number of their sick and wounded at Wilmington, where they were guarded by a force made up of a Highland regiment and some German mercenaries. On October 16 these troops marched off to Philadelphia, while the wounded were carried away on vessels. The British fleet did not gain access to Philadelphia until mid-November, when the river fortifications were finally abandoned after a long, courageous defense.

With the British fleet in complete control of the river, the threat of possible British landings daily menaced the Delaware counties, where only men of courage and strong feelings could keep the rebellion alive. In March 1778, the assembly, meeting in Dover because New Castle, beside the river, was dangerously exposed, chose Caesar Rodney as president, by twenty out of twenty-four votes, to succeed the captured McKinly. Rodney and McKean were reelected to the congressional delegation, though Rodney was too busy with affairs in Delaware to take time to go to Congress.

From October 1777 to June 1778, small parties of the British frequently landed at New Castle or Port Penn, and many farmers proved willing to sell the enemy any supplies they wanted. Washington sent troops to occupy Wilmington so the British could not use it as a base for raids, and he gave serious consideration to making it his winter headquarters before he decided upon Valley Forge. Delaware militia under Charles Pope attacked and captured near Kenton, in western Kent County, the fortified headquarters of a band of loyalists commanded by one Cheney Clow, who was himself not taken until 1782. In Sussex a riotous fight between supporters and opponents of the Revolution prevented the election from being held at its usual time in October 1777.

Gradually Rodney and other Whigs, as the supporters of the Revolution were called, gained control. A new test act, so named because it tested the loyalty of citizens by requiring them to qualify as voters by taking an oath of allegiance to the state government, was enforced at an adjourned election in Sussex County. Outspoken loyalists, such as Thomas Robinson, began to flee the state, as they could easily do with British ships constantly on the Delaware. In June the assembly confiscated the estates of forty-six specified loyalists and of anyone else found guilty of actively aiding the British unless he asked for pardon before the first of August.

By this time the military crisis had passed. In this same month of June 1778, the British evacuated Philadelphia, and thereafter the main scene of the war was at some distance from the Delaware State. British vessels off Cape Henlopen still interfered with American trade at many seasons of the year. Small boats, manned by loyalist refugees from other colonies, prowled through the bay seeking to capture shallops taking farm produce to Philadelphia. Occasionally these raiders came up the small rivers and creeks of Delaware and stole goods stored at a farm landing or looted a plantation, as they did at John Dickinson's home in August 1781. A call would go out for the militia but usually, before armed defenders could assemble, the raiders would be gone. Eventually the state of Delaware put an armed boat in the bay, commanded by Charles Pope, to give warning of the presence of enemy shipping.

Besides the loyalist refugees on the bay, loyalist sympathizers in

Thomas Robinson, of Sussex County, the most prominent Delaware loyalist. A refugee, he returned after the Revolution. Artist unknown. Photocopy from the Historical Society of Delaware, used by permission of Mrs. Thomas Robinson, Sr., Georgetown.

Delaware occasionally caused concern. In the summer of 1780 over a hundred men gathered in Sussex at a place called the Black Camp, in a counterrevolutionary protest against high taxes and militia laws. A more serious threat to the prosperity of many Delawareans was the enormous inflation that destroyed the value of paper money, whether issued by Congress or the state government.

Meanwhile a new Delaware regiment enlisted in 1776 was making a splendid record for valor. Especially in the southern campaign, these troops, a high percentage of them Scotch-Irish immigrants, distinguished themselves, though cut to pieces so badly at the Battle of Camden (where their number was reduced from 500 to 175) that they were thereafter only a company attached to a Maryland regiment. The bravery exhibited by these troops, commanded by Robert Kirkwood,* in many actions (at the Cowpens, Guilford Courthouse, Hobkirk's Hill, Ninety Six, Eutaw Springs) led to a comparison with gamecocks of a breed renowned for their valor. The men took great pride in the comparison; the term "blue hen's chickens" was eventually transferred from the handful of veterans to the people of a state that became increasingly proud of them.

Like the neighboring states of New Jersey and Maryland, Delaware was slow in ratifying the Articles of Confederation. These three states, their territories largely confined to the Atlantic Coast, objected to the western land claims of some of their neighbors, especially Virginia, which laid claim to the West and Northwest almost without limit. In a union with such a giant, Delaware would be insignificant. Since Samuel Wharton, a leading Philadelphia land speculator, had sufficient influence in the Lower Counties to be chosen to Congress in the Delaware delegation of 1782, it seems likely that speculative interests played a part in encouraging the Delaware legislature to press the states claiming western lands to cede them to the Confederation. Although Maryland held out until 1781, New Jersey and Delaware ratified the Articles in 1779 and were gratified by the cessions subsequently made.

When dissatisfaction with the Articles of Confederation led to at-

---

* David Hall, the first commander of this regiment, was furloughed home because of illness in 1779. Joseph Vaughan, who succeeded him, was captured at Camden in 1780, whereupon Kirkwood took over.

Mary Vining (1756–1821), daughter of John Vining, chief justice and speaker of the assembly, was the reigning belle of Delaware in the Revolutionary era. Her popularity is suggested by the existence of this pencil sketch by Major John André of the British army, and by her later courtship by General Anthony Wayne of the American army. Photocopy from the Historical Society of Delaware, Wilmington, used by permission of the Ridgely family, Dover.

tempts to strengthen the new government, Delaware was generally sympathetic to these efforts. The first draft of the Articles, written by Dickinson, included provision for a stronger central government than was included in the weaker version of the Articles that was finally adopted. The one concern on which Delawareans were united was that their state should remain a constitutional equal of the other states; with this equal status guaranteed, Delawareans wished to see the bonds of the union, on which they were obviously dependent, strengthened.

Attempts to strengthen the Confederation by giving Congress a revenue through tariff duties met approval in Delaware, but no amendment for this purpose ever attained the ratification by every state needed for its adoption. When James Madison, in 1786, persuaded the Virginia legislature to invite states to a conference at Annapolis to discuss enlarging the Confederation's control over commerce, Delaware cooperated cheerfully. A delegation of three men—Dickinson, Read, and Richard Bassett—represented Delaware at Annapolis when the convention officially convened on September 11, 1786. Dickinson was elected president, but since only five states were represented, the assembled delegates decided to call another convention, with expanded powers, to meet at Philadelphia in the following spring.

Dickinson, Read, Bassett, and two young men who had also been named as delegates from Delaware to the Annapolis convention but had not attended—Jacob Broom, a Wilmington merchant, and Gunning Bedford, Jr., the attorney general—were reelected to represent Delaware at the Philadelphia convention. Their instructions authorized them to discuss "alterations and further provisions . . . necessary to render the Federal Constitution adequate to the exigencies of the Union," but only so long as the provision which gave each state one vote in Congress remained inviolate.

At the meeting in Philadelphia which came to be called the Constitutional Convention, the Delaware delegates supported most provisions to strengthen the central government but were forced to oppose the initial plans of Virginians for a proportional (rather than equal) representation in Congress. Yet when the great compromise was worked out, giving the states equality in the Senate in return for proportional representation in the House of Representatives, the Delaware delegates accepted it gladly. Though it did not fit the strict letter of their instructions, they were confident it would prove acceptable in Delaware. George Read had been chairman of the committee of the Delaware legislature which drafted the delegates' instructions. Probably he had tied the hands of the delegates a little tighter than was necessary; the strict instructions had been a useful means of persuading delegates from large states to consent to less than proportional representation throughout the new Congress. With equality won in the Senate, the Delaware delegates were quite content.

So was their state. When a copy of the proposed Constitution was officially forwarded from the old Congress to the Delaware legislature, provisions were quickly adopted for a ratifying convention to be chosen by the usual voters on November 26. This convention met at Dover on Monday, December 3, 1787, and completed its sessions by ratifying the Constitution unanimously on December 7, the first state to accept the new government.

If the speed with which Delaware acted is impressive, so is the unanimity. Delaware could act quickly because it was close to Philadelphia, where the Constitution was written; the delegates could return home and begin organizing sentiment for ratification long before the Continental Congress, now meeting in New York, forwarded an official copy of the new document. Pennsylvania and New Jersey, possessing similar geographic advantages, were the second and third states to ratify, and Pennsylvania could have been the first had its convention, which met on November 21, not become involved in a lengthy debate.

What the Delaware convention did from its convening on December 3 until its action and adjournment on December 7 is not wholly known. No hint of a debate on the merits of the Constitution has survived. There was no vocal opposition to the document and probably the convention might have ratified even faster than it did had there not been an election dispute in Sussex County to consider. Unsuccessful candidates in Sussex complained of irregularities in the elections there. They explained, however, that they wished only to register their complaint; they did not ask the convention to take any action because they did not want to delay its proceedings. All of the candidates in Sussex, the victorious and the defeated, were agreed in their support of the Constitution.

So it was throughout Delaware. As in New Jersey, the third state to ratify, all thoughtful people seemed to be of one mind. The great compromise gave these small states the best agreement they could possibly hope for to assure them some guarantee of continued independence of action while attaining membership in the strong union that their future prosperity and indeed their safety demanded.

EPILOGUE

Geography and history combined to produce the anomaly of an overlooked colony that became the First State. A Swedish settlement, a Dutch and then an English conquest, made the lands on the west side of the lower Delaware an adjunct first of New York and then of Pennsylvania. A weakness in William Penn's title to the Lower Counties gave the colony an excuse to claim special treatment, but it was not the title so much as their prior settlement and the different composition of their population that led Delawareans to insist on a separate legislature so that they would not be subordinate to Quakers and other newcomers in Pennsylvania.

William Penn surrendered to the demands of his colonists in this respect as in others in 1701 because he was rushing home to England and seemed likely to lose his American properties altogether. It would be easier to plead his case in London if his colonies were calm and orderly than if they were bombarding British authorities with protests against his rule. He was unhappy about the separation of Delaware, but the leaders of the majority party in Pennsylvania were delighted, more so at first than those in the Lower Counties. Separation destroyed the negative the Lower Counties held over legislation by reason of their equal numerical power in the assembly.

Once their legislative independence from Pennsylvania was achieved, the stability of the Delaware counties was rocked by the erratic behavior of three governors—the boyish John Evans, the mad Charles Gookin, and the artful William Keith—whose administrations coincided with a series of challenges in England to the status of the proprietorship. These challenges arose from Penn's financial misfortunes and long illness and from complications concerning the inheritance of his American estate.

When the skill and wisdom of his widow finally paved the way for her three sons to enjoy their inheritance (at the same time that the Board of Trade lost its interest and its vigor), they found in the Lower Counties a cooperative assembly, because here the proprietors had retained very little power but yet were looked to as the best reliance the people had against what they regarded as the extravagant claims of Maryland. The authority of the proprietors, exercised through their deputy governor, fell so lightly upon the Delaware counties that they utterly rejected the decision of the Pennsylvania assembly to ask for a royal government. Any change of government in the Lower Counties was likely to alter what was a happy state of affairs.

On the very eve of the Revolution the long boundary controversy with Maryland was brought to a happy conclusion. The Lower Counties had no serious quarrels of their own with the English and, left to themselves, they would have been more likely to choose the loyal course of Thomas Robinson than the rebellious way of Caesar Rodney. But they were not alone. Economically and intellectually they were dependents of Philadelphia, where they sold their produce and bought their newspapers. The ideas of Philadelphia merchants regarding English policies and colonial grievances were carried to the Lower Counties as quickly as the river shallops brought imported wines, hardware, and textiles from Philadelphia wharves.

George Read and men like him sought to follow a moderate course, to keep the Lower Counties in step with their neighbors without unnecessarily upsetting the large measure of independence they already enjoyed. Men more moved by the excitement of the time or stirred, like the new Scotch-Irish element—the McKeans and Haslets—by memories of ancient wrongs, strained at the leash which Read and his cohorts held on their action. But generally the old order in Delaware—the Reads and the Bassetts—survived the stresses of Revolution and led Delaware from its old imperial haven into a new snug harbor, the Constitutional Union.

BIBLIOGRAPHY

BIBLIOGRAPHIES, LISTS, ILLUSTRATIVE MATERIALS

Fortunately an excellent bibliography exists to help readers find their way to printed Delawareana. It is entitled *A Bibliography of Delaware through 1960* and was compiled by H. Clay Reed and Marion Björnson Reed (Newark, 1966). Readers should take note that the index does not include the names of authors who have no Delaware connections themselves, but it is otherwise helpful, as is the table of contents. A supplemental *Bibliography of Delaware, 1960–1974* (Newark, 1976) was compiled by members of the reference department of the Hugh M. Morris Library at the University of Delaware and includes unpublished theses and dissertations, as well as a few printed items, of earlier date than the title indicates. *Delaware History* magazine runs a current bibliography approximately every two years; the latest installment, by Elizabeth E. Moyne, appeared in Volume 17, No. 4 (Fall-Winter, 1977), 295–308.

Arthur R. Dunlap published "A Checklist of Seventeenth-Century Maps Relating to Delaware" in *Delaware Notes,* 18: 63–76 (1945) and also a short article on "Names for Delaware" in *Names,* 3: 230–235 (1950). Harald Köhlin, "First Maps of Delaware, a Swedish Colony in North America," in *Imago Mundi,* 5: 78–80 (1948), is a well-illustrated article on pertinent Swedish maps. No list of eighteenth-century maps has appeared, though there is a good study by Lawrence Wroth of "Joshua Fisher's Chart of Delaware Bay and River" in the *Pennsylvania Magazine of History and Biography* (hereafter *PMHB*), 74: 90–109 (1950), and Pearl G. Herlihy has recently published a brief account of "The Evolution of Delaware Cartography to 1800—Early Maps," in *The Transactions of the Delaware Academy of Science,* 6: 163–188 (1975). L. W. Heck, *et al., Delaware Place Names (Geological Survey Bulletin* 1245) (Washington, 1966), is primarily a gazetteer, unlike the historical studies of names by A. R. Dunlap that are mentioned below (pp. 267–68).

There was no printing in Delaware until late in the colonial period. Once printing began, however, there is an excellent scholarly listing of the products of the press, *Printing in Delaware, 1761–1800: A Check List,* by Evald Rink (Greenville, 1969). Betty Harrington Macdonald, *Historic Landmarks of Delaware and the Eastern Shore* (Wilmington 1963; bicentennial edition, 1976) contains pen-and-ink sketches of many old Delaware buildings, with accompanying historical accounts edited by Jeannette Eckman. Other illustrative works include George Fletcher Bennett, *Early Architecture of Delaware,* with a text by Joseph L. Copeland (New York, 1932), and Harry Donaldson Eberlein and Courtlandt V. D. Hubbard, *Historic Houses and Buildings of Delaware* (Dover, 1962).

GENERAL HISTORIES

The most comprehensive history of Delaware covering the entire colonial period has long been the *History of Delaware, 1609–1888,* by J. Thomas Scharf, *et al.,* (2 vols., Philadelphia, 1888), which was photo-reproduced in 4 volumes by Xerox University Microfilms, Ann Arbor, in 1972. This is a strange work, astonishing at once for its contents, which sometimes include otherwise lost original materials, and for its omissions. Generally it approaches the history of Delaware from Pennsylvania sources, and it is never wholly dependable and seldom critical or interpretative. The index is practically useless, but fortunately a three-volume *Index,* edited by Gladys M. Coghlan and Dale Fields, was published by the Historical Society of Delaware (Wilmington 1976).

Henry C. Conrad, *History of the State of Delaware* (3 vols., Wilmington, 1908), largely follows (and sometimes copies) Scharf, but is more attractively printed and more easily used, though somewhat less comprehensive. H. Clay Reed and Marion Björnson Reed, eds., *Delaware, A History of the First State* (3 vols., New York, 1947) lacks any chronological treatment of the colonial period but has a number of chapters on various facets of colonial life that will be noted individually below. There is a good index to the first two volumes at the end of the second volume; the third volume, which the Reeds did not edit, is composed of eulogistic biographies.

The best one-volume history of Delaware is a new interpretive study by Carol E. Hoffecker, *Delaware: A Bicentennial History* (New York, 1977). More diffuse and less dependable is an older volume by Walter A. Powell, *A History of Delaware* (Boston, 1928). A new one-volume history by John A. Munroe is scheduled for publication in 1978. *Delaware, A Guide to the First State,* prepared by the Federal Writers' Project and revised by Jeannette Eckman (New York, 1955), is a mine of general information with a high degree of accuracy. W. Emerson Wilson, *Forgotten Heroes of Delaware* (Cambridge, Mass., 1969), contains short biographical sketches from all periods. Francis Vincent, *A History of . . . Delaware . . . with a Description of Its Geography and Geology* (Philadelphia, 1870), goes only to 1664; though it is labeled volume 1 there was no second volume because the author became discouraged. Benjamin Ferris, *A History of the Original Settlements on the Delaware* (Wilmington, 1846), carries its narrative only to the time of William Penn but devotes additional chapters to the ecclesiastical affairs of the Swedes and to the history of Wilmington. *The Delaware Colony* (New York, 1970), by H. Clay Reed, is directed at an adolescent audience but is nevertheless, in style and content, an excellent book for adults, too.

Of the long, comprehensive histories of all the colonies, the most dependable, by far, in terms of its references to Delaware is Charles M. Andrews, *The Colonial Period of American History* (4 vols., New Haven, 1934–1938). By contrast, references to Delaware in Herbert L. Osgood's *The American Colonies in the Seventeenth Century* (3 vols., New York, 1904–1907) and *The American Colonies in the Eighteenth Century* (4 vols., New York, 1924–1925) are frequently inaccurate.

THE SEVENTEENTH CENTURY

Indians and Prehistory

Clinton A. Weslager's *The Delaware Indians: a History* (New Brunswick, 1972) is the culminating study of years that the author has devoted to this subject. Other studies on similar subjects by Weslager include his *Red Men on the Brandywine* (Wilmington, 1953); *The Nanticoke Indians* (Harrisburg, 1948); "The Indians of the Eastern Shore of Maryland and Virginia," in Charles B. Clark, ed., *The Eastern Shore of Maryland and Virginia*, I (New York, 1950); and "The Indians of Delaware," in H. Clay Reed, *Delaware, A History of the First State*, 1: 31–62. Weslager's brief article "Who Survived the Indian Massacre at Swanendael?" in *de Halve Maen*, 40: 9–10 (1965) is notable. Weslager and Arthur R. Dunlap are co-authors of *Indian Place-Names in Delaware* (Wilmington, 1950). Other interesting publications on the Indians include William B. Marye, *Indian Towns of the Southeastern Part of Sussex County, Delaware* (Wilmingon, 1940, reprinted from volume 3 of the *Bulletin* of the Archaeological Society of Delaware), Albert Cook Myers, ed., *William Penn, His Own Account of the Lenni Lenape or Delaware Indians* (Moylan, Pa., 1937), and a new translation by C. F. Voegelin of the Lenape legend, *Walam Olum* (Indianapolis, 1954).

Clinton A. Weslager, *Delaware's Buried Past* (revised edition, New Brunswick, 1968) is an account of archaeological discoveries, as is Ronald A. Thomas's brief *The Island Field, A Prehistoric Cemetery* (Dover, 1973). Thomas is also the author of "Hunters and Fishermen of Prehistoric Delaware" in the *Delaware Conservationist*, 13: 3–12 (1968) and of "A Brief Survey of Prehistoric Man on the Delmarva Peninsula" in the *Transactions of the Delaware Academy of Science*, 5:119–140 (1974), also available as an offprint from the Hall of Records, Dover. John C. Kraft and Ronald A. Thomas combine the knowledge of a geologist and an archaeologist in their article, "Early Man at Holly Oak," in *Science*, 192: 756 (1976). Other articles on the early inhabitants of Delaware may be found in the *Bulletin* and *Papers* of the Archaeological Society of Delaware and in *Archeolog*, the journal of the Sussex Society of Archaeology and History (formerly the Sussex Archaeological Association).

Swedes and Finns

The great authority on the New Sweden colony is Amandus Johnson, whose work has maintained its splendid reputation for more than half a century. His magnum opus is *The Swedish Settlements on the Delaware, 1638–1664* (2 vols., New York, 1911); a one-volume abridgment of this work was published as *The Swedes on the Delaware* (Philadelphia, 1914), Johnson's book entitled *The Instruction for Johan Printz* (Philadelphia, 1930) is rich in primary source material, as is Peter Lindeström's *Geographia Americae* (Philadelphia, 1925), which Johnson translated and edited.

Charles de Lannoy's *History of Swedish Colonial Expansion* (Newark, 1938) was originally published in Belgium in 1921 but was translated from the French by George E. Brinton and H. Clay Reed. Two other works on the Swedish settlers that were originally published abroad are Israel Acrelius, *History of New Sweden* (Philadelphia, 1874), which emphasizes church history, and Thomas Campanius Holm, *Short Description of the Province of New Sweden,* appearing in the *Memoirs* of the Historical Society of Pennsylvania, 3: 1–166 (1834), translated respectively by William Reynolds and Peter S. Du Ponceau. Another work on the Swedes is Jehu Curtis Clay, *Annals of the Swedes on the Delaware* (2nd edition, enlarged, Philadelphia, 1858).

The Finns, who accompanied the Swedes to the New World, are discussed in Evert A. Louhi, *The Delaware Finns* (New York, 1925) and in John H. Wuorinen, *The Finns on the Delaware, 1638–1655* (New York, 1938), as well as in the article "The Finnish Language on the Delaware," by Arthur R. Dunlap and Ernest J. Moyne, in *American Speech,* 27: 81–90 (1952). Other good articles or booklets on New Sweden include Clinton A. Weslager, "Log Structures in New Sweden during the Seventeenth Century," *Delaware History,* 5: 77–95 (1952); Evelyn Page, "The First Frontier—the Swedes and the Dutch," *Pennsylvania History,* 15: 276–304 (1948); Arthur R. Dunlap, *Dutch and Swedish Place Names in Delaware* (Newark, 1956); and Arthur R. Dunlap, "Dutch and Swedish Land Records Relating to Delaware—Some New Documents and a Checklist," *Delaware History,* 6: 25–52 (1954). Harold R. Shurtleff, *The Log Cabin Myth* (Cambridge, Mass., 1939), discusses Swedish building methods, as does Clinton A. Weslager, *The Log Cabin in America* (New Brunswick, 1969) with more detail on the Delaware area. Nathaniel C. Hale, *Pelts and Palisades* (Richmond, 1959), is a popular account of the early fur trade.

The Dutch Period

Christopher Ward, *The Dutch and Swedes on the Delaware, 1609–1664* (Philadelphia, 1930), is a lively account of European settlement in the pre-English period; Ward's *New Sweden on the Delaware* (Philadelphia, 1938) is an extract from the larger work. Clinton A. Weslager with Arthur R. Dunlap, *Dutch Explorers, Traders, and Settlers in the Delaware Valley, 1609–1664* (Philadelphia, 1961), and Jeannette Eckman, "Life among the Early Dutch at New Castle," *Delaware History,* 4: 246–302 (1951) are valuable studies based on research in primary sources, as is Simon Hart, "The City-Colony of New Amstel on the Delaware," *de Halve Maen,* vols. 39 and 40, *passim* (1965). J. Franklin Jameson wrote a biography of the Dutch forefather of the Delaware settlements, *Willem Usselinx* (New York, 1887), while one of the organizers of the first settlement, David de Vries, left an autobiography, printed in the Netherlands in 1655 and 1911, which was translated by Henry C. Murphy and published in New York in 1853 (and again in the *Collections* of the New-York Historical Society, 2d ser., 3, pt. 1: 1–136, in 1857). Charles McKew Parr, *The Voyages of David de Vries* (New York, 1969), is an attractive recent recounting of these adventures. J. Franklin Jameson, ed., *Narratives of New Netherland* (New York, 1909), is of interest, as is Thomas J. Condon, *New York Beginnings: The Commercial Origins of New Netherland* (New York, 1968).

E. B. O'Callaghan, *History of New Netherland* (2 vols., New York, 1848) and especially John R. Brodhead, *History of the State of New York* (2 vols., New York, 1853–1871) discuss the settlements on the Delaware. Leland Harder and Marvin Harder, in *Plockhoy from Zurick-zee* (Newton, Kan., 1952), write of an early settler at Lewes, and Nicholas B. Wainwright, in "The Missing Evidence, Penn v. Baltimore," *PMHB,* 80: 227–235 (1956), and Arthur R. Dunlap and Clinton A. Weslager, in "More Missing Evidence: Two Depositions by Early Swedish Settlers," *PMHB,* 91: 35–45 (1967), also discuss the early settlements as does Weslager in his "Dutch Settlements on the Delaware River" in *de Halve Maen,* 37: 7–8, 13 (1962).

The great published source for the Dutch regime on the Delaware has long been the *Documents Relative to the Colonial History of the State of New York* (15 vols., Albany, 1856– 1887), of which volumes 1 and 2, *Holland Documents, 1609–1678*, and volume 3, *London Documents, 1614–1692*, all edited by E. B. O'Callaghan, and volume 12, *Documents Relating to . . . the Dutch and Swedish Settlements on the Delaware River*, edited by Berthold Fernow, are useful to students of Delaware history. Errors in the translation and transcription of materials in the last-named volume have been corrected by Charles T. Gehring in his new edition of *New York Historical Manuscripts: Dutch, . . . Delaware Papers, . . . 1664–1682* (Baltimore, 1977), which appeared too late for use in this book. Other useful primary materials are in E. B. O'Callaghan, ed., *Calendar of Historical Manuscripts in the Office of the Secretary of State* (2 vols., Albany 1865–1866); Berthold Fernow, ed., *The Records of New Amsterdam from 1653 to 1674* (7 vols., New York, 1897); A. J. F. Van Laer, ed., *Documents Relating to New Netherland, 1624–1626* (San Marino, Calif., 1924); and A. J. F. Van Laer, ed., *Van Rensselaer Bowier Manuscripts* (Albany, 1908).

Earl L. Heck's *Augustine Herrman* (Englewood, Ohio, 1941) is a biography of the founder of Bohemia Manor. In *Crane Hook on the Delaware, 1667–1699* (Newark, 1958), Jeannette Eckman has left students an excellent account of an early Swedish congregation. The permanent church that succeeded Crane Hook is described by Charles Curtis and Charles Lee Reese, Jr., in *Old Swedes Church, Wilmington, Delaware, 1698–1938* (Wilmington, 1938); also available in print are *The Records of Holy Trinity (Old Swedes) Church . . . from 1697 . . . to 1810*, translated by Horace Burr (Wilmington, 1890).

The English

Albert Cook Myers, ed., *Narratives of Early Pennsylvania, West New Jersey and Delaware, 1630–1707* (New York, 1912) is a good collection of early accounts. Clinton A. Weslager, *The English on the Delaware, 1610–1682* (New Brunswick, 1967), explores the pre-Penn period, while *Delaware's Forgotten River; the Story of the Christina* (Wilmington, 1947), by the same author, covers a long expanse of time. Bartlett B. James and J. Franklin Jameson, eds., *Journal of Jasper Danckaerts, 1679–1680* (New York, 1913), includes a description of Delaware by a Flemish missionary. Leon de Valinger, Jr., "The Burning of the Whorekill, 1673," *PMHB*, 74: 473–487 (1950), is very interesting, as is Dan Terrell, *Eight Flags over Lewes, 1609–1715* (Rehoboth Beach, 1975).

The great English compilation of source materials for this and later periods is the *Calendar of State Papers, Colonial Series, America and West Indies*, ed. by W. N. Sainsbury and others (44 vols. to date, London, 1860–1969). Closer to home, there is Delaware material, particularly regarding claims to the Delaware counties, in the *Archives of Maryland* (72 vols. to date, Baltimore, 1883–1972). *Pennsylvania Archives*, 2d ser., vol. 5 (Harrisburg, 1877) comprises *Papers Relating to the Colonies on the Delaware, 1614–1682*. A valuable work, combining documents and a historical narrative by Benjamin Nead, is the awkwardly entitled *Charter to William Penn, and Laws of the Province of Pennsylvania, Passed between 1682 and 1700, Preceded by the Duke of York's Laws, in Force from the Year 1676 to the Year 1682*, ed. by Staughton George, et al. (Harrisburg, 1879). Land records are published in *Original Land Titles in Delaware Commonly Known as the Duke of York Record . . . , 1646 to 1679* (Wilmington, 1903), and in *Walter Wharton's Land Survey Register, 1675– 1679*, ed. by Albert Cook Myers (Wilmington, 1955).

The leading student of local court records was H. Clay Reed, who discussed them in "The Court Records of the Delaware Valley," *William and Mary Quarterly*, 3d ser., 4: 192–202 (1947), and in "The Early New Castle Court," *Delaware History*, 4: 227–245 (1951), as well as in his historical introduction to *The Burlington Court Book, A Record of Quaker Jurisprudence in West New Jersey, 1680–1709* (Washington, 1944). Early court records of Delaware are published in *Records of the Court of New Castle on Delaware, 1676–1681* (Lancaster, 1904); the same title, Volume II, *1681–1699*, ed. by Albert Cook Myers (Meadville, Pa., 1935); and *Court Records of Kent County, 1680–1705*, ed. by Leon de Valinger, Jr. (Washington, 1959). De Valinger also edited a *Calendar of Kent County, Delaware, Probate Records, 1680–1800* (Dover, 1944), and a *Calendar of Sussex County, Delaware, Probate Records, 1680–1800* (Dover, 1964). The Delaware Historical Records Survey of the Works Progress Administration published an *Inventory of the County Archives of Delaware, New Castle County* (Dover, 1941), which is valuable not only for its list of public documents but because it sketches the history and functions of every county court, commission, and office. H. Clay Reed and Joseph A. Palermo, in "Justices of the Peace in Early Delaware," *Delaware History*, 14: 223–237 (1971), discuss the history of those lowly but important officials commonly called magistrates.

The Penn Proprietorship

Of many studies of Penn and his family, William I. Hull, *William Penn—A Topical Biography* (New York, 1937) is particularly helpful to a student of Delaware history, as are also Joseph E. Illick, *William Penn the Politician* (Ithaca, 1965), which explains Penn's ability to gain and hold a claim to the Lower Counties; Howard M. Jenkins, *The Family of William Penn* (Philadelphia, 1899); and Sophie H. Drinker, *Hannah Penn and the Proprietorship of Pennsylvania* (Philadelphia, 1958). The last two books help the reader understand the succession to the proprietorship.

The classic *History of Pennsylvania*, by Robert Proud (2 vols., Philadelphia, 1797–1798), is indispensable. William R. Shepherd, *History of Proprietary Government in Pennsylvania* (New York, 1896), explains some institutional arrangements. Samuel Hazard, *Annals of Pennsylvania, 1609–1682* (Philadelphia, 1850), covers a period when Delaware and Pennsylvania affairs were closely connected. Two recent studies of Pennsylvania that contain useful references to Delaware are Edwin B. Bronner, *William Penn's 'Holy Experiment,' The Founding of Pennsylvania, 1681–1701* (New York, 1962), and Gary B. Nash, *Quakers and Politics, Pennsylvania, 1681–1726* (Princeton, 1968). Useful biographical studies include Roy N. Lokken, *David Lloyd, Colonial Lawmaker* (Seattle, 1959), and Michael G. Hall, *Edward Randolph and the American Colonies, 1676–1703* (Chapel Hill, 1960). Sister Joan de Lourdes Leonard's study of "The Organization and Procedure of the Pennsylvania Assembly, 1682–1776," *PMHB*, 72: 215–239, 376–412 (1948), is partially applicable to Delaware.

The writings of the leading student of Delaware as an English colony have recently been republished (with a few sketches not printed previously) as *The Collected Essays of Richard S. Rodney on Early Delaware*, ed. by George H. Gibson (Wilmington, 1975). These essays include papers on the legislative separation from Pennsylvania, the Keith governorship, and the end of the Penn claims to Delaware, as well as biographical, ecclesiastical, and other studies. On the first of these subjects, the separation, another good essay is "The Conflict between the Three Lower Counties on the Delaware and the Province of Pennsylvania, 1682–1704," by Robert W. Johannsen, in *Delaware History*, 5: 96–132 (1952). Gary B. Nash's article on "Governor Francis Nicholson and the New Castle Expedition of 1696," *Delaware History*, 11: 229–239 (1965), applies to the same period.

THE EIGHTEENTH CENTURY

The Pennsylvania Connection

Edward Armstrong, ed., *Correspondence between William Penn and James Logan* (2 vols., Philadelphia, 1870–1872), and a further selection of Logan letters in *PMHB*, 33: 347–352 (1909) and 35: 264–275 (1911), are useful, as are the Penn letters printed in Samuel M. Janney, *The Life of William Penn* (Philadelphia, 1852). William Stevens Perry, ed., *Historical Collections Relating to the American Colonial Church* (5 vols. in 4, Hartford, 1870–1878) includes much information about colonial Delaware through the letters of Anglican clergymen to the Society for the Propagation of the Gospel. Volume 5 pertains directly to Delaware, but Volume 2, nominally consisting of Pennsylvania correspondence, and Volume 4, Maryland correspondence, also include Delaware material. An Espiscopal minister, C. H. B. Turner, assembled two collections of Sussex County documents which pertain, in part, to the colonial period; these are entitled *Some Records of Sussex County* (Philadelphia, 1909) and *Rodney's Diary and Other Delaware Records* (Philadelphia, 1911).

The Colonial Records of Pennsylvania, ed. by Samuel Hazard (10 vols., Harrisburg, 1838–1853), consist of the minutes of the Provincial Council, which in its early years had as much responsibility for Delaware as for Pennsylvania. For the minutes of the lower house in the period (1682–1701) when it represented both colonies, see *Pennsylvania Archives*, 8th ser., Vol. 1 (Harrisburg, 1931). *Pennsylvania Archives*, 4th ser., Vols. 1–3 (Harrisburg, 1900), contains some Delaware material in the papers of the Pennsylvania governors between 1681 and 1785. The minutes of the Delaware House of Assembly have been reprinted for the years 1739–1742, 1762, 1765–1770 (Dover, 1929–1931) and the journal for the years 1770–1792 is currently being edited by Harold B. Hancock and Elizabeth E. Moyne for publication by the University of Delaware Press, Newark, in 1978. *Collected Laws of the Government of New-Castle, Kent, and Sussex upon Delaware* (variant titles) were published in Philadelphia in 1741 and 1752 and in Wilmington in 1763. Occasionally session laws were also printed; a few copies have survived. An incomplete collection of the laws of 1700–1797 was published in two volumes in New Castle in 1797. The laws of 1700–1701 appear in the *Statutes at Large of Pennsylvania*, 2: 3–170 (Harrisburg, 1896).

Harold B. Hancock published "Historical Records Relating to Delaware in the British Isles," in *Delaware History*, 10: 321–360 (1963), and a selection of "Description and Travel Accounts of Delaware, 1700–1740," in *Delaware History*, 10: 115–151 (1962). Edward W. Cooch collected a number of his essays on the colonial period in *Delaware*

Historic Events (Newark, 1946). "A Nondescript Colony on the Delaware" is Chapter 8 in Lawrence H. Gipson's *British Empire before the American Revolution,* Vol. 3 (revised ed., New York, 1960). M. M. Daugherty, *Early Colonial Taxation in Delaware,* and Leon de Valinger, Jr., *Colonial Military Organization in Delaware,* are pamphlets published in Wilmington in 1938 in commemoration of the tercentennial of the Swedish settlement.

Excerpts pertaining to Delaware from colonial Philadelphia newspapers were collected by students under the direction of H. Clay Reed and are available in typescript at the Morris Library of the University of Delaware; these excerpts are particularly valuable because there were no colonial Delaware newspapers. Leon de Valinger, Jr., and Virginia Shaw made available a rich collection of contemporary material by editing *A Calendar of Ridgely Family Letters, 1742–1899, in the Delaware State Archives;* Volume 1 (Dover, 1948) consists largely of eighteenth-century material, which is accompanied by long introductory essays. Some of these letters also appeared in Mabel Lloyd Ridgely, *The Ridgelys of Delaware and Their Circle* (Portland, Me., 1949).

The Lower Counties and Their Boundary

Harold B. Hancock, ed., "Fare Weather and Good Health . . . The Journal of Caesar Rodney, 1727–1729," *Delaware History,* 10: 33–70 (1962), is a diary kept by the father of Caesar Rodney the Signer. "The Journal of Andreas Hesselius, 1711–1724," translated by Amandus Johnson, with notes by Frank Morton Jones, *Delaware History,* 2: 61–118 (1947), is the record of a Swedish pastor particularly interested in natural history. "Wertmüller's Diary: The Transformation of Artist into Farmer," ed. by Franklin D. Scott in the *Swedish Pioneer Historical Quarterly* (April 1945), is by an immigrant painter who married into the talented Hesselius family. Still another account of eighteenth-century Delaware (as well as of a larger area) by a Scandinavian is *Peter Kalm's Travels in North America,* ed. by Adolph B. Benson (2 vols., New York, 1937). In contrast, the *Journal of Benjamin Mifflin,* ed. by Victor H. Paltsits (New York, 1935), is a Quaker travel journal reprinted from the New York Public Library *Bulletin* for June 1935; Mifflin's "Journal of a Journey from Philada. to the Cedar Swamps and Back, 1764," is in *PMHB,* 52: 130–140 (1928).

A fairly voluminous literature concerns the Delaware-Maryland boundary, beginning with the journal of one of the surveyors of the Transpeninsular Line, printed as John W. Jordan, "Penn versus Baltimore: Journal of John Watson, Assistant Surveyor to the Commissioners of the Province of Pennsylvania, 1750," *PMHB,* 38: 385–406 (1914). Recently A. Hughlett Mason transcribed *The Journal of Charles Mason and Jeremiah Dixon* for publication as Volume 76 of the *Memoirs* of the American Philosophical Society (Philadelphia, 1969). Dudley Lunt, *The Bounds of Delaware* (Wilmington, 1947), is a short history of all the boundaries, while William H. Bayliff, *The Maryland-Pennsylvania and the Maryland-Delaware Boundaries* (revised, Annapolis, 1959), confines its attention to the most famous. Thomas D. Cope, "Mason and Dixon—English Men of Science," *Delaware Notes,* 22: 13–32 (1949), and Nicholas B. Wainwright, "Tale of a Runaway Cape: The Penn-Baltimore Agreement of 1732," *PMHB,* 88: 251–293 (1963), are articles of particular interest. Massive documentation produced by the boundary dispute appears in *Pennsylvania Archives,* 2d ser., Vols. 7 and 16 (Harrisburg, 1890).

Towns and Counties

On the growth of towns, a valuable article is James T. Lemon, "Urbanization and the Development of Eighteenth-Century Southeastern Pennsylvania and Adjacent Delaware," *William and Mary Quarterly,* 3rd ser., 24: 501–542 (1967). Anna T. Lincoln, *Wilmington, Delaware—Three Centuries under Four Flags* (Rutland, Vt., 1937), is detailed; Benjamin Ferris's chapters on Wilmington, in his history, cited above (p. 266), and Francis Vincent's "History of Wilmington," in *Harkness' Magazine,* 1–4: *passim* (1872–1877), might also be consulted. The Federal Writers Project volume, *New Castle on the Delaware,* ed. by Jeannette Eckman (revised by Anthony Higgins, New Castle, 1973), is attractive and dependable. *New Castle Common* (Wilmington, 1944), is an authoritative history of the river town's common land, partly written by Judge Rodney, whose *Collected Essays,* already cited (p. 270), should be consulted on New Castle history. Virginia Cullen, *History of Lewes* (Lewes, 1956), and Egbert Handy and James L. Vallandigham, *Newark, Delaware, Past and Present* (Newark, 1882), are useful. New sketches of Dover and other Kent County towns appear in the superior *History of Kent County* by Harold B. Hancock (Dover, 1975–76). Hancock's *History of Sussex County, Delaware* (Georgetown, 1976) is another excellent study of local history spawned by the bicentennial of the American Revolution. Richard R. Cooch, *History of Christiana, Delaware* (Christiana 1976) is an interesting booklet on an old village.

Mills, Farms, and Transportation

Carol E. Hoffecker, *Brandywine Village: The Story of a Milling Community* (Wilmington, 1974) is an attractive guide book as well as a history of the old mill village. Henry Seidel Canby produced two highly interesting, though not entirely dependable works that deal with the early mills and millers of this area, *The Brandywine* (New York, 1941) and *Family History* (Cambridge, Mass., 1945). Two articles by Peter C. Walsh, "The Brandywine Mills, . . . 1762–1816," *Delaware History,* 7: 17–36 (1956), and "Merchants, Millers, and Ocean Ships, . . . An Early American Industrial Town," *Delaware History,* 7: 319–336 (1957), deal with Brandywine and Wilmington respectively. Jonathan L. Fairbanks, "The House of Thomas Shipley, 'Miller at the Tide,' on the Brandywine Creek," *Winterthur Portfolio,* 2: 142–159 (1965), is an excellent study emphasizing domestic architecture and interior design. Clinton A. Weslager, "Watermills, Windmills, Horsemills— and a Tidemill: Early Colonial Grain Mills in Delaware," *Delaware History,* 14: 52–60 (1970), is a short article covering a long period.

The best survey of Delaware agriculture in the eighteenth century is "James Tilton's Notes on the Agriculture of Delaware in 1788," ed. by R. O. Bausman and John A. Munroe, *Agricultural History,* 20: 176–187 (1946). James B. Jackson, "History of a Prominent Kent County Farm," *Delaware Conservationist,* 18: 4–10 (1974), is the story of an estate called Kingston-on-Hull. John H. Powell, *The House on Jones Neck* (1955), is a well-written short account of the nearby Dickinson property. John A. H. Sweeney, *Grandeur on the Appoquinimink* (Newark, 1959) provides full and accurate information regarding a tanner's construction of a notable house at Odessa. Very interesting material from 1774 Kent County probate records has been published by Alice Hanson Jones in her

American Colonial Wealth: Documents and Methods (3 vols., New York, 1977) and in her earlier study, "Wealth Estimates for the American Middle Colonies, 1774," in *Economic Development and Cultural Change,* vol. 18, No. 2, part 2 (1970).

Ralph D. Gray, *The Nation's Waterway: A History of the Chesapeake and Delaware Canal, 1769–1965* (Urbana, Ill., 1967), is authoritative; Gray's previous study of "The Early History of the Chesapeake and Delaware Canal" appeared in *Delaware History,* 8 and 9: *passim* (1959–1960). Joshua Gilpin, *Memoir on the Rise, Progress and Present State of the Chesapeake and Delaware Canal* (Wilmington, 1821), is a classic by the son of the waterway's progenitor. David B. Tyler, *The Bay & River Delaware* (Cambridge, Md., 1955) is a popular, pictorial history of maritime affairs, while his "Shipbuilding in Delaware," *Delaware History,* 7: 207–216 (1957), is more scholarly. A genealogy by Baldwin Maull, *John Maull (1714–1753), of Lewes, Delaware* (New York, 1941), contains information about some early pilots. James M. Tunnell, Jr., "The Salt Business in Early Sussex County," *Delaware History,* 4: 48–59 (1950), tells of an industry that depended on the sea. John C. Kraft and Robert L. Caulk, *The Evolution of Lewes Harbor* (Newark, 1972), is a fascinating geological study.

Crafts, Education, and Welfare

Dorothy A. Hawkins, "James Adams, the First Printer of Delaware," *Papers of the Bibliographical Society of America,* 28: 28–63 (1934), is a good study of an early craftsman; another is Leon de Valinger, Jr., "John Janvier, Delaware Cabinetmaker," *Antiques,* 41: 37–39 (1942). Whole crafts are discussed in Charles G. Dorman, *Delaware Cabinetmakers and Allied Artisans, 1655–1855* (Wilmington, 1960), also published in *Delaware History,* 9, no. 2 (Oct. 1960); Harold B. Hancock, "Furniture Craftsmen in Delaware Records," *Winterthur Portfolio,* 9: 175–212 (1974); and Ruthanna Hindes, *Delaware Silversmiths, 1700–1850* (Wilmington, 1968), also in *Delaware History,* 12: 247–308 (1967). Some of the writers of colonial Delaware are mentioned in Augustus H. Able, III, "Delaware Literature," in H. Clay Reed, *Delaware, A History of the First State,* 2: 935–966.

Lyman P. Powell, *The History of Education in Delaware* (Washington, 1893), is still the most comprehensive study of early education. William C. Dunlap, *Quaker Education in Baltimore and Virginia Yearly Meetings, with an Account of Certain Meetings in Delaware and on the Eastern Shore* (Philadelphia, 1936) mentions the early schools kept by the Society of Friends; *Friends School in Wilmington* (Wilmington, 1948), is an account of the oldest functioning school in Delaware. William D. Lewis, "The University of Delaware: Ancestors, Friends and Neighbors," published in *Delaware Notes,* 34: 1–242 (1961) is a long, informal history. Short essays regarding the same institution include *A Brief History of the University of Delaware (Newark, 1940); Beverly McAnear, "The Charter of the Academy of Newark," *Delaware History,* 4: 149–156 (1950); George H. Ryden, "The Newark Academy of Delaware in Colonial Days," *Pennsylvania History,* 2: 205–224 (1935); and by the same author, "The Relation of the Newark Academy . . . to the Presbyterian Church and to Higher Education in the American Colonies," *Delaware Notes,* 9: 7–42 (1935). E. Miriam Lewis edited the records of another academy, "The Minutes of the Wilmington Academy, 1777–1802," *Delaware History,* 3: 181–226 (1949), and Elbert Chance wrote of an early teacher, "Matthew Wilson—Professor, Preacher, Patriot, Physician," *Delaware History,* 10: 271–284 (1963).

Decidedly the best work on care of the poor and handicapped is Elizabeth Howell Goggin's chapter on "Public Welfare in Delaware," in H. Clay Reed, *Delaware, A History of the First State*, 2: 793–820. Robert G. Caldwell, *The Penitentiary Movement in Delaware, 1776 to 1829* (Wilmington, 1946), stands alone in its field. Matthew Wilson wrote a "History of Malignant Fever in Sussex County" which appeared in the *Pennsylvania Magazine*, 1: 165–178 (1775), and James Tilton wrote about Delaware in William Currie's *Historical Account of the Climates and Diseases of the United States* (Philadelphia, 1792), 207–221. Alfred R. Shands, Jr., "James Tilton, M.D., Delaware's Greatest Physician, 1745–1822," *Delaware Medical Journal*, 46: 24–32 (1974), is the latest of several short descriptions of Tilton. Several amateur scientists and inventors are discussed in Whitfield J. Bell, Jr., "Patriot-Improvers: Some Early Delaware Members of the American Philosophical Society," *Delaware History*, 11: 195–207 (1965). An excellent short essay, with particular attention to science, is Harold B. Hancock, "The Sense of the Times: Colonial Delaware," in *Transactions of the Delaware Academy of Science*, 6: 143–162 (1975).

Religious Denominations and Ethnic Minorities

Nelson W. Rightmyer, *The Anglican Church in Delaware* (Philadelphia, 1947), is the best book on any one religious denomination in colonial Delaware. Besides the already cited collections of William Stevens Perry (p. 271) and the writings of Richard S. Rodney (p. 270) two short works of interest to students of Anglican history are Nelson Rightmyer's "Swedish-English Relations in Northern Delaware," *Church History*, 15: 101–115 (1946), and M. Catherine Downing, *Sydenham Thorne: Clergyman and Founder* (Milford, Del., 1974). The book *Friends in Wilmington* (Wilmington, 1938) contains several very interesting articles on early Quakers. Jonathan L. Fairbanks published an article with the same title in *Quaker History*, 58: 31–40 (1969). Kenneth L. Carroll, *Joseph Nichols and the Nicholites: A Look at the "New Quakers" of Maryland, Delaware, North and South Carolina* (Easton, Md., 1962) sums up work that Carroll had been publishing on this sect for a decade; a particularly pertinent article is his "Joseph Nichols, of Delaware: An Eighteenth-Century Religious Leader," *Delaware History*, 7: 37–48 (1956).

John W. Christie's chapter on "Presbyterianism in Delaware," in H. Clay Reed, *Delaware, A History of the First State*, 2: 645–658, is by an acknowledged authority. A more recent work is James H. Lappen, *Presbyterians on Delmarva: The History of the New Castle Presbytery* (Salisbury, Md., 1972). The "Records of the Presbytery of New Castle," from 1716 to 1731 have been published in the *Journal of the Presbyterian Historical Society*, 14–15 (1931–1932).

E. C. Hallman, *The Garden of Methodism* (1948), is the latest comprehensive work on Delmarva Methodism. Useful older works include Robert W. Todd, *Methodism of the Peninsula* (Philadelphia, 1886), and John D. C. Hanna, ed., *The Centennial Services of Asbury Methodist Episcopal Church* (Wilmington, 1889). Contemporary materials in print include *The Journal and Letters of Francis Asbury*, ed. by Elmer T. Clark *et al.* (3 vols., London, 1958); *The Experiences and Travels of Mr. Freeborn Garrettson*, an autobiography (Philadelphia, 1791); and *The Life, Experiences and Gospel Labors of the Rt. Rev. Richard Allen, Written by Himself* (New York, 1960).

Richard B. Cook, *The Early and Later Delaware Baptists* (Philadelphia, 1880), can be used with two Baptist documents of eighteenth-century origin: Morgan Edwards, "Materials towards a History of the Baptists in the Delaware State," *PMHB*, 9: 45–61, 197–213 (1885), and *Records of the Welsh Tract Baptist Meeting, Pencader Hundred, New Castle County* , . . . *1701 to 1828* (2 vols., Wilmington, 1904). For the Roman Catholics, see Charles H. Esling, "Catholicity in the Three Lower Counties," *Records of the American Catholic Historical Society of Philadelphia*, 1: 117–157 (1887) and Anthony F. Di Michele *et al.*, *Coffee Run, 1772–1960: The Story of the Beginnings of the Catholic Faith in Delaware* (Hockessin, 1960). Israel Acrelius's study of the Swedish Lutherans has already been cited (p. 267). Frank R. Zebley, *The Churches of Delaware, A History* (Wilmington, 1947), presents a brief account of each of about 900 churches. Martin Lodge makes only a few specific references to Delaware in his article on "The Crisis of the Churches in the Middle Colonies, 1720–1750," *PMHB*, 95: 195–210 (1971), but he is well aware of the situation in Delaware and his article is, therefore, a good general background study.

The two most important ethnic minorities in colonial Delaware were the Africans and the Scotch-Irish. In neither case is there a good history that concentrates on the group in Delaware. Unpublished master's theses by C. S. Shorter (Howard University, 1934), Helen Black Stewart (University of Delaware, 1940), and Norman W. Moore, Jr. (University of Delaware, 1965), entitled, respectively, "Slavery in Delaware," "The Negro in Delaware to 1829," and "The Anti-Slavery Movement in Delaware, 1780–1815," are beginnings, and references to colonial conditions appear in John A. Munroe, "The Negro in Delaware," *South Atlantic Quarterly*, 56: 428–444 (1957), and H. Clay Reed, "The Negro in Delaware: Legal Status," in his *Delaware, A History of the First State*, 2: 571–580, but for the most part a student must rely on general works until the completion of a study under way by Elizabeth E. Moyne at the Johns Hopkins University and the publication of readings on blacks in Delaware being compiled for the University of Delaware Press by Harold B. Hancock and James Newton. Elizabeth Donnan, ed., *Documents Illustrative of the History of the Slave Trade to America* (4 vols., Washington, 1930–1935), and W. E. B. Du Bois, *Suppression of the African Slave Trade* (New York, 1904), contain specific references to Delaware. Darold D. Wax, "Quaker Merchants and the Slave Trade in Colonial Pennsylvania," *PMHB*, 86: 144–159 (1962) does not specifically refer to Delaware but it is pertinent nonetheless.

The most useful recent works on the Scotch-Irish are James G. Leyburn, *The Scotch-Irish: A Social History* (Chapel Hill, 1962), and R. J. Dickson, *Ulster Emigration to Colonial America, 1718–1775* (London, 1966). Writings on Presbyterians in Delaware necessarily deal with this group, but not all Presbyterians were Scotch-Irish; see, for example, Henry G. Welbon, *A History of Pencader Presbyterian Church* (Welsh in origin) (Wilmington, 1936). The beginnings of local chapters of an old fraternal organization are related in Charles E. Green, *History of the M. W. Grand Lodge of Ancient, Free and Accepted Masons of Delaware* (Wilmington, 1956).

Biography and Government

There is a dearth of biographical studies of Delawareans of the late colonial and pre-Revolutionary periods. Among the few available, including sketches in Richard S. Rodney's *Collected Essays* (cited on p. 270), are Daniel F. Wolcott, "Ryves Holt, of

Lewes, Delaware, 1696–1763," *Delaware History,* 8: 3–50 (1958); J. Bennett Hill, "The Simon Kollocks of Sussex in the Eighteenth Century," *Delaware History,* 9: 51–65 (1960); and Foster Nix, "Andrew Hamilton's Early Years in the American Colonies," *William and Mary Quarterly,* 3d ser., 21: 390–407 (1964). Burton A. Konkle's *Benjamin Chew, 1722–1810* (Philadelphia, 1932) and his *Life of Andrew Hamilton, 1676–1741* (Philadelphia, 1941) are disappointingly thin in reference to the Delaware aspects of the careers of these two men.

The best studies of colonial government are two chapters in H. Clay Reed, *Delaware, A History of the First State:* the editor's essay entitled "From Dictatorship and Democracy," 1: 251–262, and Jeannette Eckman's "Colony into State," 1: 263–281. These might be read in conjunction with two other essays from the same source, H. Clay Reed, "Colonial Beginnings," 1: 63–77, and John A. Munroe, "Delaware on the Eve of the Revolution," 1: 79–94.

THE REVOLUTION

Historical Studies

The best narrative account of the role of Delaware in the Revolution is Harold B. Hancock's *Liberty and Independence* (Wilmington, 1976). A comprehensive study of the state in the revolutionary era is found in John A. Munroe, *Federalist Delaware, 1775–1815* (New Brunswick, 1954). A briefer account by Munroe is his chapter on "Revolution and Confederation," in H. Clay Reed, *Delaware, A History of the First State,* 1: 95–124. Hancock's *Delaware Loyalists* (Wilmington, 1940) has been supplanted by a new, enlarged work by the same author, *The Loyalists of Revolutionary Delaware* (Newark, 1977). Christopher Ward's *The Delaware Continentals, 1776–1783* (Wilmington, 1941), is a splendid account of the Delaware troops in the Revolution. It may be supplemented by Edward W. Cooch, *The Battle of Cooch's Bridge* (1940) and James B. Jackson, "Our Forgotten Regiment: The Second Delaware Militia, 1780," *Delaware History,* 9: 3–50 (1960).

Scholarly articles on events of the revolutionary period include Harold B. Hancock, "County Committees and the Growth of Independence in the Three Lower Counties on the Delaware, 1765–1776," *Delaware History,* 15: 269–294 (1973); H. Clay Reed, "The Delaware Constitution of 1776," *Delaware Notes,* 6: 7–42 (1930); and John A. Munroe, "Nonresident Representation in the Continental Congress: The Delaware Delegation of 1782," *William and Mary Quarterly,* 3d ser., 9: 166–190 (1952).

Social and economic history of the period is reflected in Sara G. Farris, "Wilmington's Maritime Commerce, 1775–1807," *Delaware History,* 14: 22–51 (1970); John A. Munroe, "The Philadelawareans: A Study in the Relations betweeen Philadelphia and Delaware in the Late Eighteenth Century," *PMHB,* 69: 128–149 (1945); and Elizabeth Waterston, *Churches in Delaware during the Revolution* (Wilmington, 1925). John A. Munroe, "Reflections on Delaware and the American Revolution," *Delaware History,* 17: 1–11 (1976), is an essay on factors underlying some of the actions taken by Delawareans in this period. Charles E. Green, *Delaware Heritage: The Story of the Diamond State in the Revolution* (Wilmington, 1975), and Charles J. Truitt, *Breadbasket of the Revolution: Delmarva in the War for Independence* (Salisbury, Md., 1975), cover ground familiar to scholars.

Printed Contemporary Materials

The leading contemporary history of Delaware politics is a partisan tract by James Tilton under the pen name of Timoleon, republished as *Timoleon's Biographical History of Dionysius, Tyrant of Delaware*, John A. Munroe, ed. (Newark, 1958), reprinted with an index from *Delaware Notes*, 31 (1958). Important official records in print include the *Minutes of the Council of the Delaware State, 1776 to 1792* (Dover, 1886); *Proceedings of the* [Constitutional] *Convention of the Delaware State. . . , 1776* (Wilmington, 1927); Leon de Valinger, Jr., ed., "Minutes of the Delaware Council of Safety," *Delaware History*, 1: 55–78 (1946); and *Delaware Archives* (5 vols., Wilmington, 1911–1916), consisting of military and naval records going back to colonial wars. Harold B. Hancock has published a selection of "Revolutionary War Period Material in the Hall of Records, 1775–1787," in *Delaware History*, 17: 54–85 (1976). Delaware state constitutions and colonial charters may be examined in Francis N. Thorpe, ed., *Federal and State Constitutions, Colonial Charters, and Other Organic Laws*, Vol. 1 (Washington, 1909). *Laws of the State of Delaware*, ed. by George Read (2 vols., New Castle, 1797), already mentioned, cover this period.

A great collection of primary material of a personal nature appears in *Letters to and from Caesar Rodney, 1756–1784*, ed. by George H. Ryden (Philadelphia, 1933), which should be supplemented by Rodney letters edited by Leon de Valinger, Jr., and Harold B. Hancock that were published in *Delaware History*, 1: 99–110 (1946), 3: 105–115 (1948), and 12: 54–76 and 147–168 (1966). Letters of Thomas Rodney, younger brother of Caesar, appear in *PMHB*, ed. by Simon Gratz, 43–45, *passim* (1919–1921) and a *Diary of Thomas Rodney, 1776–1777*, was published in the *Papers of the Historical Society of Delaware*, No. 8 (Wilmington, 1888). *The Political Writings of John Dickinson* were collected by the firm of Bonsall and Niles and printed in Wilmington in two volumes in 1801, and a selection of Dickinson's political writings, 1764–1774, edited by Paul Leicester Ford, was published in Philadelphia in 1895. H. Trevor Colbourn edited Dickinson's London letters, 1754–1756, under the title "A Pennsylvania Farmer's Letters at the Court of King George," in *PMHB*, 86: 241–286, 417–453 (1962). Leon de Valinger, Jr., plans a complete edition of Dickinson's letters.

Hilda Justice, ed., *Life and Ancestry of Warner Mifflin* (Philadelphia, 1905), includes an autobiography and other contemporary material. Lynn Perry, ed., *Some Letters of and Concerning Major William Peery* (Strasburg, Va., 1935); Harold B. Hancock, "The Revolutionary War Diary of William Adair," *Delaware History*, 13: 154–165 (1968); and John A. H. Sweeney, "The Norris-Fisher Correspondence: A Circle of Friends, 1779–1782," *Delaware History*, 6: 187–232 (1955) present original materials of the period. Harold B. Hancock, "A Loyalist in Sussex County: The Adventures of J. F. D. Smyth in 1777," *Delaware History*, 16: 323–336 (1975), is an excerpt from the published reminiscences of a British soldier. Several accounts of military service by Delawareans have been published, including the *Personal Recollections of Captn Enoch Anderson*, edited by Henry H. Bellas (Wilmington, 1896); the "Journal of Lieutenant Thomas Anderson, 1780–1782," *Historical Magazine*, n.s., 1: 207–211 (1867); the "Orderly Book of Caleb Prew Bennett at the Battle of Yorktown," ed. by Charles W. Dickens, *Delaware History*, 4: 105–148 (1950); *The Journal and Order Book of Captain Robert Kirkwood of the Delaware Regiment of the Continental Line* (Wilmington, 1910), ed.

by Joseph Brown Turner as No. 56 in the *Papers of the Historical Society of Delaware;* and William Seymour, *Journal of the Southern Expedition, 1780–1783* (Wilmington, 1896), No. 15 in the *Papers* just mentioned.

Biographies

Besides data accompanying some of the contemporary writings cited in the preceding two paragraphs, there are several good biographies of Delawareans of the revolutionary period. William Thompson Read, *Life and Correspondence of George Read* (Philadelphia, 1870), is an old-fashioned work but full of original material relating not only to Read but also to some of his contemporaries. John M. Coleman, *Thomas McKean, Forgotten Leader of the Revolution* (Rockaway, N. J., 1975) is also a storehouse of information; though it traces McKean's life only to 1780 it covers the years when he was most active in Delaware. Several good essays on McKean have been published recently by G. S. Rowe: "A Valuable Acquisition in Congress: Thomas McKean, Delegate from Delaware to the Continental Congress, 1774–1783," *Pennsylvania History,* 38: 225–264 (1971); "Thomas McKean and the Coming of the Revolution," *PMHB,* 96: 3–47 (1972); and "The Legal Career of Thomas McKean, 1750–1775," *Delaware History,* 16: 22–46 (1974). There is a brief sketch of Caesar Rodney by George H. Ryden in the latter's collection of Rodney letters, already cited in the previous section. A booklet by William P. Frank, *Caesar Rodney, Patriot* (Wilmington, 1975) incorporates the latest information. *Thomas Rodney, Revolutionary and Builder of the West* (Durham, 1953), is a brief biography by William B. Hamilton that also appears in his *Anglo-American Law on the Frontier* of the same date.

John Dickinson so far lacks an adequate biography, for Charles J. Stillé, *Life and Times of John Dickinson* (Philadelphia, 1891), is unsatisfactory. John H. Powell, who never published his Iowa doctoral dissertation on the young Dickinson, wrote several excellent articles on this statesman, including his "Speech of John Dickinson Opposing the Declaration of Independence, 1 July, 1776," *PMHB,* 65: 458–481 (1941); and "John Dickinson, President of the Delaware State, 1781–1782," *Delaware History,* 1: 1–54,[1] 111–134 (1936). Other useful articles include James M. Tunnell, Jr., "John Dickinson and the Federal Constitution," *Delaware History,* 6: 288–293 (1955); Frederick B. Tolles, "John Dickinson and the Quakers," in *"John and Mary's College"; the Boyd Lee Spahr Lectures at Dickinson College* (Westfield, N. J., 1956), 67–88; Richard M. Gummere, "John Dickinson, the Classical Penman of the Revolution," *Classical Journal,* 52: 81–88 (1960); David L. Jacobson, "John Dickinson Fights against Royal Government, 1764," *William and Mary Quarterly,* 3d ser., 19: 64–85 (1962); Edwin Wolf, II, "The Authorship of the 1774 Address to the King Restudied," *William and Mary Quarterly,* 3d ser., 22: 1–36 (1965); and Milton E. Flower, "John Dickinson, Delawarean," *Delaware History,* 17: 12–25 (1976). David L. Jacobson, *John Dickinson and the Revolution in Pennsylvania, 1764–1776* (Berkeley, 1965), like some of the articles listed above, shows little interest in Dickinson's Delaware connections. A book-length study of Dickinson by Milton E. Flower is expected to be published soon.

"Who Was Colonel John Haslet of Delaware?" by Ernest J. Moyne, *Delaware History,* 13: 283–300 (1969), is a model of excellence, both in research and in writing. Greville and Dorothy Bathe, *Oliver Evans: A Chronicle of Early American Engineering* (Philadelphia,

1935), is a good biography of a Delaware mechanical genius who began his career in this period; "Oliver Evans' Memoir 'On the Origin of Steam Boats and Steam Waggons,'" ed. by Arlan K. Gilbert, *Delaware History,* 7: 142–167 (1956) is interesting. John Walton, *John Filson of Kentucke* (Lexington, 1956) is the biography of a Wilmington schoolteacher who became famous in the West. An interesting recent article is "The Travail of John McKinly, First President of Delaware," by G. S. Rowe, in *Delaware History,* 17: 26–36 (1976).

INDEX